THE WIT
AND WISDOM OF
GANDHI

THE WIT
AND WISDOM OF
GANDHI

MOHANDAS GANDHI

Edited by
Homer A. Jack

Preface by
John Haynes Holmes

DOVER PUBLICATIONS, INC.
Mineola, New York

Bibliographical Note

This Dover edition, first published in 2005, is an unabridged republication of
the work originally published in 1951 by The Beacon Press, Boston.

Library of Congress Cataloging-in-Publication Data

Gandhi, Mahatma, 1869–1948.
   [Selections. 1951]
   The wit and wisdom of Gandhi / Mohandas Gandhi ; edited by Homer A.
Jack ; preface by John Haynes Holmes.
     p. cm.
   Reprint. Originally published: Boston : Beacon Press, 1951.
   Includes bibliographical references and index.
   ISBN 0-486-43992-5 (pbk.)
   1. Jack, Homer Alexander. II. Title.

DS481.G3A25 2005
954.03'5'092—dc22

2004065695

Manufactured in the United States of America
Dover Publications, Inc., 31 East 2nd Street, Mineola, N.Y. 11501

To my mother

PREFACE

GANDHI was a voluminous writer on a vast variety of topics. I doubt if even the prodigious Voltaire could rival him. For years he wrote innumerable letters, composed editorials and articles regularly each week for his famous newspapers, *Young India*, *Navajivan*, and *Harijan*, published books, and in 1927 crowned his literary labors with his two-volume autobiography, *The Story of My Experiments with Truth*. In addition there were endless interviews, public addresses, prayer talks, even casual conversations, which were taken down and printed verbatim in the daily press in India and beyond. There was never anything like it! Pyarelal Nayyar, the Mahatma's official biographer, may well feel himself daunted by the ocean of material that stretches before him.

Gandhi's literary achievement is the more remarkable in view of the fact that he was never, in any sense of the phrase, a literary man. Unlike his great contemporary, Rabindranath Tagore, and his accomplished successor, Pandit Nehru, the Mahatma had no especial grace of style. Seldom, if ever, in his writings, did he rise to heights of eloquence and beauty. Memorable passages—i.e., memorable for their own sake—are rarely found. Gandhi's interests were never aesthetic, but rather pragmatic. He had no desire or ambition, no time, to be an artist. His one thought was of his own people, and his struggle to make them free. So he wrote with disciplined simplicity, seeking only to make himself clearly understood. The result was the one most important quality of literary art—namely, clarity. I doubt if, in all his works, Gandhi ever wrote a sentence which failed to express with utter precision the thought he had in mind to convey. Gandhi mastered his medium. He wrought a style which was perfect for his purpose of communication. To read his writings is to think of content and not of style—which means a triumph in the adaptation of means to ends.

It is into this vast Gandhian sea that Homer Jack has had the courage to plunge. Like the sponge-diver, he has sought and brought to the surface the best of the myriad growths which would have otherwise been lost. Like the chemist in his laboratory, he has analyzed the compound before him, and produced a distillation of all the most precious elements therein concealed. Or, dropping all more or less artificial figures of speech, Mr. Jack has performed the stupendous task of reading great masses of Gandhi's writing, and bringing to us the winnowing for our inspection. What we would never have done ourselves, he has done for us. We can now peruse this book with the serene content that the best that Gandhi ever wrote and said is here before us.

What impresses me, in this anthology of Gandhi's mind, is the excellence of the selections. There are more gems of wit and wisdom here than I supposed would have been found. Mr. Jack has been wise enough to make his quotations short rather than long, and therefore to the point. The temptation must have been strong upon him to float along the easy current of the Mahatma's thought. But this would have buried the Mahatma anew in the sheer mass of his writings. With excellent judgment, Mr. Jack has made his pieces brief and incisive, and therewith has increased rather than diminished the effectiveness of Gandhi's thought. Nowhere do I find any evidence of skimping the material—least of all, any abuse of context. I count this editorial work of a high order.

The same is true of the classification of material. This has been done with skill and impeccable good taste. Religion, theology, personal ethics, social ethics (love), service, international affairs, political affairs, the family, education, culture and the professions, Indian problems, Gandhi himself—these are the topics chosen, and all are clarified and illuminated by the cogency of Gandhi's words. Who can doubt the greatness of Gandhi's spirit, and the lucidity and power of his mind, as here revealed in the ever-recurring flashes of his genius?

I count it a privilege to commend this book to what I hope will be a host of readers. My feeling is that numberless persons who have known nothing of Gandhi will here discover him, and therewith enrich their lives. Those who have long known and revered the Mahatma will here refresh themselves as at some wayside shrine. In either case, Mr. Jack as editor may well feel rewarded for his labors.

JOHN HAYNES HOLMES

New York, N. Y.

ACKNOWLEDGMENTS

The quotations from Gandhi used in this book are reprinted with the permission of the Navajivan Trust of Ahmedabad, India, in which the copyright of all of M. K. Gandhi's writings are vested. Grateful acknowledgment is also made for permission from the following publishers to reprint copyright material:

Abingdon-Cokesbury Press, Nashville, Tenn., for quotations from *Mahatma Gandhi: An Interpretation*, by E. Stanley Jones.

Allen & Unwin, Ltd., London, for quotations from *Mahatma Gandhi's Ideas*, by C. F. Andrews.

Appleton-Century-Crofts, Inc., New York City, for quotations from *Mahatma Gandhi*, by Romain Rolland:

Doubleday and Company, Inc., Garden City, New York, for quotations from *Great Soul: The Growth of Gandhi*, by Herrymon Maurer.

Duell, Sloan and Pearce, New York City, for quotations from *A Week with Gandhi*, by Louis Fischer (copyright 1942 by Louis Fischer).

Harper and Brothers, New York City, for quotations from *The Life of Mahatma Gandhi*, by Louis Fischer and *Gandhi's Letters to a Disciple*.

G. A. Natesan and Co., Madras, India, for quotations from *Gandhi's Speeches and Writings*.

Oxford University Press, New York City, for quotations from *What Does Gandhi Want?* by T. A. Raman.

Public Affairs Press, Washington, D. C., for quotations from *Gandhi's Autobiography: The Story of My Experiments with Truth*, by M. K. Gandhi.

Random House, Inc., New York City, for quotations from *Lead, Kindly Light*, by Vincent Sheean.

Henry Regnery Company, Chicago, Illinois, for quotations from *Satyagraha: The Power of Truth*, by R. R. Diwakar.

D. G. Tendulkar of Bombay, India, for quotations from *Gandhiji: His Life and Work*.

The editor is deeply grateful to John Haynes Holmes for writing the preface and, more than anybody else, for helping him to understand Gandhi. The editor acknowledges his indebtedness to the staff of the Beacon Press for aid in the publication of this volume. Without time taken from his parish and especially from his family, the editor would never have completed this task.

CONTENTS

THE WIT
AND WISDOM OF
GANDHI

Introduction

ORIGINALITY is for the gods—not even for the saints. Mohandas K. Gandhi's ideas were not completely original. Indeed, in developing his most original concept, group non-violent direct action—*satyagraha*—Gandhi repeatedly acknowledged the insights he obtained from Count Leo Tolstoy, Henry D. Thoreau, the Sermon on the Mount, and Hindu scriptures.

In many respects, Gandhi was an unusual blend of the East and the West. Born in India, he had less training in his native culture than he later wished, for his early education was conditioned, as he often regretted, by his having had to study in English. By the time he was nineteen years old, he was in England studying law—and learning Western ways as only a non-Westerner can. Gandhi stayed only briefly in India upon his return from England, and for twenty years was an expatriate in South Africa, working for the civil rights of the large Indian colony there. Here again, he was able to study Western culture and the Western mind. He was also able, for the first time, to make a careful study of his own people and their culture.

If Gandhi condemned, as he often did, the English system of education prevailing in India until 1947 and the whole of Western civilization, he also admitted—on other occasions—his deep indebtedness to the West. Much of Gandhi's greatness lies in his very eclecticism. He carefully selected what he felt to be truth in the cultures and religions of both the West and the East. Because of Gandhi's well-known condemnation of the West, he was often charged with being old-fashioned and indeed reactionary. He repeatedly denied, however, that he was interested in the old merely because it was old. He was preoccupied, for example, with reviving the old spinning wheel, because of its economic fitness for an impoverished rural people with much spare time. He took not too kindly to machines, because he saw their viciousness in the hands of capital—foreign and indigenous—which treated the men who manned them also like machines.

Gandhi once wrote that people would be surprised at the few books he read. For one thing, with all his political activity, he had little time. He looked forward to jail in order to have time to catch up with his reading! He wrote about his imprisonment in 1913 in South Africa: "I never had had time for study for years together, particularly since 1893, and the prospect of uninterrupted study for a year filled me with joy." [1]

In London, Gandhi studied Western legal theory and made some casual attempts to study Christian literature. In South Africa, however, he made a determined effort to study Christianity. During his first year there he read "quite eighty" books. Two books which especially impressed him were Leo Tolstoy's *The Kingdom of God Is Within You* and John Ruskin's *Unto This Last*. He later wrote how, upon reading Ruskin, he "arose with the dawn, ready to reduce [his] principles to practice"—which characteristically he did! (His translation of this book by Ruskin into Gujarati, entitled *Sarvodaya*—the "Welfare of All"—was published and distributed in 1919 to offer civil disobedience against proscribed literature in Bombay.)

While in South Africa, Gandhi was able for the first time to study his own Indian culture, partly through Theosophy and partly through other English interpretations. In his *Autobiography*, he tells of reading Max Müller's *India—What Can It Teach Us?* and the translations of the *Upanishads* published by the Theosophical Society. In this period, too, he read Washington Irving's *Life of Mohammed and His Successors* and Carlyle's essay on Mohammed in his *Heroes and Hero Worship*. Throughout his life, Gandhi continued to read selected volumes published in the West. During his last imprisonment in the Aga Khan's palace, beginning in 1942, he read portions of Karl Marx's *Das Kapital*.

Gandhi himself was a prolific writer—although he apparently

[1] Supernumerals refer to Sources beginning on page 217.

never accepted a royalty or honorarium for his writings.[2] His first known publication was a pamphlet entitled *An Appeal to Every Briton in South Africa.* This contained a "statement, supported by evidence, of the general condition of Natal Indians" and was issued in South Africa in 1894. On a voyage from London back to South Africa in 1909, Gandhi wrote *Hind Swaraj* or *Indian Home Rule.* This brief work became the basis for his subsequent thirty-year campaign for Indian freedom. Widely reprinted, *Hind Swaraj* was issued in 1938 with a new introduction by Gandhi who then asserted, "I have seen nothing to make me alter the views expanded in it."

Gandhi early appreciated the necessity of a medium of communication for his political work and in 1904 established *Indian Opinion* written in English and Gujarati. Gandhi wrote about this periodical: "It was a mirror of part of my life. . . . Week after week I poured out my soul in its columns. I cannot recall a word in those articles set down without thought or deliberation, or a word of conscious exaggeration, or anything merely to please." The essay *Hind Swaraj* appeared serially in *Indian Opinion*, as did many articles on dietetics which later appeared in book form in English as *A Guide to Health.* Gandhi ceased editing *Indian Opinion* when he left South Africa in 1914. By a curious repetition of history, a Gandhi—his son, Manilal—is still publishing and editing *Indian Opinion* in Natal and it is still attacking the bitter racism of the Union of South Africa.

In 1919, Gandhi helped establish the English *Young India* and the Gujarati *Navajivan.* In 1933, *Young India* became *Harijan*—the latter word being the term Gandhi used in speaking of the untouchables. That these modest-appearing weeklies had tremendous political influence can be seen from the fact that *Harijan*, in the early nineteen-forties, was issued in a total of twelve editions in nine languages and that Gandhi's most important articles were reprinted the next day by all the newspapers of India, then numbering 37 in English and 115 in Indian languages.

In the early twenties Gandhi wrote *Satyagraha in South Africa.* This was written principally while he was in Yeravda prison and was first published serially in *Navajivan*. Also in this period he was persuaded to write his unusually frank autobiography which he chose to call *The Story of My Experiments with Truth*. Written in Gujarati, it was also composed partly in prison. It appeared chapter by chapter each week in *Navajivan*. Mahadev Desai, Gandhi's personal secretary, translated the chapters of the auto-biography into English, with Mirabehn (Madeleine Slade) often making corrections. This English translation appeared serially in *Young India* and in John Haynes Holmes's *Unity* magazine in the United States. The complete autobiography was not pub-lished in book form in the United States until 1948, although C. F. Andrews published portions of it in America in 1930.

Much of Gandhi's later writing was in the form of articles and interviews printed in *Young India, Navajivan,* or *Harijan*. These writings were collected in various ways. Three separate volumes of his writings in *Young India* were, for example, published in America in the nineteen-twenties. Separate excerpts of his writings on missions, untouchability, home industry, etc., have appeared—sometimes under his own editorship, at other times edited by his close associates. Most "official" collections of Gandhi's articles have been published by the Navajivan Pub-lishing House at Ahmedabad.

From 1918 to his death in 1942, Mahadev Desai was con-stantly at Gandhi's elbow. He has been called "Gandhi's Bos-well." He published several volumes, including *Gandhiji in Indian Villages* and *Gandhiji in Ceylon*. Pyarelal, who was his secretary when Gandhi died in 1948, has also written several volumes and is now at work in India on a monumental, multi-volume biog-raphy of Gandhi.

Gandhi was no great literary craftsman—at least he does not appear to be so in English translation. He could write (and speak) English with great facility, but preferred on many occasions to use Gujarati as part of his campaign for the use of indigenous languages. John Haynes Holmes observes of his writing: "Gandhi was not distinguished as a writer. . . . He touched no heights of eloquence and beauty. For one thing, he was concerned not with style but with meaning. Writing to him was not an art, but rather a practical medium of expression. He had something to say, and he must say it as quickly and clearly as possible." [3]

Gandhi, for all the grim battle he was waging, combined wit with his wisdom. If humor and satire were not exactly full-fledged weapons in his non-violent arsenal, they were often used in his personal relations with friends. He could frequently see humorous situations in his own life and would seldom hesitate to point these out to others. In his *Autobiography* he recalls how, after surreptitiously tasting goat meat as a boy, he dreamed that evening of goats bleating in his stomach! He also wrote that "the woes of *Mahatmas* are known to *Mahatmas* alone." [4] Once he revealed to Louis Fischer the motivation for his mystical practice of a weekly day of silence: "I was working very hard. . . . I wanted to rest for one day a week. So I instituted a day of silence. Later of course I clothed it with all kinds of virtues and gave it a spiritual cloak. But the motivation was really nothing more than that I wanted to have a day off." [5]

Gandhi, unlike Stalin, never attended a seminary. Gandhi, like Jesus, was no systematic theologian—yet his whole life and message was based on an intense personal faith. His message like his life was basically religious. He did not succumb to the rather persistent efforts to convert him to Christianity, but he incorporated a few of the insights of Christianity into his own religion— a very eclectic Hinduism. He was critical of the excrescences of Hinduism, especially the concept and practice of untouchability.

Gandhi's greatest social invention was *satyagraha*—group non-violent direct action or soul force. This new weapon he forged in opposing the racist oppression of the Indians in South Africa, and he perfected it in opposing British imperialism in India. He couldn't dissociate *satyagraha* from his religious orientation, and indeed one grew out of the other.

As Horace Alexander has wisely observed, Gandhi's whole life was "a kind of dialectic," first preparing his people for freedom and then helping them attain it. [6] The preparation, called "the constructive program," dealt at various times with Moslem-Hindu communal unity, home industry, protection of women, educational reform, prohibition, and the removal of untouchability. As progress was made in the constructive program, Gandhi would launch a campaign of non-violent direct action to attain the freedom for which he had better prepared his countrymen. That alternation of effort contributed to the catholicity of Gandhi's interests—and writings.

Gandhi's message transcended religion, theology, *satyagraha*, Indian independence, and domestic political affairs. For one thing, he developed a rich code of personal and social ethics, including well-developed if controversial convictions about dieting, continence, and non-possession. His emphasis on poverty was a function of his concept of leadership for community service. Gandhi was less vocal on international affairs than one might suppose, although in later life he did symbolize the movement against war as an instrument of national policy in accord with his disavowal of violence and hate as instruments of domestic policy.

Much has already been written analyzing Gandhi's ideas, beginning with the first biography by the Rev. Joseph J. Doke (which Gandhi himself modestly sent to Tolstoy), the early sermons by John Haynes Holmes, and the well-known biography by Romain Rolland. Since then the "Gandhi literature" has increased to huge proportions, the bibliography of Gandhiana now containing more than 1,400 references to books in English alone. Some of the best interpretations of Gandhi's ideas have come from his long-time associate, the versatile, wandering English missionary, C. F. Andrews. Separate volumes are being published evaluating Gandhi's specific ideas. Especially valuable are Gopi N. Dhawan's *The Political Philosophy of Mahatma Gandhi*, Richard Gregg's *The Power of Non-Violence*, and R. R. Diwakar's *Satyagraha: The Power of Truth*.

Gandhi was father to the children of Mother India and, as a typical Eastern father, he offered all kinds of advice to his progeny. Gandhi could discourse in abstruse Hindu theology and, often in the same article, could give some very practical advice on marriage, diet, or spinning. Some Westerners see something of the faddist in Gandhi—his denunciation of vivisection and smoking and his firm support of vegetarianism and earth-cures. Gandhi admitted being a quack! He was an inveterate experimenter in all aspects of living, insisting that his philosophy was all of a piece. Today, most of us will have reservations in our estimate of Gandhi's competence in certain areas—and that is our privilege. As Pandit Nehru implied that Gandhi's political wisdom was right *in the end* when it appeared until the end to be wrong, so perhaps are Gandhi's opinions even on what we in the West would dismiss as his nostrums. Acharya Kripalani once told E. Stanley Jones in another connection: "The *Mahatma* is more right when he is wrong than we are when we are right." [7]

Apart from certain personal topics, such as diet, and certain areas of special Indian concern, such as *Swaraj*, the question remains—is Gandhi's message universal and timeless? Only history can answer this question, although many have predicted that the like of Gandhi will not be duplicated on this earth in a thousand years. As Albert Einstein wrote of Gandhi on the latter's seventy-fifth birthday: "Generations to come will scarce believe that such a one as this ever in flesh and blood walked upon this earth." [8]

Gandhi was not always consistent in his speeches and writings. Much has been made of this apparent inconsistency. Yet what appears to be an inconsistency may be the treatment of a subject from a different point of view—or it may represent a growth in time. Louis Fischer, after spending a week with Gandhi in 1942, observed the ease with which "Gandhi can be mischievously misquoted out of context"; and he recounted the many facets in Gandhi's thinking: "Part of the pleasure of intimate intellectual contact with Gandhi is that he really opens his mind and allows the interviewer to see how the machine inside works. When most people talk they try to bring their ideas out in final, perfect form so that they are least exposed to attack. Not so with Gandhi. He gives immediate expression to each step in his thinking. . . . Actually, he thinks aloud, and the entire process is for the record. This confuses some people and impels others to say he contradicts himself. Maybe he is too old and impersonal and not of this world to bother about the impression he makes." [9]

But Gandhi was human enough to answer his critics occasionally. Once he admitted: "I have never made a fetish of consistency." [10] Elsewhere he stated: "My aim is not to be consistent with my previous statements on a given question, but to be consistent with truth as it may present itself to me at a given moment. The result has been that I have grown from truth to truth; I have saved my memory an undue strain, and what is more, whenever I have been obliged to compare my writing even of fifty years ago with the latest, I have discovered no inconsistency between the two. But friends who observe inconsistency will do well to take the meaning that my latest writing may yield, unless, of course, they prefer the old. But before making the choice, they should try to see if there is not an underlying abiding consistency between the two seeming inconsistencies." [11]

Gandhi's insistence on truth permeated his whole existence. Not by accident did he entitle his autobiography *The Story of My Experiments with Truth*. In the early twenties he stated that "my uniform experience has convinced me that there is no other God than Truth." [12] In 1931, he asserted: "Truth is God." [13] Truth and non-violence constituted "the essence of his faith—twin suns round which all the lesser planets of his life and thought revolved." [14]

The quotations which comprise this book are, the editor believes, representative of Gandhi's total thinking; but they are not exhaustive. The selection is necessarily subjective and in some ways arbitrary. Nothing, however, has been omitted because of the editor's prejudices or because of the mark of time. Many important quotations no doubt have been omitted because of the inaccessibility to the editor of some of Gandhi's writings.

The topics or divisions of the chapters have been made as obvious as possible, but the reader should initially refer to the table of contents in order to obtain a perspective of the whole work. It has sometimes been difficult to make logcial separations between topics. It has been especially difficult to separate Indian problems from the more universal ones, and it has been impossible to disentangle Gandhi's reminiscences from his opinions of various topics. The penultimate chapter does, however, deal especially with Indian problems and the last chapter deals with his more obviously autobiographical wit and wisdom.

The quotations are generally arranged in the order of their publication. The fullest possible source for each quotation is given in the Notes and Sources at the end of the volume.

The wit and wisdom of Gandhi is for us to live by and not merely to quote. In 1940 Gandhi said: "If Gandhism is another name for sectarianism, it deserves to be destroyed. If I were to know, after my death, that what I stood for had degenerated into sectarianism, I should be deeply pained. . . . Let no one say that he is a follower of Gandhi . . . but fellow students, fellow pilgrims, fellow seekers." [15] In fact, Gandhi wished that his "writings should be cremated with my body—what I have done will endure, not what I have said and written." [16]

The wit and wisdom of Gandhi can be lived not only by saints, but also by sinners, by those of us who are average, as Gandhi insisted he was average: "I have not the shadow of a doubt that any man or woman can achieve what I have, if he or she would make the same effort and cultivate the same hope and faith." [17] To those who felt overwhelmed by his divine standards, Gandhi warned that "to dismiss my evidence as useless, because I am popularly regarded as a *Mahatma*, is not proper in a serious inquiry." [18] And yet to those who automatically accepted his standards, Gandhi had the last word when he warned: "Never take anything for gospel truth even if it comes from a *Mahatma*." [19]

HOMER A. JACK

Evanston, Illinois

GLOSSARY OF INDIAN TERMS

Ahimsa   Non-violence (*a*, privative; *himsa*, violence). This is an ancient Hindu precept, proclaimed by Buddha, by disciples of Vishnu, and by Mahavira, founder of Jainism.

Ashram   Religious community or institution or school; place of discipline and service.

Ba   Familiar title for mother in Gujarati. Used as a title of respect for Mrs. Gandhi.

Bai, Behn   A kindly way of addressing a woman.

Bapu   Familiar title for father in Gujarati. Used throughout India as a title of respect for Gandhi.

Bhagavad Gita   The Song of the Divine Lord. This is a poem of 700 stanzas and part of the *Mahabharata*.

Bhai   A kindly way of addressing a man.

Brahmacharya   Continence, sexual self-restraint. Literally, conduct that leads one to God.

Brahmin   The highest caste in Hinduism; when spelled *Brahman* it refers to the essence of godhead.

Charkha   The hand spinning wheel.

Congress   The Indian National Congress.

Darshan   A form of spiritual happiness induced by being in the presence of a cherished person, place, or thing.

Dharma   Religion or religious duty. See *Sanatana Dharma* and *Varnashrama Dharma*.

Gandhiji   A title of respect for Gandhi, the *ji* corresponding to *sir* or *mister*. Sometimes the word *Mahatmaji* was used.

Gita   Song. See *Bhagavad Gita*.

Gujarati   Language spoken in the province of Gujarat, India, in which Gandhi was born.

Guru   A spiritual guide.

Gurudeva   Revered teacher. This title was used for Rabindranath Tagore, although Gandhi often called him simply "The Poet."

Harijans   A term given by Gandhi to the untouchables (*hari*, God's; *jan*, people).

Hartal   Cessation of work. (A Hindustani word of Moslem origin.)

Himsa   Violence, hate. See *Ahimsa*.

Hind Swaraj   Indian self-government. See *Swaraj*.

Hindi   The language of North India, with Sanskrit roots.

Hindustani   A language which is a blend of Hindi and Urdu.

Khaddar (khadi)   Hand-spun or home-spun cloth.

Mahabharata	The national epic of which Krishna is the divine hero. The *Bhagavad Gita* is part of this epic.
Mahatma	Great soul (*maha*, great; *atma*, soul).
Muslim	Indian spelling and pronunciation of the word *Moslem*.
Pandit	A learned man or teacher, especially a Brahmin, in Hindu religion, law, and science.
Puranas	Sacred Hindu legends.
Ramayana	The sacred epic of North India, of which Rama is the divine hero. This has been translated into Hindi.
Rupee	The monetary unit of India. Four *pice* equal one *anna*. Sixteen annas equal one rupee. A *lakh* equals 100,000 rupees and a *crore* equals 100 lakhs or 10,000,000 rupees. In 1951 a rupee was worth about 21¢.
Sanatana Dharma	Orthodox Hindu religion.
Sanatani	An orthodox Hindu.
Satyagraha	Truth-force or soul-force (*sat*, truth; *agraha*, firmness). Non-violent direct action or "passive resistance."
Satyagrahi	One who practices truth-force.
Swadeshi	Belonging to, or made in, one's own country (*swa*, self; *deshi*, country).
Swaraj	Self-government; independence (*swa*, self; *raj*, government).
Upanishads	Hindu religious philosophical discourses.
Urdu	A language based on Hindi, with a Persian and Arabic vocabulary.
Varnashrama Dharma	Religion of caste (*varna*, color; *ashrama*, place of discipline).
Vedanta	An important Hindu philosophical system.
Vedas	Earliest Hindu religious hymns.

1. Religion

RELIGION

Religions are different roads converging to the same point. What does it matter that we take different roads, so long as we reach the same goal? In reality, there are as many religions as there are individuals.

Humbug there undoubtedly is about all religions. Where there is light, there is also shadow.

It is not the Hindu religion which I certainly prize above all other religions, but the *religion* which transcends Hinduism, which changes one's very nature, which binds one indissolubly to the truth within and which ever purifies.

Religion which takes no account of practical affairs and does not help to solve them is no religion.

I came to the conclusion that all religions were right, and every one of them imperfect, because they were interpreted with our poor intellects, sometimes with our poor hearts, and more often misinterpreted. In all religions I found to my grief that there were various and even contradictory interpretations of some texts.

A man who aspires after [Truth] cannot afford to keep out of any field of life. That is why my devotion to Truth has drawn me into the field of politics; and I can say without the slightest hesitation, and yet in all humility, that those who say that religion has nothing to do with politics do not know what religion means.

The test of the possession of the religious sense really consists in one's being able to pick out the "rightest" thing out of many things which are all "right" more or less.

The study of other religions besides one's own will give a grasp of the rock-bottom unity of all religions and afford a glimpse also of the universal and absolute truth which lies beyond the "dust of creeds and faiths." Let no one even for a moment entertain the fear that a reverent study of other religions is likely to weaken or shake one's faith in one's own.

After long study and experience, I have come to the conclusion that (1) all religions are true; (2) all religions have some error in them; (3) all religions are almost as dear to me as my own Hinduism, in as much as all human beings should be as dear to one as one's own close relatives.

One's own religion is after all a matter between oneself and one's Maker.

If we are imperfect ourselves, religion as conceived by us must also be imperfect. We have not realized religion in its perfection, even as we have not realized God. Religion of our conception, being thus imperfect, is always subject to a process of evolution and reinterpretation. Progress towards Truth, towards God, is possible only because of such evolution.

For me religion is one in essence, but it has many branches, and if I, the Hindu branch, fail in my duty to the parent trunk, I am an unworthy follower of that one indivisible, visible religion.

A religion has to be judged not by its worst specimens but by the best it might have produced. For that and that alone can be used as the standard to aspire to, if not to improve upon.

Religion deals with the science of the soul.

The most spiritual act is the most practical in the true sense of the term.

I cannot conceive politics as divorced from religion. Indeed religion should pervade every one of our actions. Here religion does not mean sectarianism. It means a belief in ordered moral government of the universe. . . . This religion transcends Hinduism, Islam, Christianity, etc. It does not supersede them. It harmonizes them and gives them reality.

Religions are not for separating men from one another, they are meant to bind them. It is a misfortune that today they are so distorted that they have become a potent cause of strife and mutual slaughter.

His own religion is the truest to every man even if it stands low in the scales of philosophic comparison.

ATHEISM

[God] is even the atheism of the atheist.

There are some who in the egotism of their reason declare that they have nothing to do with religion. But it is like a man saying that he breathes but that he has no nose. Whether by reason, or by instinct, or by superstition, man acknowledges some sort of relationship with the Divine. The rankest agnostic or atheist does acknowledge the need of moral principle, and associates something good with its observance and something bad with its non-observance. . . . Even a man who disowns religion cannot, and does not, live without religion.

It is the fashion, now-a-days, to dismiss God from life altogether and insist on the possibility of reaching the highest kind of life without the necessity of a living faith in a living God.

TOLERANCE

I tolerate unreasonable religious sentiment when it is not immoral.

Intolerance is a species of violence and therefore against our creed.

Intolerance betrays want of faith in one's cause.

The golden rule of conduct is mutual toleration, seeing that we will never all think alike and we shall see Truth in fragments and from different angles of vision. Conscience is not the same thing for all. Whilst, therefore, it is a good guide for individual conduct, imposition of that conduct upon all will be an insufferable interference with everybody's freedom of conscience.

If you cannot feel that the other faith is as true as yours, you should feel at least that the men are as true as you.

So long as there are different religions, every one of them may need some outward distinctive symbol. But when the symbol is made into a fetish and an instrument of proving the superiority of one's religion over others, it is fit only to be discarded.

Just as preservation of one's own culture does not mean contempt for that of others, but requires assimilation of the best that there may be in all the other cultures, even so should be the case with religion.

Even as a tree has a single trunk, but many branches and leaves, so there is one true and perfect religion, but it becomes many, as it passes through the human medium. The one religion is beyond all speech. Imperfect men put it into such language as they can command, and their words are interpreted by other men equally imperfect. Whose interpretation is to be held to be the right one? Everybody is right from his own standpoint, but it is not possible that everybody is wrong. Hence the necessity of tolerance, which does not mean indifference to one's own faith, but a more intelligent and purer love for it. . . . True knowledge of religion breaks down the barriers between faith and faith.

I do not like the word tolerance. . . . Tolerance may imply a gratuitous assumption of the inferiority of other faiths to one's own, whereas *ahimsa* teaches us to entertain the same respect for the religious faiths of others as we accord to our own, thus admitting the imperfections of the latter.

If all faiths outlined by men are imperfect, the question of comparative merit does not arise. All faiths constitute a revelation of Truth, but all are imperfect and liable to error. Reverence for other faiths need not blind us to their faults. We must be keenly alive to the defects of our own faith also, yet not leave it on that account, but try to overcome those defects. Looking at all religions with an equal eye, we would not only not hesitate, but would think it our duty, to blend into our faith every acceptable feature of other faiths.

CONVERSION

See also the section on "Missionaries" in Chapter 12.

Many of the "conversions" are only so-called. In some cases the appeal has gone not to the heart but to the stomach; and in every case a conversion leaves a sore behind it.

Converts are those who are "born again" or should be. A higher standard is expected of those who change their faith, if the change is a matter of the heart and not of convenience.

I do not believe in people telling others of their faith, especially with a view to conversion. Faith does not admit of telling. It has to be lived and then it becomes self-propagating.

A convert's enthusiasm for his new religion is greater than that of a person who is born in it.

I should not think of embracing another religion before I had fully understood my own.

My own veneration for other faiths is the same as that for my own faith; therefore no thought of conversion is possible.

We do not need to proselytize either by our speech or by our writing. We can only do so really with our lives. Let our lives be open books for all to study.

If a person, through fear, compulsion, starvation or for material gain or consideration, goes over to another faith, it is a misnomer to call it conversion. Real conversion springs from the heart and at the prompting of God, not of a stranger. The voice of God can always be distinguished from the voice of man.

SCRIPTURES

Scriptures cannot transcend reason and truth. They are intended to purify reason and illuminate truth.

Spirituality is not a matter of knowing scriptures and engaging in philosophical discussions.

Divine knowledge is not borrowed from books. It has to be realized in oneself. Books are at best an aid, often a hindrance.

Error can claim no exemption even if it can be supported by the scriptures of the world.

Knowledge of religious books is not equivalent of that religion.

Nothing can be accepted as the word of God which cannot be tested by reason or be capable of being spiritually experienced. . . . Learning . . . lives in the experiences of its saints and seers, in their lives and sayings. When all the most learned commentators of the scriptures are utterly forgotten, the accumulated experience of the sages and saints will abide and be an inspiration for ages to come.

Truth is the exclusive property of no single scripture.

HINDUISM

See also Chapter 12; and the section on "Religious Faith" in Chapter 13.

Hinduism . . . is the most tolerant creed because it is non-proselytizing and it is as capable of expansion today as it has been found to be in the past. It has succeeded, not in driving out (as I think it has been erroneously held), but in absorbing Buddhism. By reason of the *Swadeshi* spirit a Hindu refuses to change his religion, not necessarily because he considers it to be the best, but because he knows that he can complement it by introducing reforms.

Unfortunately, Hinduism seems to consist today merely in eating and not eating. . . . Hinduism is in danger of losing its substance if it resolves itself into a matter of elaborate rules as to what and with whom to eat.

Hinduism is not an exclusive religion. In it, there is room for the worship of all the prophets of the world. It is not a missionary religion in the ordinary sense of the term. ... Hinduism tells everyone to worship God according to his own faith or *dharma*, and so it lives at peace with all religions.

A man may not believe even in God and still call himself a Hindu. Hinduism is a relentless pursuit after Truth and if today it has become moribund, inactive, irresponsive to growth, it is because we are fatigued and as soon as the fatigue is over, Hinduism will burst forth upon the world with a brilliance perhaps unknown before.

Hinduism is like the Ganges, pure and unsullied at its source, but taking in its course the impurities in the way. Even like the Ganges it is beneficent in its total effect. It takes a provincial form in every province, but the inner substance is retained everywhere.

The *Gita* is, in my opinion, a very easy book to understand. ... The general trend of the *Gita* is unmistakable. It is accepted by all Hindu sects as authoritative. It is free from any form of dogma. In a short compass it gives a complete, reasoned, moral code. It satisfies both the intellect and the heart. It is thus both philosophical and devotional. Its appeal is universal. The language is incredibly simple.

Brahmanism that can tolerate untouchability, virgin widowhood, spoliation of virgins, stinks in my nostrils. It is a parody of Brahmanism. There is no knowledge of *Brahman* therein. There is no true interpretation of the scriptures. It is undiluted animalism. Brahmanism is made of sterner stuff.

The *Gita* is the Universal Mother. She turns away nobody. Her door is wide open to anyone who knocks. A true votary of the *Gita* does not know what disappointment is. He ever swells in perennial joy and peace that passeth understanding.

Hinduism is not a religion. . . . It is a way of life. Many who do not practice formal religion are nearer to this way of life than some who do.

CHRISTIANITY

See also the section on "Missionaries" in Chapter 12.

God did not bear the Cross only 1,900 years ago, but He bears it today and He dies and is resurrected from day to day. It would be poor comfort to the world if it had to depend upon a historical God who died 2,000 years ago. Do not then preach the God of history, but show Him as He lives today through you.

I have not been able to see any difference between the Sermon on the Mount and the *Bhagavad Gita*. What the Sermon describes in a graphic manner, the *Bhagavad Gita* reduces to a scientific formula. It may not be a scientific book in the accepted sense of the term, but it has argued out the law of love—the law of abandon as I would call it—in a scientific manner. The Sermon on the Mount gives the same law in a wonderful language. The New Testament gave me comfort and boundless joy, as it came after the repulsion that parts of the Old had given me. Today, supposing I was deprived of the *Gita*, and forgot all its contents but had a copy of the Sermon, I should derive the same joy from it as I do from the *Gita*.

My difficulties [with Christianity] lay deeper. It was more than I could believe that Jesus was the only incarnate son of God, and that only he who believed in him would have everlasting life. If God could have sons, all of us were His sons. If Jesus was like God, or God Himself, then all men were like God and could be God Himself. My reason was not ready to believe literally that Jesus by his death and by his blood redeemed the sins of the world. Metaphorically there might be some truth in it. Again, according to Christianity only human beings had souls, and not other living beings, for whom death meant complete extinction; while I held a contrary belief. I could accept Jesus as a martyr, an embodiment of sacrifice, and a divine teacher, but not as the most perfect man ever born. His death on the Cross was a great example to the world, but that there was anything like a mysterious or miraculous virtue in it my heart could not accept. The pious lives of Christians did not give me anything that the lives of men of other faiths had failed to give. I had seen in other lives just the same reformation that I had heard of among Christians. Philosophically there was nothing extraordinary in Christian principles. From the point of view of sacrifice, it seemed to me that the Hindus greatly surpassed the Christians. It was impossible for me to regard Christianity as a perfect religion or the greatest of all religions.

For many years I have regarded Jesus of Nazareth as one among the mighty teachers that the world has had, and I say this in all humility. I claim humility for this expression because this is exactly what I feel. Of course, Christians claim a higher place for Jesus of Nazareth than I, as a non-Christian and a Hindu, am able to feel. I purposely use the word "feel" instead of "give" because I consider that neither I nor anybody else can possibly arrogate to himself the claim of *giving* a place to a great man. . . . Jesus occupies in my heart the place of one of the great teachers who have made a considerable influence on my life.

Do not confuse Jesus' teaching with what passes as modern civilization.

If Jesus came to earth again, he would disown many things that are being done in the name of Christianity.

He [Jesus] affects my life no less because I regard him as one among many begotten Sons of God. The adjective "begotten" has for me a deeper, possibly a grander meaning than its literal meaning. For me it implies spiritual birth. In his own times he was the nearest to God.

Christianity became disfigured when it went to the West. It became the religion of kings.

2. Theology

GOD

There can be but one universal creed for man, that is loyalty to God. It includes, when it is not inconsistent, loyalty to King, Country, and Humanity. But it, equally often, excludes all else.

God is the greatest Revolutionist the world has ever known or will know. He sends deluges. He sends storms where a moment ago there was calm. He levels down mountains which He builds with exquisite care and infinite patience.

God is that indefinable something which we all feel but which we do not know. To me God is Truth and Love. God is ethics and morality. God is fearlessness, God is the source of light and life and yet He is above and beyond all these. God is conscience. . . . He transcends speech and reason. He is a personal God to those who need His touch. He is the purest essence. He simply Is to those who have faith. He is long suffering. He is patient but He is also terrible. He is the greatest democrat the world knows. He is the greatest tyrant ever known. We are *not*. He alone *Is*.

The contents of the richest word—God—are not the same to every one of us. They will vary with the experience of each.

Mankind is notoriously too dense to read the signs that God sends from time to time. We require drums to be beaten into our ears before we should wake from our trance and hear the warning and see that to lose oneself in all is the only way to find oneself.

I see the same God in the *Bhagavad Gita* as I see in the Bible and the Koran.

God is a very hard taskmaster. He is never satisfied with fireworks display. His mills although they grind surely and incessantly grind excruciatingly slow and He is never satisfied with hasty forfeitures of life. It is a sacrifice of the purest that He demands, and so you and I have prayerfully to plod on, live out the life so long as it is vouchsafed to us to live it.

He who would be friends with God must remain alone, or make the whole world his friend.

The voice of the people is the voice of God.

I have not seen Him, neither have I known Him. I have made the world's faith in God my own, and as my faith is ineffaceable, I regard that faith as amounting to experience. However, as it may be said that to describe faith as experience is to tamper with truth, it may perhaps be more correct to say that I have no word for characterizing my belief in God.

Let no one [say] that God can never be partial, and that He has no time to meddle with the humdrum affairs of men. I have no other language to express the fact of the matter, to describe this uniform experience of mine. Human language can but imperfectly describe God's ways. I am sensible of the fact that they are indescribable and inscrutable. But if mortal man will dare to describe them, he has no better medium than his own inarticulate speech.

There is an indefinable mysterious power that pervades everything. I feel it, though I do not see it. It is this unseen power that makes itself felt and yet defies proof, because it is so unlike all that I perceive through my senses. It transcends reason. But it is possible to reason out the existence of God to a limited extent.

I do dimly perceive that whilst everything around me is ever changing, ever dying, there is underlying all that change a living power that is changeless, that holds all together, that creates, dissolves and recreates. That informing power or spirit is God. And since nothing else I see merely through the senses can or will persist, He alone is. And is this power benevolent or malevolent? I see it as purely benevolent, for I can see that in the midst of death life persists, in the midst of untruth truth persists, in the midst of darkness light persists. Hence I gather that God is Life, Truth, Light. He is Love. He is the supreme Good.

God seems to be as cruel as he is merciful.

We may each of us be putting our own interpretation on the word "God." We must of necessity do so; for God embraces not only this tiny globe of ours, but millions and billions of such globes and worlds beyond worlds. How can we, little crawling creatures, possibly measure His greatness, His boundless love, His infinite compassion? So great is His infinite love and pity that He allows man insolently to deny Him, to wrangle about Him, and even to cut the throat of his fellow-man!

I would say with those who say God is Love, God is Love. But deep down in me I used to say that though God may be Love, God is Truth, above all. . . . I went a step further and said Truth is God. . . . When you want to find Truth as God the only inevitable means is Love, i.e., non-violence, and since I believe that ultimately means and ends are convertible terms, I should not hesitate to say that God is Love.

God keeps an accurate record of all things good and bad. There is no better accountant on earth.

Perfection is the attribute of the Almighty, and yet what a great democrat He is! What an amount of wrong and humbug he suffers on our part! He even suffers insignificant creatures of His to question His very existence, though He is in every atom about us, around us and within us. But He has reserved to Himself the right of becoming manifest to whomsoever He chooses. He is a Being without hands and feet and other organs, yet he can see Him to whom He chooses to reveal Himself.

God is not a Power residing in the clouds. God is an unseen Power residing within us and nearer to us then finger-nails to the flesh.

God may be called by any other name so long as it connotes the living Law of Life.

There is orderliness in the universe; there is an unalterable Law governing everything and every being that exists or lives. It is not a blind law; for no blind law can govern the conduct of living beings. . . . The Law which governs all life is God. Law and the lawgiver are one. I may not deny the Law or the Law-Giver because I know so little about It or Him.

I believe in an inscrutable Providence that presides over our destinies—call it God or by any name you like.

MAN AND HUMAN NATURE

I refuse to suspect human nature. It will, is bound to respond to any noble and friendly action.

No matter how timid a man is, he is capable of the loftiest heroism when he is put to the test.

No human being is so bad as to be beyond redemption, no human being is so perfect as to warrant his destroying him whom he wrongly considers to be wholly evil.

On God's earth nobody is low and nobody is high. We are all His creatures; and just as in the eyes of parents all their children are absolutely equal, so also in God's eyes all His creatures must be equal.

Man will ever remain imperfect, and it will always be his part to try to be perfect. Perfection in love or non-possession will remain an unattainable ideal as long as we are alive, but towards which we must ceaselessly strive.

I positively refuse to judge man from the scanty material furnished to us by history.

I have an undying faith in the responsiveness of human nature.

I have discovered that man is superior to the system he propounds.

Man's upward progress means ever-increasing difficulty which is to be welcomed.

I have been convinced more than ever that human nature is much the same, no matter under what clime it flourishes, and that if you approached people with trust and affection you would have ten-fold trust and thousand-fold affection returned to you.

Mankind would die if there were no exhibition any time and anywhere of the divine in man.

You must not lose faith in humanity. Humanity is an ocean. If a few drops of the ocean are dirty, the ocean does not become dirty.

PRAYER

Virtue lies in being absorbed in one's prayers in the presence of din and noise.

Prayer . . . is a yearning of the heart to be one with the Maker, an invocation for His blessing. It is . . . the attitude that matters, not words uttered or muttered. . . . The utterance of the word *Rama* will instantaneously affect millions of Hindus when the word God, although they may understand the meaning, will leave them untouched. Words, after all, acquire a power by a long usage and sacredness associated with their use.

There can be no fixed rule laid down as to the time . . . devotional acts should take. It depends upon individual temperament. These are precious moments in one's daily life. . . . There are moments when one reviews his immediate past confessing one's weakness, asks for forgiveness and strength to be and do better. One minute may be enough for some, twenty-four hours may be too little for others.

For those who are filled with the presence of God in them, to labor is to pray. Their life is one continuous prayer, or act of worship.

Prayer needs no speech. It is in itself independent of any sensuous effort. I have not the slightest doubt that prayer is an unfailing means of cleansing the heart of passions. But it must be combined with the utmost humility.

God never answers the prayers of the arrogant, nor the prayers of those who bargain with Him.

Prayer is no mere exercise of words or of the ears; it is no mere repetition of empty formula. Any amount of repetition of *Ramanama* is futile, if it fails to stir the soul. . . . Even as a hungry man relishes a hearty meal, a hungry soul will relish a heartfelt prayer. . . . He who has experienced the magic of prayer may do without food for days together, but not a single moment without prayer.

We should be offering our prayers every minute of our lives. There is no doubt about it. But we erring mortals, who find it difficult to retire within ourselves for inward communion even for a single moment, will find it impossible to remain perpetually in communion with the divine. We, therefore, fix some hours when we make a serious effort to throw off the attachments of the world for a while; we make a serious endeavor to remain, so to say, out of the flesh.

Do not worry about the form of prayer. Let it be any form; it should be such as can put us in communion with the Divine. Only, whatever be the form, let not the spirit wander while the words of prayer run on out of your mouth.

But why pray at all? . . . God needs no reminder. He is within everyone. Nothing happens without His permission. Our prayer is a heart search. It is a reminder to ourselves that we are helpless without His support. No effort is complete without prayer—without a definite recognition that the best human endeavor is of no effect if it has not God's blessing behind. Prayer is a call to humility. It is a call to self-purification, to inward search.

My faith is increasing in the efficacy of silent prayer. It is by itself an art—perhaps, the highest art requiring the most refined diligence.

I feel life more in tune with the infinite when I am silent, though I agree that we should always be in tune with it, whether we are silent or speaking, whether we are in the solitude or in a bustling crowd.

Prayer is the key to the morning and the bolt of the evening.

It is better in prayer to have a heart without words, than words without heart.

WORSHIP

I do not disbelieve in idol worship. An idol does not excite any feeling of veneration in me. But I think that idol worship is part of human nature. . . . Images are an aid to worship. No Hindu considers an image to be God. I do not consider idol worship a sin.

A congregational prayer is a mighty thing. What we do not often do alone, we do together. . . . All who flock to churches, temples or mosques are not scoffers or humbugs. They are honest men and women. For them congregational prayer is like a daily bath, a necessity of their existence. These places of worship are not a mere idle superstition to be swept away at the opportunity. They have survived all attacks up to now and are likely to persist to the end of time.

Worshipping God is singing the praise of God. Prayer is a confession of one's own unworthiness and weakness. God has a thousand names, or, rather, He is nameless. We may worship or pray to Him by whichever name we please. Some call Him *Rama*, some Krishna, others call Him God. All worship the same Spirit. But as all foods do not agree with all, so all names do not appeal to all. Each chooses the name according to his own associations; and He being the In-Dweller, the All-Powerful, the Omniscient, knows our innermost feelings and responds to us according to our deserts. Worship and prayer, therefore, are not to be performed with the lips but with the heart. That is why they can be performed equally by the dumb and the stammerer, by the ignorant and the stupid; and the prayers of those whose tongues are nectared, but whose hearts are full of poison, are never heard. He, therefore, who would pray to God must cleanse his heart.

It depends on our mental condition whether we gain something or do not gain something by going to the temples. We have to approach these temples in a humble and penitent mood. They are so many homes of God. Of course God resides in every human form, indeed every particle of His creation, everything that is on this earth. But since we very fallible mortals do not appreciate the fact that God is everywhere we impute special sanctity to temples and think that God resides there.

Idolatry is bad—not so idol worship. An idolator makes a fetish of his idol. An idol worshipper sees God even in a stone and, therefore, takes the help of an idol to establish his union with God. . . . A book, a building, a picture, a carving are, surely, all images in which God does reside, but they are not God. He, who says they are, errs.

Churches, mosques and temples which cover so much hypocrisy and humbug and shut the poorest out of them seem but a mockery of God and His worship when one sees the eternally renewed temple of worship under the vast blue canopy inviting every one of us to real worship, instead of abusing His name by quarreling in the name of religion.

SALVATION

Man alone can worship God with knowledge and understanding. Where devotion to God is void of understanding, there can be no true salvation, and without salvation there can be no true happiness.

God ultimately saves him whose motive is pure.

Of the thing that sustains him through trials, man has no inkling, much less knowledge, at the time. If an unbeliever, he will attribute his safety to chance. If a believer, he will say God saved him. He will conclude, as well he may, that his religious study or spiritual discipline was at the back of the state of grace within him. But in the hour of his deliverance he does not know whether his spiritual discipline or something else saves him. Who that has prided himself on his spiritual strength has not seen it humbled to the dust? A knowledge of religion, as distinguished from experience, seems but chaff in such moments of trial.

I do not seek redemption from the consequences of my sin. I seek to be redeemed from sin itself, or rather from the very thought of sin. Until I have attained that end, I shall be content to be restless.

I know that I have still before me a difficult path to traverse. I must reduce myself to zero. So long as a man does not of his own free will put himself last among his fellow creatures, there is no salvation for him.

If one is to find salvation, he must have as much patience as a man who sits by the seaside and with a straw picks up a single drop of water, transfers it, and thus empties the ocean.

CONFESSION

Confession of error is like a broom that sweeps away dirt and leaves the surface cleaner than before. It is a million times better to *appear* untrue before the world than to *be* untrue to ourselves.

There [is] not . . . a cleansing without a clean confession.

A clean confession, combined with a promise never to commit the sin again, when offered before one who has the right to receive it, is the purest type of repentance.

There is no discredit greater than the refusal to acknowledge errors.

There is no defeat in the confession of one's error. The confession itself is a victory.

DEATH

The brave meet death with a smile on their lips, but they are circumspect all the same. There is no room for foolhardiness.

Death is as necessary for man's growth as life itself.

We are living in the midst of death. What is the value of "working for our own schemes" when they might be reduced to naught in the twinkling of an eye, or when we may equally swiftly and unawares be taken away from them? But we may feel strong as a rock, if we could truthfully say "we work for God and His schemes." Then nothing perishes. All perishing is then only what seems. Death and destruction have *then, but only then*, no reality about them. For death and destruction is then but a change.

Death is no fiend, he is the truest of friends. He delivers us from agony. He helps us against ourselves. He ever gives us new chances, new hopes. He is like sleep a sweet restorer.

We really live through and in our work. We perish through our perishable bodies, if instead of using them as temporary instruments, we identify ourselves with them. . . . Sorrow over separation and death is perhaps the greatest delusion. To realize that it is a delusion is to become free. There is no death, no separation of the substance. And yet the tragedy of it is that though we love friends for the substance we recognize in them, we deplore the destruction of the insubstantial that covers the substance for the time being.

Whom the Gods love die young.

For many years I have accorded intellectual assent to the proposition that death is only a big change in life and nothing more, and should be welcome whenever it arrives. I have deliberately made a supreme attempt to cast out from my heart all fear whatsoever including the fear of death. Still I remember occasions in my life when I have not rejoiced at the thought of approaching death as one might rejoice at the prospect of meeting a long lost friend. Thus man often remains weak notwithstanding all his efforts to be strong.

It is better to leave a body one has outgrown. To wish to see the dearest ones as long as possible in the flesh is a selfish desire and it comes out of weakness or want of faith in the survival of the soul after the dissolution of the body. The form ever changes, ever perishes, the informing spirit neither changes nor perishes. True love consists in transferring itself from the body to the dweller within and then necessarily realizing the oneness of all life inhabiting numberless bodies.

Both birth and death are great mysteries. If death is not a prelude to another life, the intermediate period is a cruel mockery. We must learn the art of never grieving over death, no matter when and to whom it comes. I suppose that we shall do so when we have really learned to be utterly indifferent to our own, and the indifference will come when we are every moment conscious of having done the task to which we are called.

[Death] is such a sweet sleep that the body has not to wake again and the dead load of memory is thrown overboard. So far as I know, happily there is no meeting in the beyond as we have it today. When the isolated drops melt, they share the majesty of the ocean to which they belong. In isolation they die but to meet the ocean again.

IMMORTALITY

Why should we be upset when children or young men or old men die? Not a moment passes when some one is not born or is not dead in this world. We should feel the stupidity of rejoicing in a birth and lamenting a death. Those who believe in the soul—and what Hindu, Mussalman or Parsi is there who does not?—know that the soul never dies. The souls of the living as well as of the dead are all one. The eternal processes of creation and destruction are going on ceaselessly. There is nothing in it for which we might give ourselves up to joy or sorrow. Even if we extend the idea of relationship only to our countrymen and take all the births in the country as taking place in our own family, how many births shall we celebrate? If we weep for all the deaths in our country, the tears in our eyes would never dry. This train of thought should help us to get rid of all fear of death.

Transmigration and rebirth are not mere theories with me, but facts as patent as the daily rise of the sun.

Man hankers also after posthumous fame based on power.

It is nature's kindness that we do not remember past births. Where is the good either of knowing in detail the numberless births we have gone through? Life would be a burden if we carried such a tremendous load of memories. A wise man deliberately forgets many things.

Our existence as embodied beings is purely momentary: what are a hundred years in eternity? But if we shatter the chains of egotism, and melt into the ocean of humanity, we share its dignity. To feel that we are something is to set up a barrier between God and ourselves; to cease feeling that we are something is to become one with God. A drop in the ocean partakes of the greatness of its parent, although it is unconscious of it. But it is dried up as soon as it enters upon an existence independent of the ocean. We do not exaggerate, when we say that life is a mere bubble.

Nothing but fixed faith that death for the good is a translation to a better state, and for the evil a beneficent escape, can reconcile us to the mystery of death.

I have no fear of death. I would regard it with relief and satisfaction. But it is impossible for me to think that that is the end. I have no proof. People have tried to demonstrate that the soul of a dead man finds a new home. I do not think this is capable of proof. But I believe it.

FAITH

One's faith in one's plans and methods is truly tested when the horizon before one is the blackest.

It is poor faith that needs fair weather for standing firm. That alone is true faith that stands the foulest weather.

Learning takes us through many stages in life but it fails us utterly in the hour of danger and temptation. Then faith alone saves.

Someone has to make a beginning with a faith that will not flinch.

Faith only begins where reason stops.

A man cannot borrow faith or courage from others.

The man who has faith in him and the strength which flows from faith does not care if he is looked down upon by others. He relies solely upon his internal strength.

Faith is evidence of things unseen and unseeable.

It is faith that steers us through the stormy seas, faith that moves mountains, and faith that jumps across the ocean. That faith is nothing but a living, wide-awake consciousness of God within. He who has achieved that faith wants nothing.

Those who have faith have all their cares lifted from off their shoulders. You cannot have faith and tension at the same time.

God is the hardest taskmaster I have known on earth, and He tries you through and through. And when you find that your faith is failing or your body is failing you, and you are sinking, He comes to your assistance somehow or other and proves to you that you must not lose your faith and that He is always at your beck and call, but on His terms, not on your terms.

The fullest life is impossible without an immovable belief in a Living Law in obedience to which the whole universe moves. A man without that faith is like a drop thrown out of the ocean bound to perish. Every drop in the ocean shares its majesty and has the honor of giving us the ozone of life.

Faith can only grow from within; it cannot be acquired vicariously. Nothing great in this world was ever accomplished without a living faith.

Meetings and group organizations are all right. They are of some help, but very little. . . . The thing that really matters is an invincible faith that cannot be quenched.

Faith is a function of the heart. It must be enforced by reason. The two are not antagonistic as some think. The more intense one's faith is, the more it whets one's reason. When faith becomes blind it dies.

REASON

Every formula of every religion has in this age of reason to submit to the test of reason and universal assent.

Ultimately one is guided not by the intellect but by the heart. The heart accepts the conclusions for which the intellect subsequently finds the reasoning. Argument follows conviction. Man finds reason in support of whatever he does or wants to do.

Experience has humbled me enough to let me realize the specific limitations of reason. Just as matter misplaced becomes dirt, reason misused becomes lunacy. . . . Rationalists are admirable beings. Rationalism is a hideous monster when it claims for itself omnipotence. Attribution of omnipotence to reason is as bad a piece of idolatry as a worship of stick and stone, believing it to be God.

I plead, not for the suppression of reason, but for a due recognition of that in us which sanctifies reason itself.

Knowledge which stops at the head and does not penetrate into the heart is of but little use in the critical times of living experience.

If you want something really important to be done, you must not merely satisfy reason, you must move the heart also.

To renounce the sovereignty of reason over the blind instincts is to renounce a man's estate. In man, reason quickens and guides the feeling; in brute, the soul lies ever dormant. To awaken the heart is to awaken the dormant soul, to awaken reason, and to inculcate discrimination between good and evil.

There are subjects where reason cannot take us far and we have to accept things on faith. Faith then does not contradict reason but transcends it. Faith is a kind of sixth sense which works in cases which are without the purview of reason.

I cannot grasp the position by the intellect; the heart must be touched. Saul became Paul, not by an intellectual effort, but by something touching his heart.

FREE WILL

He is the greatest tyrant ever known, for He often dashes the cup from our lips and under the cover of free will leaves us a margin so wholly inadequate as to provide only mirth for Himself at our expense.

One's life is not a single straight line; it is a bundle of duties very often conflicting. And one is called upon continually to make one's choice between one duty and another.

Man is higher than the brute in his moral instincts and moral institutions. The law of nature as applied to the one is different from the law of nature as applied to the other. Man has reason, discrimination, and free will such as it is. The brute has no such thing. It is not a free agent, and knows no distinction between virtue and vice, good and evil. Man, being a free agent, knows these distinctions, and when he follows his higher nature shows himself far superior to the brute, but when he follows his baser nature can show himself lower than the brute.

Fatalism has its limits. We leave things to Fate after exhausting all the remedies.

As we know that a man often succumbs to temptation, however much he may resist it, we also know that Providence often intercedes and saves him in spite of himself. How all this happens—how far a man is free and how far a creature of circumstances—how far free will comes into play and where fate enters on the scene—all this is a mystery and will remain a mystery.

I had inured myself to an uncertain life. I think it is wrong to expect certainties in this world, where all else but God that is Truth is an uncertainty. All that appears and happens about and around us is uncertain, transient. But there is a Supreme Being hidden therein as a Certainty, and one would be blessed if one could catch a glimpse of that Certainty and hitch one's wagon to it. The quest for that Truth is the *summum bonum* of life.

Man can change his temperament, can control it, but cannot eradicate it. God has not given him so much liberty. If the leopard can change his spots then only can man modify the peculiarities of his spiritual constitution.

Manliness consists in making circumstances subservient to ourselves.

Accidents will happen in the best of all possible worlds. There is no such thing as accident in God's dictionary. The world is a chapter of accidents. For accidents are events which we cannot control and often can't find causes for even after they have occurred.

We cannot command results, we can only strive.

The free will we enjoy is less than that of a passenger on a crowded deck.

We shall err, and sometimes grievously in our application. But man is a self-governing being, and self-government necessarily includes the power as much to commit errors as to set them right as often as they are made.

Man is the maker of his own destiny in the sense that he has freedom of choice as to the manner in which he uses that freedom. But he is no controller of results. The moment he thinks he is, he comes to grief.

GOOD AND EVIL

In order to overcome evil one must stand wholly outside it, that is, on the firm solid ground of unadulterated good.

Evil in itself is sterile. It is self-destructive; it exists and flourishes through the implication of good that is in it.

Evil does not cease to be such because of lapse of time.

He is the greatest democrat the world knows, for He leaves us unfettered to make our own choice between evil and good.

I cannot account for the existence of evil by any rational method. To want to do so is to be co-equal with God. I am therefore humble enough to recognize evil as such; and I call God long-suffering and patient precisely because He permits evil in the world. I know that He has no evil in Himself; and yet if there is evil He is the author of it and yet untouched by it.

Vice pays a homage to virtue, and sometimes the way it chooses is to expect virtue not to fall from its pedestal, even while vice is rampant round about.

There is an eternal struggle raging in man's breast between the powers of darkness and of light, and he, who has not the sheet-anchor of prayer to rely upon, will be a victim to the powers of darkness.

Man must choose either of the two courses, the upward or the downward; but as he has the brute in him, he will more easily choose the downward course than the upward, especially when the downward course is presented to him in a beautiful garb. Man easily capitulates when sin is presented in the garb of virtue.

Man's estate is one of probation. During that period he is played upon by evil forces, as well as good. He is ever prey to temptations. He has to prove his manliness by resisting and fighting temptations. He is no warrior who fights outside foes of his imagination, and is powerless to lift his little finger against the innumerable foes within, or what is worse, mistakes them for friends.

There is nothing in the world that in human hands does not lend itself to abuse. The human being is a mixture of good and evil, Jekyll and Hyde. But there is the least likelihood of abuse when it is a matter of self-suffering.

In God's world unmixed evil never prospers. God rules even where Satan holds sway because the latter exists only on His sufferance.

It is always possible by correct conduct to lessen an evil and eventually even to bring good out of evil.

3. Personal Ethics

MORALITY

Good travels at a snail's pace. Those who want to do good are not selfish, they are not in a hurry, they know that to impregnate people with good requires a long time.

Immorality is often taught in the name of morality.

Civilization is that mode of conduct which points out to man the path of duty. Performance of duty and observance of morality are convertible terms. To observe morality is to attain mastery over our mind and our passions. So doing, we know ourselves.

There is no such thing as religion overriding morality.

To say what offends another is against ethics and certainly against spirituality if the saying is not required in the interest of truth.

The most practical, the most dignified way of going on in the world is to take people at their word, when you have no positive reason to the contrary.

A negative injunction without a positive obligation is like body without soul, worthy to be consigned to the flames.

Trivialities possess deadly potentialities.

Any tradition, however ancient, if inconsistent with morality, is fit to be banished from the land.

One thing took deep root in me—the conviction that morality is the basis of things, and that truth is the substance of all morality.

It has always been a mystery to me how men can feel themselves honored by the humiliation of their fellow-beings.

Hypocrisy [presses] political theory into service in order to make out a plausible case. . . . The human intellect delights in inventing specious arguments in order to support injustice itself.

The world learns to apply to a man the standards which he applies to himself.

Duty well done undoubtedly carries rights with it, but a man who discharges his obligations with an eye upon privileges generally discharges them indifferently and often fails to attain the rights he might have expected, or when he succeeds in gaining them they turn out to be burdens.

Life is governed by a multitude of forces. It would be smooth sailing if we could determine the course of action only by one general principle, whose application at a given time was too obvious to need even a moment's reflection. But I cannot recall a single act which could be so easily determined.

Satan's snares are most subtly laid, and they are the most tempting, when the dividing line between right and wrong is so thin as to be imperceptible.

There are some who think that morality has nothing to do with politics. We do not concern ourselves with the character of our leaders. The democracies of Europe and America steer clear of any notion of morality having anything to do with politics.

For the morals, ethics and religion are convertible terms. A moral life, without reference to religion, is like a house built upon sand. And religion, divorced from morality, is like "sounding brass, good only for making a noise and breaking heads."

To err, even grievously, is human. But it is human only if there is determination to mend the error and not to repeat it. The error will be forgotten if the promise is fully redeemed.

The motive will determine the quality of the act.

HONESTY

If I believe that honesty is the best policy, surely whilst I so believe, I must be honest in thought, word and deed; otherwise I become an impostor.

Ultimately a deceiver only deceives himself.

Cunning is not only morally wrong but also politically inexpedient, and [I] have always discountenanced its use even from the practical standpoint.

A cause can only lose by exaggeration.

Any departure, conscious or unconscious, from the laws of Nature is a lie. A conscious departure from the known laws is a lie that hurts our moral fibre, not so, or not to the same extent, an unconscious departure.

HUMILITY

I feared humility would cease to be humility the moment it became a matter of vow. The true connotation of humility is self-effacement. Self-effacement is salvation, and whilst it cannot, by itself, be an observance, there may be other observances necessary for its attainment. If the acts of an aspirant after salvation or a servant have no humility or selflessness about them, there is no longing for salvation or service. Service without humility is selfishness and egotism.

It is only when one sees one's own mistakes with a convex lens, and does just the reverse in the case of others, that one is able to arrive at a just relative estimate of the two.

Truth is not to be found by anybody who has not got an abundant sense of humility. If you would swim on the bosom of the ocean of Truth you must reduce yourself to zero.

To cultivate humility is tantamount to cultivating hypocrisy.

A life of service must be one of humility. He, who could sacrifice his life for others, has hardly time to reserve for himself a place in the sun. . . . True humility means most strenuous and constant endeavor entirely directed towards the service of humanity.

SILENCE

Experience has taught me that silence is a part of the spiritual discipline of a votary of truth. Proneness to exaggerate, to suppress or modify truth, wittingly or unwittingly, is a natural weakness of man, and silence is necessary in order to surmount it. A man of few words will rarely be thoughtless in his speech; he will measure every word.

Silence is a great help to a seeker after truth. In the attitude of silence the soul finds the path in a clearer light and what is elusive and deceptive resolves itself into crystal clearness. Our life is a long and arduous quest after Truth, and the soul requires inward restfulness to attain its full height.

I wanted to rest for one day a week. So I instituted the day of silence. Later of course I clothed it with all kinds of virtues and gave it a spiritual cloak. But the motivation was really nothing more than that I wanted to have a day off. . . . Silence is very relaxing. It is not relaxing in itself. But when you can talk and don't, it gives you great relief—and there is time for thought.

FRIENDSHIP

It is the special privilege of a friend to own the other's faults and redeclare his affection in spite of faults.

Real friendship should be used to reach the whole through the fragment.

One earns the right of fiercest criticism when one has convinced one's neighbors of one's affection for them and one's sound judgment and when one is sure of not being in the slightest degree ruffled if one's judgment is not accepted or enforced. In other words, there should be love faculty for clear perception and complete toleration to enable one to criticize.

True friendship is an identity of souls rarely to be found in this world. Only between like natures can friendship be altogether worthy and enduring. Friends react on one another. Hence in friendship there is very little scope for reform.

Even in offering battle to the adversary one does not learn the valuable lessons which come home to oneself while thus dealing with misunderstandings and strivings between friends. There is a sort of intoxication and exultation in fighting the adversary. But misunderstandings and differences between friends are rare phenomena and are therefore all the more painful. Yet it is only on such occasions that one's mettle is put to a real test.

When a slave salutes a master and a friend salutes a friend, the form is the same in either case, but there is a world of difference between the two, which enables the detached observer to recognize the slave and the friend at once.

There should be a definite realization that personal friends and relations are no greater friends than strangers of the human family and birds, beasts and plants. They are all one, and they are all an expression of God if we would but realize the fact. Such definite realization assuages all craving for seeing outside friends when we are inside prison walls.

Friendship cannot be bought by bribery.

A friendship which exacts oneness of opinion and conduct is not worth much. Friends have to tolerate one another's ways of life and thought, even though they may be different, except where the difference is fundamental.

Cooperation that needs consideration is a commercial contract and not friendship.

Adversity is the crucible in which friendship is tested.

FEARLESSNESS

Those who defy death are free from all fear.

If we trust and fear God, we shall have to fear no one, not Maharajahs, not Viceroys, not the detectives, not even King George.

Let us fear God and we shall cease to fear man. If we grasp the fact that there is divinity within us which witnesses everything we think or do and which protects us and guides us along the true path, it is clear that we shall cease to have any other fear on the face of the earth save the fear of God. Loyalty to the Governor of governors supersedes all other loyalty and gives an intelligent basis to the latter.

Fearlessness should never mean want of due respect or regard for the feelings of others.

Fearlessness is the first requisite of spirituality. Cowards can never be moral.

Courteousness must not be mistaken for flattery nor impudence for fearlessness.

A man who fears no one on earth would consider it troublesome even to summon up anger against one who is vainly trying to injure him.

When we fear God, then we shall fear no man, however highly-placed he may be; and if you want to follow the vow of truth, then fearlessness is absolutely necessary.

Passive resistance cannot proceed a step without fearlessness. Those alone can follow the path to the end who are free from fear, whether as to their possessions, their false honor, their relatives, the government, bodily injuries, or death.

Fearlessness connotes freedom from all external fear—fear of disease, bodily injury and death, of dispossession, of losing one's nearest and dearest, of losing reputation or giving offense, and so on.

Fear has no place in our hearts, when we have shaken off the attachment for wealth, for family and for the body. . . . When we cease to be masters, and reduce ourselves to the rank of servants, humbler than the very dust under our feet, all fears will roll away like mists.

DETERMINATION

Strength does not come from physical capacity. It comes from an indomitable will.

The best and the most solid work was done in the wilderness of minority.

Strength in numbers is the delight of the timid. The valiant of spirit glory in fighting alone.

If a single *satyagrahi* holds out to the end, victory is absolutely certain.

In every great cause it is not the number of fighters that counts, but it is the quality of which they are made that becomes the deciding factor. The greatest prophets, Zoroaster, Buddha, Jesus, Mahommed—they all stood alone. . . . But they had living faith in themselves and their God, and believing as they did that God was on their side, they never felt lonely.

Performance of one's duty should be independent of public opinion. . . . One is bound to act according to what appears to oneself to be right, even though it may appear wrong to others. . . . If a man fails to follow the light within for fear of public opinion, or any other similar reason, he would never be able to know right from wrong, and in the end lose all sense of distinction between the two.

The example of a few true men or women if they have fully imbibed the spirit of non-violence is bound to infect the whole mass in the end.

A small body of determined spirits fired by an unquenchable faith in their mission can alter the course of history.

In *satyagraha* it is never the numbers that count; it is always the quality, more so when the forces of violence are uppermost.

RESOLUTION

Interpretation of pledges [resolutions] has been a fruitful source of strife all the world over. No matter how explicit the pledge, people will turn and twist the text to suit their own purposes. . . . Selfishness turns them blind, and by a use of the ambiguous middle they deceive themselves and seek to deceive the world and God. One golden rule is to accept the interpretation honestly put on the pledge by the party administering it. Another is to accept the interpretation of the weaker party, where there are two interpretations possible. Rejection of these two rules gives rise to strife and iniquity, which are rooted in untruthfulness. He who seeks truth alone easily follows the golden rule. He need not seek learned advice for interpretation.

A vow, far from closing the door to real freedom, opens it. I had not met with success because the will had been lacking, because I had had no faith in myself, no faith in the grace of God, and therefore, my mind had been tossed on the boisterous sea of doubt. I realized that in refusing to take a vow man was drawn into temptation. . . . Where therefore the desire is gone, a vow of renunciation is the natural and inevitable fruit.

The ideal of truth requires that vows taken should be fulfilled in the spirit as well as in the letter.

Failure to observe resolutions on the part of persons agreeing thereto are ordinary experiences of public life all the world over. But no one ever imports the name of God into such resolutions. In the abstract there should not be any distinction between a resolution and an oath taken in the name of God. When an intelligent man makes a resolution deliberately he never swerves from it by a hair's breadth. With him his resolution carries as much weight as a declaration made with God as witness does. But the world takes no note of abstract principles and imagines an ordinary resolution and an oath in the name of God to be as poles asunder. A man who makes an ordinary resolution is not ashamed of himself when he deviates from it, but a man who violates an oath administered to him is not only ashamed of himself, but is also looked upon by society as a sinner.

Pledges and vows are, and should be, taken on rare occasions. A man who takes a vow every now and then is sure to stumble.

The taking of a vow does not mean that we are able to observe it completely from the very beginning; it does mean constant and honest effort in thought, word and deed with a view to its fulfillment. We must not practice self-deception by resorting to some make-believe.

A life without vows is like a ship without an anchor or like an edifice that is built on sand instead of a solid rock. A vow imparts stability, ballast and firmness to one's character.

One never can achieve anything lasting in this world by being irresolute.

Moderation and sobriety are of the very essence of vow-taking. The taking of vows that are not feasible or that are beyond one's capacity would betray thoughtlessness and want of balance. Similarly a vow can be made conditional without losing any of its efficacy or virtue.

A vow can never be used to support or justify an immoral action. A vow must lead one upwards, never downwards toward perdition.

RESTRAINT

He who has conquered his senses has really conquered the whole world, and he becomes a part of God.

Restraint is the law of our being. For highest perfection is unattainable without highest restraint.

Morally I have no doubt that all self-denial is good for the soul.

Identification with everything that lives is impossible without self-purification; without self-purification the observance of the law of *ahimsa* must remain an empty dream; God can never be realized by one who is not pure of heart. Self-purification, therefore, must mean purification in all walks of life. And purification being highly infectious, purification of oneself necessarily leads to the purification of one's surroundings. But the path of self-purification is hard and steep. To attain to perfect purity one has to become absolutely passion-free in thought, speech, and action; to rise above the opposing currents of love and hatred, attachment and repulsion. I know that I have not in me as yet that triple purity in spite of constant ceaseless striving for it.

To conquer the subtle passions seems to me to be harder far than the physical conquest of the world by the force of arms.

Never go beyond your capacity. That too is a breach of truth.

It is discipline and restraint that separate us from the brute. If we will be men walking with our heads erect, and not walking on all fours, let us understand and put ourselves under voluntary discipline and restraint.

SIMPLICITY

India's salvation consists in unlearning what she has learned during the past fifty years. . . . The so-called upper classes have to learn consciously, religiously, and deliberately the simple peasant life, knowing it to be a life giving true happiness.

I preach against the modern artificial life of sensual enjoyment, and ask men and women to go back to the simple life. . . . Without an intelligent return to simplicity, there is no escape from our descent to a state lower than brutality.

Europeans themselves will have to remodel their outlook, if they are not to perish under the weight of the comforts to which they are becoming slaves.

In this country of semi-starvation of millions and insufficient nutrition of practically eighty per cent of the people, the wearing of jewellery is an offence to the eye. . . . The wearing of expensive jewellery is a distinct loss to the country. It is so much capital locked up or, worse still, allowed to wear away.

A certain degree of physical harmony and comfort is necessary, but above that level, it becomes a hindrance instead of help. The ideal of creating an unlimited number of wants and satisfying them seems to be delusion and a snare.

Speed is not the end of life. Man sees more and lives more truly by walking to his duty.

There is no question of loin-cloth civilization. The adoption of the loin-cloth was for me a necessity. But in so far as the loin-cloth also spells simplicity let it represent Indian civilization.

HEALTH

It is far easier and safer to prevent illness by the observance of the laws of health than to set about curing the illness which has been brought on by our own ignorance and carelessness.

Illness is the result not only of our actions but also of our thoughts.

There is nothing so closely connected with us as our body, but there is also nothing perhaps of which our ignorance is so profound, or our indifference so complete.

[It is a] fatal delusion that no disease can be cured without medicine.

When once a bottle of medicine gets itself introduced into a home, it never thinks of going out, but only goes on drawing other bottles in its train.

Disease increases in proportion to the increase in the number of doctors in a place.

The relation between the body and the mind is so intimate that, if either of them got out of order, the whole system would suffer. Hence it follows that a pure character is the foundation of health in the real sense of the term; and . . . all evil thoughts and evil passions are but different forms of disease.

Our aim should be to attain the maximum of health by all legitimate means; we should not be content merely to live anyhow.

Our passion for exercise should become so strong that we could not bring ourselves to dispense with it on any account. We hardly realize how weak and futile is our mental work when unaccompanied by hard physical exercise.

Our body has been given to us on the understanding that we should render devoted service to God with its aid. It is our duty to keep it pure and unstained from within as well as from without, so as to render it back to the Giver, when the time comes for it, in the state of purity in which we got it. If we fulfill the terms of the contract to God's satisfaction, He will surely reward us, and make us heirs to immortality.

If we knew all the laws of nature or having known, had the power to obey them in thought, word and deed, we would be God Himself and not need to do anything at all. As it is, we hardly know the laws and have little power to obey them. Hence disease and all its effects. It is, therefore, enough for us to realize that every illness is but a breach of some unknown law of nature and to strive to know the laws and pray for power to obey. Heart prayer, therefore, whilst we are ill, is both work and medicine.

Cigars and cigarettes, whether foreign or indigenous, must be avoided. Cigarette smoking is like an opiate, and the cigars that you smoke have a touch of opium about them. They get to your nerves and you cannot leave them afterwards. How can a single [person] foul his mouth by converting it into a chimney?

If it is necessary to take coffee or tea to keep awake, let them not drink coffee or tea but go to sleep. We must not become slaves to these things. But the majority of the people, who drink coffee or tea, are slaves to them.

No matter what amount of work one has, one should always find some time for exercise, just as one does for one's meals. It is my humble opinion that, far from taking away from one's capacity for work, it adds to it.

In trying to cure one old disease, we give rise to a hundred new ones; in trying to enjoy the pleasures of sense, we lose in the end even our capacity for enjoyment.

DIET

Abstemiousness from intoxicating drinks and drugs and from all kinds of foods, especially meat, is undoubtedly a great aid to the evolution of the spirit, but it is by no means an end in itself. Many a man eating meat and dining with everybody, but living in the fear of God, is nearer his freedom than a man religiously abstaining from meat and many other things but blaspheming God in every one of his acts.

It is impossible to lay down hard and fast, rules in the matter of food. . . . Although, however, it is impossible to say conclusively what sort of food we should eat, it is the clear duty of every individual to bestow serious thought on the matter.

Man is not born to eat, nor should he live to eat. His true function is to know and serve his Maker; but, since the body is essential to this service, we have perforce to eat.

A calm reflection will show that all sins like lying, cheating and stealing are ultimately due to our subjection to the palate. He who is able to control the palate will easily be able to control the other senses.

If we enquire minutely into the methods of preparation of all our articles of food, we shall have to give up 90 per cent of them!

There is no fear at all of men ruining their health by eating too little; the great need is for a reduction in the quantity of food that we generally take.

True happiness is impossible without true health, and true health is impossible without a rigid control of the palate.

To sum up all religion in terms of diet, as is often done in India, is as wrong as it is to disregard all restraint in regard to diet and to give full rein to one's appetite.

Many ... experiments taught me that the real seat of taste was not the tongue but the mind.

It is part of my religious conviction that man may not eat meat, eggs, and the like. There should be a limit even to the means of keeping ourselves alive. Even for life itself we may not do certain things.

It is not what you put inside from without, but what you express outwardly from within, that matters. ... For the seeker who would live in fear of God and who would see Him face to face, restraint in diet both as to quantity and quality is as essential as restraint in thought and speech.

All food should be taken as medicine. ... Medicine need not be nasty to taste; nor is it taken for the pleasure of the palate. Food should be treated exactly in the same manner, i.e., suitable food, in suitable proportion, in suitable manner and at suitable times.

A "full" meal is ... a crime against God and man—the latter because the full-mealers deprive their neighbors of their portion. God's economy provides from day to day just enough food for all in just medicinal doses. We are all of the tribe of full-mealers. Instinctively to know the medicinal dose required is a Herculean task, for by parental training we are gluttons. Then, when it is almost too late, it dawns upon some of us that food is made not to enjoy but to sustain the body as our slave. It becomes from that moment a grim fight against inherited and acquired habit of eating for pleasure. Hence the necessity for a complete fast at intervals and partial fasts forever.

More people are weak through overfeeding or wrong feeding than through underfeeding. It is wonderful, if we chose the right diet, what extraordinary small quantity would suffice.

I do not regard flesh-food as necessary for us at any stage and under any clime in which it is possible for human beings ordinarily to live. I hold flesh-food to be unsuited to our species. We err in copying the lower animal world, if we are superior to it. For one thing the tremendous vested interests that have grown round the belief in animal food prevent the medical profession from approaching the question with complete detachment.

The choice of one's diet is not a thing to be based on faith. It is a matter for every one to reason out for himself.

There is a great deal of truth in the saying that man becomes what he eats. The grosser the food the grosser the body.

FASTING

The mental attitude is everything. Just as prayer may be merely a mechanical intonation as of a bird, so may a fast be a mere mechanical torture of the flesh. Neither will touch the soul within.

For me there is nothing so cleansing as a fast. A fast undertaken for fuller self-expression, for attainment of the spirit's supremacy over the flesh, is a most powerful factor in one's evolution.

The public will have to neglect my fasts and cease to worry about them. They are a part of my being. I can as well do without my eyes, for instance, as I can without fasts. What the eyes are for outer world, fasts are for the inner. And much as I should like the latest fast to be the very last in my life, something within me tells me that I might have to go through many such ordeals and, who knows, much more trying.

Fasting of the body has to be accompanied by fasting of *all* the senses.

Under certain circumstances [fasting] is the one weapon which God has given us for use in times of utter helplessness. We do not know its use or fancy that it begins and ends with mere deprivation of physical food. It is nothing of the kind. Absence of food is an indispensable but not the largest part of it. The largest part is the prayer—communion with God. It more than adequately replaces physical food.

Fasting is not for everyone and for every occasion. Fasting without faith may even lead to disastrous consequences. All such spiritual weapons are dangerous when handled by unqualified persons.

EXPERIMENTATION

Evolution is always experimental. All progress is gained through mistakes and their rectification. No good comes fully fashioned, out of God's hand, but has to be carved out through repeated experiments and repeated failures by ourselves. This is the law of individual growth. The same law controls social and political evolution also. The right to err, which means the freedom to try experiments, is the universal condition of all progress.

If we may make new discoveries and inventions in the phenomenal world, must we declare our bankruptcy in the spiritual domain?

He who would go in for novel experiments must begin with himself. That leads to a quicker discovery of truth, and God always protects the honest experimenter.

Whether I will or not, I must involve in my own experiment the whole of my kind. Nor can I do without experiment. Life is but an endless series of experiments.

We have had saints who have worn out their bodies, and laid down their lives in order to explore the secrets of the soul.

As I have all along believed that what is possible for one is possible for all, my experiments have not been conducted in the closet, but in the open.

CONTINENCE (*BRAHMACHARYA*)

Chastity is one of the greatest disciplines without which the mind cannot attain requisite firmness. A man who is unchaste loses stamina, becomes emasculated and cowardly.

Continence . . . is an ideal state which is rarely realized. It is almost like Euclid's line which exists only in imagination, never capable of being physically drawn. It is nevertheless an important definition in geometry yielding great result. So may a perfect celibate exist only in imagination. But if we did not keep him constantly before our mind's eye, we should be like a rudderless ship. The nearer the approach to the imaginary state, the greater the perfection.

Incontinence is the root-cause of all the vanity, anger, fear and jealousy in the world.

Realization of God is impossible without complete renunciation of the sexual desire.

When your heart is not pure, and you cannot master your passions, you cease to be an educated man.

In *brahmacharya* lies the protection of the body, the mind and the soul. For *brahmacharya* was now no process of hard penance, it was a matter of consolation and joy. Every day revealed a fresh beauty in it. But if it was a matter of ever-increasing joy, let no one believe that it was an easy thing for me. . . . It is like walking on the sword's edge, and I see every moment the necessity for eternal vigilance.

A mind consciously unclean cannot be cleansed by fasting. Modifications in diet have no effect on it. The concupiscence of the mind cannot be rooted out except by intense self-examination, surrender to God and, lastly, grace. There is an intimate connection between the mind and the body, and the carnal mind always lusts for delicacies and luxuries. . . . For those whose minds are working towards self-restraint, dietetic restrictions and fasting are very helpful. In fact, without their help, concupiscence cannot be completely rooted out of the mind.

The aim of human life is deliverance . . . freedom from birth, by breaking the bonds of the flesh, by becoming one with God. Now marriage is a hindrance in the attainment of this supreme object, inasmuch as it only tightens the bonds of flesh. Celibacy is a great help, inasmuch as it enables one to lead a life of full surrender to God.

Protestantism did many good things; but one of its few evils was that it ridiculed celibacy.

It is celibacy that has kept Catholicism green up to the present day.

How to use the organs of generation? By transmitting the most creative energy that we possess from creating counterparts of our flesh into creating constructive work for the whole of life, i.e., for the soul. We have to rein in the animal passion and change it into celestial passion.

Observance of the law of continence is impossible without a living faith in God, which is living Truth.

*B*rahmacharya [means] that conduct which puts one in touch with God. The conduct consists in the fullest control over all the senses. . . . Popularly it has come to mean mere physical control over the organ of generation. . . . Control over the organ of generation is impossible without proper control over all the senses. They are all interdependent. . . . Without control over the mind mere physical control, even if it can be attained for a time, is of little or no use.

We cannot properly control or conquer the sexual passion by turning a blind eye to it. I am, therefore, strongly in favor of teaching young boys and girls the significance and right use of their generative organs. . . . Sex education. . . . must have for its object the conquest and sublimation of the sex passion.

4. Social Ethics

LOVE

Love never claims, it ever gives. Love ever suffers, never resents, never revenges itself.

Love is the strongest force the world possesses and yet it is the humblest imaginable.

If we have no love for our neighbors, no change, however revolutionary, can do us any good.

I know that nothing is impossible for pure love.

Where love is, there God is also.

A love that is based on the goodness of those you love is a mercenary affair; whereas, true love is self-effacing and demands no consideration.

Blind surrender to love is often more mischievous than a forced surrender to the lash of the tyrant.

The sword of the *satyagrahi* is love and the unshakable firmness that comes from it.

TRUTH

There is not truth in a man who cannot control his tongue.

Truth is by nature self-evident. As soon as you remove the cobwebs of ignorance that surround it, it shines clear.

Truth is the sovereign principle which includes numerous other principles. This truth is not only truthfulness in word, but truthfulness in thought also, and not only the relative truth of our conception, but the Absolute Truth, the Eternal Principle, that is God.

The instruments for the quest of truth are as simple as they are difficult. They may appear quite impossible to an arrogant person, and quite possible to an innocent child. The seeker after truth should be humbler than the dust.

Truth is like a vast tree, which yields more and more fruit, the more you nurture it. The deeper the search in the mine of truth, the richer the discovery of the gems buried there, in the shape of openings for an ever greater variety of service.

A devotee of Truth may not do anything in deference to convention. He must always hold himself open to correction, and whenever he discovers himself to be wrong he must confess it at all costs and atone for it.

My uniform experience has convinced me that there is no other God than Truth. . . . The only means for the realization of Truth is *ahimsa*. . . . However sincere my strivings after *ahimsa* may have been, they have still been imperfect and inadequate. The little fleeting glimpses, therefore, that I have been able to have of Truth can hardly convey an idea of the indescribable lustre of Truth, a million times more intense than that of the sun we daily see with our eyes. In fact what I have caught is only the faintest glimmer of that mighty effulgence. . . . I can say with assurance, as a result of all my experiments, that a perfect vision of Truth can only follow a complete realization of *ahimsa*. To see the universal and all-pervading Spirit of Truth face to face one must be able to love the meanest of creation as oneself.

Truth ... is what the voice within tells you. ....
What may be truth for one may be untruth for another.

Devotion to. ... Truth is the sole justification
for our existence.

Truth is not truth merely because it is ancient.
Nor is it necessarily to be regarded with suspicion because it is
ancient.

In violence truth is the greatest sufferer; in non-
violence, truth is ever triumphant.

When it is relevant, truth has to be uttered,
however unpleasant it may be.

JUSTICE

We who seek justice will have to do justice to
others.

Justice that love gives is a surrender, justice that
law gives is a punishment. What a lover gives transcends justice.
And yet it is always less than he wishes to give because he is
anxious to give more and frets that he has nothing left.

We win justice quickest by rendering justice to
the other party.

No tyrant has yet lived who has not paid for the
suffering he has caused. No lover has ever given pain without
being more pained.

Justice without generosity may easily become
Shylock's justice.

Even [the bully] is entitled to justice, for immediately you brush aside the bully and be unjust to him, you justify his bullying.

Even as justice to be justice has to be generous, generosity in order to justify itself has got to be strictly just.

REVERENCE FOR LIFE

Complete non-violence is complete absence of ill-will against all that lives. It therefore embraces even sub-human life, not excluding noxious insects or beasts. They have not been created to feed our destructive propensities. If we only knew the mind of the Creator, we should find their proper place in His creation. Non-violence is therefore in its active form good-will towards all life.

The central fact of Hinduism is cow protection. Cow protection, to me, is one of the most wonderful phenomena in human evolution. It takes the human being beyond his species. The cow, to me, means the entire subhuman world. . . . The cow is a poem on pity. One reads pity in the gentle animal. She is the mother to millions of Indian mankind. Protection of the cow means protection of the whole creation of God.

It is a primary duty to go about without hurting even an ant. A man who proudly struts about regardless of the numerous insects and living things that he treads upon deliberately commits sin and chooses the pathway to perdition. He cannot at all be placed side by side with the comparatively innocent agriculturist.

Spiritual progress does demand at some stage that we should cease to kill our fellow creatures for the satisfaction of our bodily wants.

To my mind the life of a lamb is no less precious than that of a human being. I should be unwilling to take the life of a lamb for the sake of the human body. I hold that, the more helpless a creature, the more entitled it is to protection by man from the cruelty of man.

By unnecessarily exercising ourselves over conundrums about the justifiability of man's killing creatures and animals of a lower order, we often seem to forget our primary duties. Everyone of us is not faced every day with the question of killing obnoxious animals. Most of us have not developed courage and love enough to practice *ahimsa* with regard to dangerous reptiles. We do not destroy the vipers of ill-will and anger in our own bosom, but we dare to raise futile discussions about the propriety of killing obnoxious creatures, and we thus move in a vicious circle. We fail in the primary duty and lay the unction to our souls that we are refraining from killing obnoxious life. One who desires to practice *ahimsa* must, for the time being, forget all about snakes, etc. Let him not worry if he cannot avoid killing them, but try for all he is worth to overcome the anger and ill-will of men by his patient endeavor as a first step toward cultivating universal love.

I know how in the name of truth and science inhuman cruelties are perpetrated on animals when men perform vivisection.

We have here [in Yervada prison] learned to recognize friends among animals. We have a cat who is a revelation. And if we had vision enough, we should appreciate the language of trees and plants and value their friendship.

NON-POSSESSION AND POVERTY

See also the section on "Simplicity" in Chapter 3.

Happiness is largely a mental condition. A man is not necessarily happy because he is rich, or unhappy because he is poor. The rich are often seen to be unhappy, the poor to be happy.

We are thieves in a way. If I take anything that I do not need for my own immediate use, and keep it, I thieve it from somebody else. It is the fundamental law of Nature, without exception, that Nature produces enough for our wants from day to day, and if only everybody took enough for himself and nothing more, there would be no pauperism in this world, there would be no man dying from starvation in this world. . . . I do not want to dispossess anybody. . . . If somebody else possesses more than I do, let him. But as far as my own life has to be regulated, I do say that I dare not possess anything which I do not want. . . . You and I have no right to anything that we really have until [the] millions are clothed and fed better. You and I, who ought to know better, must adjust our wants, and even undergo voluntary starvation in order that they may be nursed, fed and clothed.

The greater the possession of riches, the greater . . . the [moral] turpitude.

The golden rule . . . is resolutely to refuse to have what the millions cannot. . . . The first thing is to cultivate the mental attitude that we will not have possessions or facilities denied to millions, and the next immediate thing is to rearrange our lives as fast as possible in accordance with that mentality.

I had long learned the principle of never having more money at one's disposal than necessary.

I understood the *Gita* teaching of non-possession to mean that those who desired salvation should act like the trustee who, though having control over great possessions, regards not an iota of them as his own. It became clear to me as daylight that non-possession and equability presupposed a change of heart, a change of attitude.

Increase of material comforts, it may be generally laid down, does not in any way whatsoever conduce to moral growth.

The richest gifts must be destroyed without compensation and hesitation if they hinder one's moral progress.

[To the custom's inspector in Marseilles:] I am a poor mendicant. All of my earthly possessions consist of these spinning wheels, some dishes, a can of goat's milk, six homespun loincloths, a towel and my reputation, which can't be worth much.

It is possible to conceive a person not being poor in spirit though he may have nothing, because he is jealous of those who possess. He has nothing, but feels the deprivation. Another may have by him a golden footstool which he is seen using in order to save his feet from treading on hot ashes, but which he converts into cash for the poor the very next moment and feels the delight of dispossession.

Perfect fulfillment of the ideal of non-possession requires that man should, like the birds, have no roof over his head, no clothing and no stock of food for the morrow.

Non-possession is a principle applicable to thoughts as well as to things. One, who fills his brain with useless knowledge, violates that inestimable principle. Thoughts, which turn us away from God, or do not turn us towards Him, constitute impediments in our way.

The use of [soul-] force requires the adoption of poverty, in the sense that we must be indifferent whether we have the wherewithal to feed or clothe ourselves.

It is more blessed to be poor than to be rich. The uses of poverty are far sweeter than those of riches.

BODY LABOR

Monotony is the law of nature. Look at the monotonous manner in which the sun rises. And imagine the catastrophe that would befall the universe if the sun became capricious and went in for a variety of pastime. But there is a monotony that sustains and a monotony that kills. The monotony of necessary occupation is exhilarating and life-giving.

I can only think of spinning as the fittest and most acceptable body labor. I cannot imagine anything nobler . . . than for one hour in the day we should all do the labor that the poor must do, and thus identify ourselves with them and through them with all mankind. I cannot imagine better worship of God than that in His name I should labor for the poor even as they do. The spinning wheel spells a more equitable distribution of the riches of the earth.

Ruskin's *Unto This Last* . . . was impossible to lay aside, once I had begun it. It gripped me. . . . I determined to change my life in accordance with the ideals of the book. . . . [It] brought about an instantaneous and practical transformation in my life. . . . The teachings of *Unto This Last* I understood to be: 1. That the good of the individual is contained in the good of all; 2. That a lawyer's work has the same value as the barber's, inasmuch as all have the same right of earning their livelihood from their work; 3. That a life of labor, i.e., the life of the tiller of the soil and the handicraftsman, is the life worth living. . . . I arose with the dawn, ready to reduce these principles to practice.

It is only when a man or woman has done body labor for the sake of service that he or she has a right to live.

The divine law [is] that man must earn his bread by laboring with his own hands. . . . How can a man, who does not do body labor, have the right to eat? . . . if every one, whether rich or poor, has to take exercise in some shape or form, why should it not assume the form of productive, i.e., bread labor? . . . more than nine-tenths of humanity lives by tilling the soil. How much happier, healthier and more peaceful would the world become, if the remaining tenth followed the example of the overwhelming majority, at least to the extent of laboring enough for their food! Invidious distinctions of rank would be abolished, when every one without exception acknowledged the obligation of bread labor. . . . Bread labor is a veritable blessing to one who would observe non-violence, worship Truth, and make the observance of *brahmacharya* a natural act. . . . A person can therefore spin or weave, or take up carpentry or smithery, instead of tilling the soil, always regarding agriculture however to be the ideal. Every one must be his own scavenger. . . . We are all scavengers. . . . Every one who has realized this [should] commence bread labor as a scavenger. Scavenging, thus intellectually taken up, will help one to a true appreciation of the equality of man.

If all labored for their bread and no more, then there would be enough food and enough leisure for all. Then there would be no cry of overpopulation, no disease and no such misery as we see around. Such labor will be the highest form of sacrifice. Men will no doubt do many other things either through their bodies or through their minds, but all this will be labor of love for the common good. There will then be no rich and no poor, none high and none low, no touchable and no untouchable. This may be an unattainable ideal. But we need not, therefore, cease to strive for it. . . . We should eat to live, not live to eat. . . . May not men earn their bread by intellectual labor? No. The needs of the body must be supplied by the body.

5. Service

REFORM

Discontent is a very useful thing. As long as a man is contented with his present lot, so long is it difficult to persuade him to come out of it. Therefore it is that every reform must be preceded by discontent.

It is simple impertinence for any man, or any body of men, to begin, or to contemplate, reform of the whole world.

A movement lacks sincerity when it is supported by unwilling workers under pressure.

Power that comes from service faithfully rendered ennobles. Power that is sought in the name of service and can only be obtained by a majority of votes is a delusion and a snare to be avoided.

It is not legislation that will cure a popular evil; it is enlightened public opinion that can do it. I am not opposed to legislation in such matters, but I do lay greater stress on cultivation of public opinion.

To give a little bit of money is easy enough, to do a little thing one's self is more difficult.

I could not so easily count on the help of the community in getting it to do its own duty as I could in claiming for it rights.

I have always been loath to hide or connive at the weak points of the community or to press for its rights without having purged it of its blemishes.

Even where the end might be political, but where the cause was non-political, one damaged it by giving it a political aspect and helped it by keeping it within its non-political limit.

I have noticed this characteristic difference in the popular attitude—partiality for exciting work, dislike for quiet constructive work. The difference has persisted to this day.

A chronic and long standing social evil cannot be swept away at a stroke; it always requires patience and perseverance.

Put your talents in the service of the country instead of converting them into pounds, shillings, and pence.

Service, which has not the slightest touch of self in it, is itself the highest religion.

We won't find the remedy for human ills by losing patience and by rejecting everything that is old because it is old. Our ancestors also dreamed, perhaps vaguely, the same dreams that fire us with zeal.

Man's ultimate aim is the realization of God, and all his activities, social, political, religious, have to be guided by the ultimate aim of the vision of God. The immediate service of all human beings becomes a necessary part of the endeavor, simply because the only way to find God is to see Him in His creation and be one with it. This can be done by service to all. . . . I cannot find Him apart from the rest of humanity.

Reform cannot be rushed; if it is to be brought about by non-violent means, it can only be done by education both of the haves and have-nots.

All reforms owe their origin to the initiation of minorities in opposition to majorities.

No cause that is intrinsically just can ever be described as forlorn.

LEADERSHIP

Those who want to do good are not selfish, they are not in a hurry, they know that to impregnate people with good requires a long time. But evil has wings.

Courage, endurance, fearlessness and above all self-sacrifice are the qualities of our leaders.

A reformer's business is to make the impossible possible by giving an ocular demonstration of the possibility in his own conduct.

I am used to misrepresentation all my life. It is the lot of every public worker. He has to have a tough hide. . . . It is a rule of life with me never to explain misrepresentations except when the cause required correction.

More is always expected from those who give much.

Service can have no meaning unless one takes pleasure in it. When it is done for show or for fear of public opinion, it stunts the man and crushes his spirit. Service which is rendered without joy helps neither the servant nor the served. But all other pleasures and possessions pale into nothingness before service which is rendered in a spirit of joy.

Without infinite patience it was impossible to get the people to do any work. It is the reformer who is anxious for the reform, and not society, from which he should expect nothing better than opposition, abhorrence and even mortal persecution. Why may not society regard as retrogression what the reformer holds dear as life itself?

A public worker should accept no costly gifts.

Even a man's reforming zeal ought not to make him exceed his limits.

A public worker should not make statements of which he has not made sure. Above all, a votary of truth must exercise the greatest caution. To allow a man to believe a thing which one has not fully verified is to compromise truth.

[In] service of the community . . . winning the confidence of the people was an indispensable condition.

An aspirant after a life exclusively devoted to service must lead a life of celibacy [and] accept poverty as a constant companion through life.

It is always difficult for followers to sustain a conflict in the absence of their leader, and the shock is all the greater when the leader has disgraced himself.

It is in the interest of reform for reformers to avoid hysterics and exaggerations.

The reformer's path is strewn not with roses, but with thorns, and he has to walk warily. He can but limp, dare not jump.

I regard it as self-delusion if not worse, when a person says he is wearing himself away in service. Is such service preferred by God to service steadily and detachedly performed? [The] body is like a machine requiring to be well kept for full service.

It is the duty of him who claims to serve humanity not to be angry with those whom he is serving.

One, who has consecrated his life to service, cannot lie idle for a single moment. But one has to learn to distinguish between good activity and evil activity.

No matter how insignificant the thing you have to do, do it as well as you can, give it as much of your care and attention as you would give to the thing you regard as most important. For it will be by those small things that you shall be judged.

No reform has ever been brought about except through intrepid individuals breaking down inhuman customs or usages.

A voice in the wilderness has a potency which voices uttered in the midst of "the madding crowd" lack. For, the voice in the wilderness has meditation, deliberation, and unquenchable faith behind it, whilst the babel of voices has generally nothing, but the backing of the experience of personal enjoyment.

In every branch of reform, constant study giving one a mastery over one's subject is necessary. Ignorance is at the root of failures, partial or complete, of all reform movements whose merits are admitted. For every project masquerading under the name of reform is not necessarily worthy of being so designated.

There is no one without faults, not even men of God. They are men of God not because they are faultless but because they know their own faults, they strive against them, they do not hide them and are ever ready to correct themselves.

Where is the reformer who has not a price put upon his head?

IDENTIFICATION WITH POOR

We should be ashamed of resting or having a square meal so long as there is one able-bodied man or woman without work or food.

Whenever I see an erring man, I say to myself: "I have also erred;" when I see a lustful man, I say to myself: "So was I once;" and in this way I feel kinship with everyone in the world and feel that I cannot be happy without the humblest of us being happy.

Service of the poor has been my heart's desire, and it has always thrown me amongst the poor and enabled me to identify myself with them.

Educated men should make a point of travelling third class and reforming the habits of the people, as also of never letting the railway authorities rest in peace, sending in complaints wherever necessary, never resorting to bribes or any unlawful means for obtaining their own comforts, and never putting up with infringements of rules on the part of anyone concerned. . . . My serious illness in 1918–19 unfortunately compelled me practically to give up third class travelling, and it has been a matter of constant pain and shame to me.

I had altered my style of dress so as to make it more in keeping with that of the indentured laborers.

If I am to identify myself with the grief of the least in India, aye, if I have the power, the least in the world, let me identify myself with the sins of the little ones who are under my care.

ORGANIZATIONAL WORK

I myself have been "fed up" with speeches and lectures. . . . We have now reached almost the end of our resources in speech making, and it is not enough, that our ears have feasted, that our eyes are feasted, but it is necessary that our hearts have got to be touched and that our hands and feet have got to be moved. . . . If we are to retain our hold upon the simplicity of Indian character . . . our hands and feet should move in unison with our heart.

Every good movement passes through five stages: indifference, ridicule, abuse, repression, and respect.

I share to the fullest extent Panditji's [Nehru's father's] horror of conferences. Not that they are always useless. They were absolutely necessary at a certain stage in our career. But they have in their present form almost outgrown their usefulness. Even when they do no other harm, they mean waste of money and time. The public spirit awakened by them needs to be consolidated into efficient work which can best be done by small committees. These latter to be useful must be harmonious and ever responsive to and by their solidly active work in touch with the general public. Abandonment of conferences should never be due to public apathy, but it should be because the public is more usefully engaged.

In England and other Western countries there is one, in my view, barbarous custom of inaugurating movements at dinners.

The greater the organization, the less felt is the effect of corruption, because it is so widely distributed.

I have my own organization, myself. I am a man possessed by an idea. If such a man cannot get an organization, he becomes an organization.

ORGANIZATIONAL FINANCING

I have learned to be shameless in emptying the pockets of the poor for the benefit of those who are poorer than they.

Though I have had to handle public funds amounting to *lakhs*, I have succeeded in exercising strict economy in their disbursement, and instead of outstanding debts have had invariably a surplus balance in respect to all the movements I have led.

I had learned at the onset not to carry on public work with borrowed money. One could rely on people's promises in most matters except in respect to money.

Economy is essential for every organization, and yet I know that it is not always exercised. . . . Carefully kept accounts are a *sine qua non* for any organization. Without them it falls into disrepute. Without properly kept accounts it is impossible to maintain truth in its pristine purity.

It is not good to run public institutions on permanent funds. A permanent fund [endowment] carries in itself the seed of moral fall of the institution. . . . Institutions maintained on permanent funds are often found to ignore public opinion, and are frequently responsible for acts contrary to it. . . . The ideal is for public institutions to live, like nature, from day to day. . . . The subscriptions that an institution annually receives are a test of its popularity and the honesty of its management. . . . The current expenditure should be found from subscriptions voluntarily received from year to year. . . . I can recollect times when I did not know what would happen the next day if no subscriptions came in.

I do not think anyone can beat me in my passion for guarding and expending public money like a miser. The reason is obvious. Public money belongs to the poor public of India than whom there is none poorer on earth.

No movement or activity that has the sure foundation of the purity of character of its workers is ever in danger to come to an end for want of funds. . . . We must not always depend only on our monied men. We have to tap humbler resources. Our middle classes and even poor classes support so many beggars, so many temples, why will they not support a few good workers?

I have always felt that when a religious organization has more money than it requires, it is in peril of losing its faith in God and pinning its faith on money. . . . The moment financial stability is assured, spiritual bankruptcy is also assured.

If we are prepared to sacrifice our lives for the cause, money is nothing.

6. *Satyagraha*

ORIGINS

The principle called *satyagraha* came into being before that name was invented. Indeed when it was born, I myself could not say what it was. . . . When in a meeting of Europeans I found that the term "passive resistance" was too narrowly construed, that it was supposed to be a weapon of the weak, that it could be characterized by hatred, and that it could finally manifest itself as violence, I had to demur to all these statements and explain the real nature of the Indian movement. It was clear that a new word must be coined by the Indians to designate their struggle. But I could not . . . find out a new name and therefore offered a nominal prize. . . . As a result, Maganlal Gandhi coined the word "*Sadagraha*" (*Sat*, truth; *Agraha*, firmness). . . . In order to make it clearer I changed the word to "*Satyagraha*" which has since become current in Gujarati as a designation for the struggle.

Satyagraha is essentially different from what people generally mean in English by the phrase passive resistance.

When I read in the Sermon on the Mount such passages as "Resist not him that is evil; but whosoever smiteth thee on thy right cheek, turn to him the other also," and "Love your enemies; pray for them that persecute you, that ye may be sons of your Father which is in Heaven," I was simply overjoyed, and found my own opinion confirmed where I least expected it. The *Bhagavad Gita* deepened the impression, and Tolstoy's *The Kingdom of God Is Within You* gave it a permanent form.

Passive resistance . . . in the vernacular rendered into English means Truth-Force. I think Tolstoy called it also Soul-Force or Love-Force.

The statement that I derived my idea of civil disobedience from the writings of Thoreau is wrong. The resistance to authority in South Africa was well advanced before I got the essay of Thoreau on civil disobedience. But the movement was then known as passive resistance. As it was incomplete, I had coined the word *satyagraha* for the Gujarati readers. When I saw the title of Thoreau's great essay, I began the use of the phrase to explain our struggle to the English readers. But I found that even civil disobedience failed to convey the full meaning of the struggle. I therefore adopted the phrase "civil resistance." Non-violence was always an integral part of our struggle.

MEANS AND ENDS

That there is no connection between the means and the end is a great mistake. Through that mistake even men who have been considered religious have committed grievous crimes. . . . The means may be likened to a seed, the end to a tree; and there is just the same inviolable connection between the means and the end as there is between the seed and the tree.

They say "means are after all means." I would say "means are after all everything." As the means so the end. There is no wall of separation between means and end. . . . Realization of the goal is in exact proportion to that of the means. This is a proposition that admits of no exception.

Means and ends are convertible terms in my philosophy of life.

There is a law of nature that a thing can be retained by the same means by which it has been acquired. A thing acquired by violence can be retained by violence alone, while one acquired by truth can be retained only by truth.

Our progress toward the goal will be in exact proportion to the purity of our means. This method may appear to be long, perhaps too long, but I am convinced that it is the shortest.

Means to be means must always be within our reach. . . . If we take care of the means, we are bound to reach the end sooner or later.

If one takes care of the means, the end will take care of itself.

Means are not to be distinguished from ends. If violent means are used there will be a bad result. . . . The terms are convertible. No good act can produce an evil result. Evil means, even for a good end, produce evil results.

Fairest means cease to be fair when the end sought is unfair.

I am an uncompromising opponent of violent methods even to serve the noblest of causes.

SACRIFICE

Gift of life is the greatest of all gifts; a man who gives it in reality disarms all hostility.

Forced sacrifice is no sacrifice.

A nation that is capable of limitless sacrifice is capable of rising to limitless heights. The purer the sacrifice, the quicker the progress.

Self-sacrifice of one innocent man is a million times more potent than the sacrifice of [a] million men who die in the act of killing others.

The willing sacrifice of the innocent is the most powerful retort to insolent tyranny that has yet been conceived by God or man.

No sacrifice is worth the name unless it is a joy. Sacrifice and a long face go ill together. Sacrifice is "making sacred." He must be a poor specimen of humanity who is in need of sympathy for his sacrifice.

There should be no sorrow felt over one's sacrifice. That sacrifice causes pain, loses its sacred character and will break down under stress. One gives up things that one considers to be injurious and, therefore, there should be pleasure attendant upon the giving up.

The mice which helplessly find themselves between the cat's teeth acquire no merit from their enforced sacrifice.

In true sacrifice all the suffering is on one side— one is required to master the art of getting killed without killing, of gaining life by losing it.

A *satyagrahi* must always be ready to die with a smile on his face, without retaliation and without rancor in his heart.

SUFFERING

The mother suffers so that her child may live. Life comes out of death. The condition of wheat growing is that the seed grain should perish. No country has ever risen without being purified through the fire of suffering. . . . It is impossible to do away with the law of suffering which is the one indispensable condition of our being. Progress is to be measured by the amount of suffering undergone. . . . The purer the suffering, the greater is the progress.

The secret of non-violence and non-cooperation lies in our realizing that it is through suffering that we are to attain our goal. . . . That preliminary renunciation is a prelude to the larger suffering—the hardships of a jail life and even the final consummation on the gallows if need be. The more we suffer and the more of us suffer, the nearer we are to our cherished goal.

Suffering cheerfully endured ceases to be suffering and is transmuted into an ineffable joy. The man who flies from suffering is the victim of endless tribulation before it has come to him, and is half dead when it does come. But one who is cheerfully ready for anything and everything that comes, escapes all pain; his cheerfulness acts as an anaesthetic.

The salvation of the people depends upon themselves, upon their capacity for suffering and sacrifice.

Real suffering bravely borne melts even a heart of stone.

Suffering has its well-defined limits. Suffering can be both wise and unwise, and when the limit is reached, to prolong it would be not unwise but the height of folly.

People who voluntarily undergo a course of suffering raise themselves and the whole of humanity.

Things of fundamental importance to the people are not secured by reason alone but have to be purchased with their suffering. Suffering is the law of human beings; war is the law of the jungle. Suffering is infinitely more powerful than the law of the jungle for converting the opponent and opening his ears, which are otherwise shut to the voice of reason.

FASTING

See also the section on "Fasting" in Chapter 3.

Whenever there is distress which one cannot remove, one must fast and pray.

Fasting unto death is an integral part of [the] *satyagraha* program, and it is the greatest and most effective weapon in its armory under given circumstances. Not everyone is qualified for undertaking it without a proper course of training.

In the very nature of things, fasting for any selfish gain puts itself out of court. The *satyagrahi* must not fast to get himself released from jail, or have other benefits conferred upon him while in jail.

It is our duty to strengthen by our fasting those who hold the same ideals but are likely to weaken under pressure.

IMPRISONMENT

See also the section on "Crime" in Chapter 10; and the section on "Jail Experiences" in Chapter 13.

If one has committed an offense, he must plead guilty and suffer the penalty. If he has not and is still found guilty, imprisonment for him is no disgrace. And if he is a *satyagrahi*, he has no business to fear the hardships of jail life.

We are not to seek imprisonment out of bravado. The jail is the gateway to liberty and honor, when innocence finds itself in it.

Not all prisoners feel like me and enjoy solitary confinement. It is as inhuman as it is unnecessary. It could be avoided by a proper distribution of the prisoners. . . . Prisons are abused for political ends, and, therefore, the political prisoner is not safe from persecution even within their walls.

The shame lies not so much in going to jail as in committing the offence. . . . Imprisonment you should regard as a penance. The real penance lies in resolving never to [do wrong] again.

Jail-going was understood to be the normal lot of *satyagrahis.*

When the fear of jail disappears, repression puts heart into the people.

It is easy to get into prison by committing a crime but it is difficult to get in in spite of one's innocence. As the criminal works to escape arrest, the police pursue and arrest him. But they lay their hands upon the innocent man who courts arrest of his own free will only when they cannot help it.

Prison life . . . is a good discipline in patience.

Over fifty years ago prisoners could not receive visitors or write letters. Ordinary prison life now-a-days has lost all its terrors. . . . The day is not far distant when prisons will be rechristened and persons will be merely detained so as to be unable to do harm, whether moral, social, or political, in accordance with the conception of respective states. But we have to rejoice whatever the conditions of jail life, trying nevertheless to secure relief whenever possible.

A *satyagrahi* goes to prison, not to embarrass the authorities but to convert them by demonstrating to them his innocence.

We must widen the prison gates and we must enter them as a bridegroom enters the bride's chamber. Freedom is to be wooed only inside prison walls and sometimes on gallows, never in the council chambers, courts, or the schoolroom.

THE OPPONENT

Passive resistance . . . blesses him who uses it and him against whom it is used.

Whilst we may attack measures and systems, we may not, must not, attack men. Imperfect ourselves, we must be tender toward others and be slow to impute motives.

We must be ever courteous and patient with those who do not see eye to eye with us. We must resolutely refuse to consider our opponents as enemies.

Immediately we begin to think of things as our opponents think of them we shall be able to do them full justice. . . . Three-fourths of the miseries and misunderstandings of the world will disappear if we step into the shoes of our adversaries and understand their standpoint.

Let us honor our opponents for the same honesty of purpose and patriotic motives that we claim for ourselves.

Man and his deed are two distinct things. Whereas a good deed should call forth approbation and a wicked deed disapprobation, the doer of the deed, whether good or wicked, always deserves respect or pity as the case may be. "Hate the sin and not the sinner" is a precept which, though easy enough to understand, is rarely practised, and that is why the poison of hatred spreads in the world. . . . It is quite proper to resist and attack a system, but to resist and attack its author is tantamount to resisting and attacking oneself. For we are all tarred with the same brush, and are children of one and the same Creator, and as such the divine powers within us are infinite. To slight a simple human being is to slight those divine powers, and thus to harm not only that being but with him the whole world.

A *satyagrahi* bids goodbye to fear. He is therefore never afraid to trust the opponent. Even if the opponent plays him false twenty times, the *satyagrahi* is ready to trust him the twenty-first time, for an implicit trust in human nature is the very essence of his creed.

A *satyagrahi* must never forget the distinction between evil and the evil-doer. He must not harbor ill-will or bitterness against the latter. He may not even employ needlessly offensive language against the evil person, however unrelieved his evil might be. . . . There is no one so fallen in this world but can be converted by love. A *satyagrahi* will always try to overcome evil by good, anger by love, untruth by truth, *himsa* by *ahimsa*. There is no other way of purging the world of evil.

I am transferring the ill-will from men to things.

As no human being is so bad as to be beyond redemption, no human being is so perfect as to warrant his destroying him whom he wrongly considers to be wholly evil.

The idea underlying *satyagraha* is to convert the wrongdoer, to awaken the sense of justice in him, to show him also that without the cooperation direct or indirect of the wronged, the wrongdoer cannot do the wrong intended by him.

It is never the intention of a *satyagrahi* to embarrass the wrongdoer. The appeal is never to his fear; it is, must be, always to his heart. The *satyagrahi's* object is to convert, not to coerce, the wrongdoer.

One must believe in the possibility of every person, however depraved, being reformed under humane and skilled treatment.

When it is a question of choice between killing oneself or the assailant, I have no doubt in my mind that the first should be the choice.

Whenever you are confronted with an opponent, conquer him with love.

In the dictionary of *satyagraha* there is no enemy.

NON–COOPERATION

Every citizen silently but none the less certainly sustains the government of the day in ways of which he has no knowledge. Every citizen therefore renders himself responsible for every act of his government. And it is quite proper to support it so long as the actions of the government are bearable. But when they hurt him and his nation, it becomes his duty to withdraw his support.

Non-cooperation is not a passive state, it is an intensely active state—more active than physical resistance or violence. Passive resistance is a misnomer.

Non-cooperation is an attempt to awaken the masses to a sense of their dignity and power. This can only be by enabling them to realize that they need not fear brute force, if they would but know the soul within.

A non-cooperationist strives to compel attention and to set an example not by his violence, but by his unobtrusive humility. He allows his solid action to speak for his creed. His strength lies in his reliance upon the correctness of his position.

The sole justification for the existence of the State is the assumption that it promotes the well-being of the people. This alone constitutes its claim to the allegiance of its subjects. Therefore, it goes without saying that, as soon as it begins to fail in its duty or begins to pass measures and frame laws which are contrary to the conscience and the best interests of the people, it loses its right to their allegiance, and it not only becomes necessary but a matter of religious duty for the people to withdraw their support from the State when the dictates of conscience require it.

Non-cooperation does not in any way mean anarchy or absence of order. For non-cooperation with the State means a closer cooperation among the people themselves. Thus non-cooperation is a process of evolution; it has most aptly been described as evolutionary revolution.

The primary motive of non-cooperation is self-purification by withdrawing cooperation from an unrighteous and unrepentant government. The secondary object is to rid ourselves of the feeling of helplessness by being independent of all government control or supervision, i.e., to govern ourselves in all possible affairs, and in fulfilling both the objects, to refrain from doing or promoting injury, or violence, to any individual or property.

Non-cooperation, when its limitations are not recognized, becomes a license instead of being a duty and therefore becomes a crime.

Non-cooperation with evil is as much a duty as is cooperation with good. In the past, non-cooperation has been deliberately expressed in violence to the evil-doer. I am endeavoring to show to my countrymen that violent non-cooperation only multiplies evil and that, as evil can only be sustained by violence, withdrawal of support of evil requires complete abstention from violence.

My non-cooperation has its roots not in hatred, but in love.

Non-cooperation in itself is unnatural, vicious, and sinful. But non-violent non-cooperation, I am convinced, is a sacred duty at times.

My non-cooperation is with methods and systems, never with men.

CIVIL DISOBEDIENCE

When we do not like certain laws, we do not break the heads of the law-givers but we suffer and do not submit to the laws. That we should obey laws whether good or bad is a new-fangled notion. There was no such thing in former days. The people disregarded those laws they did not like and suffered the penalties for their breach. It is contrary to our manhood if we obey laws repugnant to our conscience.

If our rulers are doing what in our opinion is wrong, and if we feel it our duty to let them hear our advice even though it may be considered sedition, I urge you to speak sedition—but at your peril, you must be prepared to suffer the consequences. And, when you are ready to suffer the consequences and not hit below the belt, then I think you will have made good your right to have your advice heard even by the Government.

Only he who has mastered the art of obedience to law knows the art of disobedience to law.

Those only can take up civil disobedience who believe in willing obedience even to irksome laws imposed by the State so long as they do not hurt their conscience or religion, and are prepared equally willingly to suffer the penalty of civil disobedience.

Complete civil disobedience is rebellion without the element of violence in it. An out-and-out civil resister simply ignores the authority of the State. . . . He never uses force and never resists force when it is used against him. In fact, he invites imprisonment and other uses of force against himself. . . . Submission to the State law is the price a citizen pays for his personal liberty. Submission, therefore, to a State law wholly or largely unjust is an immoral barter for liberty. A citizen who thus realizes the evil nature of a State is not satisfied to live on its sufferance, and therefore appears to the others who do not share his belief to be a nuisance to society whilst he is endeavoring to compel the State, without committing a moral breach, to arrest him. . . . A body of civil resisters is like an army subject to all the discipline of a soldier's life. . . . One *perfect* civil resister is enough to win the battle of right against wrong.

NON–VIOLENCE (*AHIMSA*)

If I am a follower of *ahimsa*, I must love my enemy. I must apply the same rules to the wrong-doer who is my enemy or a stranger to me as I would to my wrong-doing father or son. . . . A man cannot practice *ahimsa* and be a coward at the same time. The practice of *ahimsa* calls forth the greatest courage.

Ahimsa, truly understood, is in my humble opinion a panacea for all evils mundane and extra-mundane. We can never overdo it.

Non-violence is the law of our species as violence is the law of the brute.

Non-violence . . . is a conscious, deliberate restraint put upon one's desire for vengeance.

It is no easy thing to walk on the sharp swordedge of *ahimsa* in this world which is full of *himsa*. . . . Anger is the enemy of *ahimsa;* and pride is a monster that swallows it up.

Ahimsa is uttermost selflessness. Selflessness means complete freedom from a regard of one's body. If man desired to realize himself, i.e., Truth, he could do so only by being completely detached from the body, i.e., by making all other beings feel safe from him. That is the way of *ahimsa*. *Ahimsa* does not simply mean non-killing.

Participation in war could never be consistent with *ahimsa*. . . . A votary of truth is often obliged to grope in the dark. . . . The saying that life lives on life has a deep meaning in it. Man cannot for a moment live without consciously or unconsciously committing outward *himsa*. The very fact of his living —eating, drinking and moving about—necessarily involves some *himsa*, destruction of life, be it ever so minute. A votary of *ahimsa*

therefore remains true to his faith if the spring of all his actions
is compassion, if he shuns to the best of his ability the destruction
of the tiniest creature, tries to save it, and thus incessantly strives
to be free from the deadly coil of *himsa*. He will be constantly
growing in self-restraint and compassion but he can never become
entirely free from outward *himsa*.

*A*himsa is a weapon of matchless potency. It
is the *summum bonum* of life. It is an attribute of the brave; in
fact, it is their all. It does not come within reach of the coward.
It is no wooden or lifeless dogma, but a living and life-giving
force. It is the special attribute of the soul.

There is no zest in killing one who welcomes
death. . . . If the mouse did not flee before the cat, the cat would
be driven to seek another prey. If all lambs voluntarily lay with
the lion, the lion would be compelled to give up feasting upon
lambs. Great hunters would give up lion hunting if the lion took
to non-resistance.

*A*himsa means "non-killing." . . . It really means
that you may not offend anybody; you may not harbor an unchar-
itable thought, even in connection with one who may consider
himself to be your enemy. . . . If you express your love—*ahimsa*
—in such a manner that it impresses itself indelibly upon your
so-called enemy, he must return that love.

Those who have to bring about radical changes
in human conditions and surroundings cannot do it except by
raising a ferment in society. There are only two methods of
doing this, violent and non-violent. Violent pressure is felt on
the physical being, and it degrades him who uses it as it depresses
the victim, but non-violent pressure exerted through self-suffering, as by fasting, works in an entirely different way. It touches
not the physical body, but it touches and strengthens the moral
fiber of those against whom it is directed.

Non-violence in action cannot be sustained unless it goes hand in hand with non-violence in thought.

They must be ready to face bullets without flinching but also without lifting their little finger in so-called self-defense. A *satyagrahi* abjures the right of self-defense.

Non-violence is like radium in its action. An infinitesimal quantity of it embedded in a malignant growth acts continuously, silently and ceaselessly till it has transformed the whole mass of the diseased tissue into a healthy one. Similarly, even a little of true non-violence acts in a silent, subtle, unseen way and leavens the whole society.

Non-violence is never a method of coercion; it is one of conversion.

Prolonged training of the individual soul is an absolute necessity so that a perfect passive resister has to be almost, if not entirely, a perfect man. We cannot all suddenly become such men ... but the greater the spirit of passive resistance in us, the better men we will become. ... There never will be an army of perfectly non-violent people. It will be formed of those who will honestly endeavor to observe non-violence.

We are constantly being astonished these days at the amazing discoveries in the field of violence. But I maintain that far more undreamt of and seemingly impossible discoveries will be made in the field of non-violence.

Non-violence does not work in the same way as violence. It works in the opposite way. An armed man naturally relies on arms. A man who is intentionally unarmed relies upon the unseen force called God by poets, but called the unknown by scientists. But that which is unknown is not necessarily non-existent. God is the Force among all forces known and unknown. Non-violence without reliance upon that Force is poor stuff to be thrown in the dust.

The votary of *ahimsa* has only one fear—that is God.

He who perishes sword in hand is no doubt brave; but he who faces death without raising his little finger and without flinching is braver.

Non-violence begins and ends by turning the searchlight inward.

A non-violent fight is as sharp as the edge of the sword—sharpened on the whetstone of the heart.

Passive resistance is an all-sided sword; it can be used any how; it blesses him who uses it and also against whom it is used, without drawing a drop of blood. It produces far-reaching results. It never rusts, and it cannot be stolen. The sword of passive resistance does not require a scabbard, and one cannot be forcibly dispossessed of it. . . . It is quite plain that passive resistance thus understood is infinitely superior to physical force, and that it requires greater courage than the latter.

VIOLENCE AND HATE (*HIMSA*)

We shall have to give up even verbal violence and learn dignified ways of dealing with our opponents.

I do believe that, where there is only a choice between cowardice and violence, I would advise violence.

Terrorism and deception are weapons not of the strong but of the weak.

The end of hatred is never justice; it is retaliation; it is blind fury.

Violence is suicide.

Violence flourishes on response, either by submission to the will of the violator, or by counter-violence.

I object to violence because when it appears to do good, the good is only temporary; the evil it does is permanent.

History teaches one that those who have, no doubt with honest motives, ousted the greedy by using brute force against them, have in their turn become a prey to the disease of the conquered.

The sin of *himsa* consists not in merely taking life, but in taking life for the sake of one's perishable body. . . . The destruction of bodies of tortured creatures . . . cannot be regarded as *himsa*. . . . Taking life may be a duty. We do destroy as much life as we think necessary for sustaining our body. Thus for food we take life, vegetable and other, and for health we destroy mosquitoes and the like by the use of disinfectants, etc., and we do not think that we are guilty of irreligion in doing so. . . . Even man-slaughter may be necessary in certain cases.

Those who seek to destroy men rather than manners, adopt the latter and become worse than those whom they destroy under the mistaken belief that the manners will die with the man.

In *satyagraha* physical force is forbidden even in the most favorable circumstances.

Not only has hatred no place in *satyagraha*, but is a positive breach of its ruling principle.

If light can come out of darkness, then alone can love emerge from hatred.

We can only win over the opponent by love, never by hate. Hate is the subtlest form of violence.

A *satyagrahi* is always prepared for but does not anticipate repression. He imputes no evil to his opponent.

Hatred injures the hater, never the hated.

METHODOLOGY

The religion of non-violence is not meant merely for the . . . saints. It is meant for the common people as well.

The danger is the greatest when victory seems the nearest. No victory worth the name has ever been won without a final effort, more serious than all the preceding ones. God's last test is ever the most difficult. Satan's last temptation is ever the most seductive. We must stand God's last test and resist Satan's last temptation if we would be free.

There is no time limit for a *satyagrahi* . . . hence there is no such thing as defeat in *satyagraha*.

Every piece of work in connection with the struggle is just as important as any other piece.

You need not be afraid that the method of non-violence is a slow long-drawn out process. It is the swiftest the world has seen, for it is the surest.

Since *satyagraha* is one of the most powerful methods of direct action, a *satyagrahi* exhausts all other means before he resorts to *satyagraha*. . . . When he has found the impelling call of the inner voice within him and launches out upon *satyagraha* he has burned his boats and there is no receding.

Satyagraha could not be conducted simply by means of money. Money is the thing that it least needs.

Civility [must be combined] with fearlessness. ... If they resorted to incivility it would spoil their *satyagraha*, like a drop of arsenic in milk. ... Civility does not mean the mere outward gentleness of speech cultivated for the occasion, but an inborn gentleness and desire to do the opponent good. These should show themselves in every act of a *satyagrahi*.

The beauty of *satyagraha* [is that] it comes up to oneself; one has not to go out in search for it.

It is only when the *satyagrahi* feels quite helpless, is apparently on his last legs and finds utter darkness all around him, that God comes to the rescue.

A *satyagraha* struggle depends but little upon help from outside, and it is only internal remedies that are effective.

The *satyagrahis* were strongly of the opinion that they not only must not entertain any ill-will against those who did not join the struggle whether for want of faith or weakness or any other reason whatever, but must maintain their present friendly relations with them unimpaired and even work side by side with them in all other movements except the *satyagraha* struggle.

Secrecy had no place in a movement, where one could do no wrong, where there was no scope for duplicity or cunning, and where strength constituted the single guarantee of victory.

In *satyagraha* ... there is no question of retreat, and the only movement possible is an advance. In other struggles, even when they are righteous, the demand is first pitched a little higher so as to admit of future reduction.

Satyagraha against *satyagraha* is impossible.

A *satyagraha* struggle is impossible without capital in the shape of character. As a splendid palace deserted by its inmates looks like a ruin, so does a man without character, all his material belongings notwithstanding.

In a pure fight the fighters would never go beyond the objective fixed when the fight began even if they received an accession to their strength in the course of the fighting, and on the other hand they could not give up their objective if they found their strength dwindling away.

The humility of a *satyagrahi* knows no bounds. He does not let slip a single opportunity for settlement, and he does not mind if any one therefore looks upon him as timid.

A *satyagrahi* fights for essentials alone.

No matter how often a *satyagrahi* is betrayed, he will repose his trust in the adversary so long as there are not cogent grounds for distrust. Pain to a *satyagrahi* is as pleasure. He will not therefore be misled by the mere fear of suffering into groundless distrust. On the other hand, relying as he does upon his own strength, he will not mind being betrayed by the adversary, will continue to trust in spite of frequent betrayals, and will believe that he thereby strengthens the forces of truth and brings victory nearer.

Satyagraha is a priceless and matchless weapon, and those who wield it are strangers to disappointment or defeat.

I do not wish to disparage the strength of numbers. It has its use, but only when it is backed by the latent spirit force. Millions of ants can kill an elephant by together attacking it in a vulnerable place. Their sense of solidarity, consciousness of oneness of spirit in spite of the diversity of bodies, in other words their spirit force, makes the ants irresistible. Even so, the moment we develop a sense of mass unity like the ants, we, too, shall become irresistible and shall free ourselves from our chains.

The end of non-violent "war" is always an agreement, never dictation, much less humiliation of the opponent.

Truth-Force . . . is independent of pecuniary or other material assistance. . . . It is a force that may be used by individuals as well as by communities. It may be used as well in political as in domestic affairs. Its universal applicability is a demonstration of its permanence and invincibility. It can be used alike by men, women and children. It is totally untrue to say that it is a force to be used only by the weak so long as they are not capable of meeting violence by violence. . . . Only those who realize that there is something in man which is superior to the brute nature in him, and that the latter always yields to it, can effectively be passive resisters. This force is to violence and, therefore, to all tyranny, all injustice, what light is to darkness. In politics, its use is based upon the immutable maxim that government of the people is possible only so long as they consent either consciously or unconsciously to be governed.

7. International Affairs

GREAT BRITAIN AND THE BRITISH

The English are both a timid and a brave nation. England is, I believe, easily influenced by the use of gunpowder.

I bear no enmity towards the English but I do towards their civilization.

Look at the history of the British Empire and the British nation; freedom-loving as it is, it will not be party to give freedom to a people who will not take it themselves.

Superiority of race is a passion, has become almost a religion, with the average Englishman. Nor does he strive to conceal it from view.

I did not consider Englishmen nor do I now consider them as particularly bad or worse than other human beings. I considered and still consider them to be as capable of high motives and actions as any other body of men and equally capable of making mistakes.

The color prejudice that I saw in South Africa was, I thought, quite contrary to British traditions, and I believed that it was only temporary and local. I therefore vied with Englishmen in loyalty to the throne.

As the elephant is powerless to think in the terms of the ant, in spite of the best intentions in the world, even so is the Englishman powerless to think in terms of, or legislate for, the Indian.

I knew the difference in status between an Indian and an Englishman, but I did not believe that we had been quite reduced to slavery. I felt then that it was more the fault of individual British officials than of the British system, and that we could convert them by love. Though the system was faulty, it did not seem to me to be intolerable as it does today.

Under the British constitution, if the policy of the Government is liberal, the subjects receive the utmost advantage of its liberality. On the other hand if their policy is oppressive or niggardly, the subjects feel the maximum weight of their heavy hand.

I discovered that the British Empire had certain ideals with which I have fallen in love, and one of those ideals is that every subject of the British Empire has the freest scope possible for his energies and honor, and whatever he thinks is due to his conscience. I think that this is true of the British Empire as it is not true of any other government. I feel, as you here perhaps know, that I am no lover of any government, and I have more than once said that that government is best which governs least; and I have found that it is possible for me to be governed least under the British Empire. Hence my loyalty to the British Empire.

An Englishman never respects you till you stand up to him. Then he begins to like you.

In a free India, Englishmen will come out to India either in a spirit of adventure, or from penance, and willingly serve on a small salary and put up with the rigors of Indian climate instead of being a burden on poor India, whilst they draw inordinately large salaries and try to live there in extra English extravagance, and reproduce even the English climate.

In the matter of capacity for detachment, Englishmen are far in advance of us. . . . They are not unnerved in the face of dangers or impending calamity.

The news about the destruction in England is heart-rending. The Houses of Parliament, the Abbey, the Cathedral seemed to be immortal. And yet there is no end.

Though I do not wish any humiliation to Britain —and therefore, no defeat—my mind refuses to give her any moral support [in World War II].

The British must go. I do not say that the British are worse than the Japanese. . . . I do not wish to exchange one master for another.

Britain often cloaks herself in a cloth of hypocrisy, promising what she later doesn't deliver.

THE UNITED STATES

When Americans come and ask me what service they can render, I tell them: If you dangle your millions before us, you will make beggars of us and demoralize us. But in one thing I do not mind being a beggar. I would beg of you your scientific talent. You can ask your engineers and agricultural experts to place their services at our disposal. They must not come to us as our lords and masters but as voluntary workers.

American tradition singles her out as an arbitrator and mediator between warring nations. By her territorial vastness, amazing energy, unrivalled financial status and owing to the composite character of her people, she is the one country which could have saved the world from the unthinkable butchery that is going on [in World War II].

Americans [do] not listen to others; they . . . lionize people but they . . . go their own way. It is difficult to wean the golden calf from the worshippers of Mammon.

It was a wrong thing for America and unfortunate for the world peace that America, instead of working—as she could have worked—for peace, identified herself with war [in World War II].

America and Britain are very great nations but their greatness will count as dust before the bar of dumb humanity, whether African or Asiatic. . . . They have no right to talk of human liberty and all else unless they have washed their hands clean of the pollution.

America is too big financially, intellectually, and in scientific skill to be subdued by any nation or even combination. Hence, my tears over her throwing herself in a caldron [of World War II].

[To Stanley Jones:] I have not seen the American people, but give them my love.

SOVIET RUSSIA AND COMMUNISM

Bolshevism is the necessary result of modern materialistic civilization. Its insensate worship of matter has given rise to a school which has been brought up to look upon materialistic advancement as the goal and which has lost all touch with the final things of life.

I am yet ignorant of what exactly Bolshevism is. I have not been able to study it. I do not know whether it is for the good of Russia in the long run. But I do know that in so far as it is based on violence and denial of God, it repels me. I do not believe in short-violent-cuts to success. Those Bolshevik friends who are bestowing their attention on me should realize that however much I may sympathize with and admire worthy motives, I am uncompromisingly an opponent of violent methods even to serve the noblest of causes.

From what I know of Bolshevism, it not only does not preclude the use of force, but freely sanctions it for the expropriation of private property and maintaining the collective state ownership of the same. And if that is so, I have no hesitation in saying that the Bolshevik regime, in its present form, cannot last long. For ... nothing enduring can be built on violence.

All communists are not bad, as all Congressmen are not angels. I have, therefore, no prejudice against communists as such. Their philosophy, as they have declared it to me, I cannot subscribe to.

What does communism mean in the last analysis? It means a classless society—an ideal that is worth striving for. Only I part company with it when force is called to aid for achieving it. ... The idea of inequality, of "high and low" is an evil, but I do not believe in eradicating evil from the human breast at the point of the bayonet.

Communism of the Russian type, that is communism which is imposed on a people, would be repugnant to India. If Communism came without violence, it would be welcome. For then no property would be held by anybody except on behalf of the people and for the people.

GERMANY AND HITLER

I do not believe that the Germans are the fiends the English press has made them out to be, nor do I believe that the world would have come to an end if they had won [World War I].

The Jews . . . have been the untouchables of Christianity. . . . The German persecution of the Jews seems to have no parallel in history. The tyrants of old never went so mad as Hitler seems to have done. If there ever could be a justifiable war in the name of and for humanity, war against Germany to prevent the wanton persecution of a whole race would be completely justified. But I do not believe in any war.

[To Adolf Hitler:] You are today the one person in the world who can prevent a war which may reduce humanity to the savage state. Must you pay that price for an object however worthy it may appear to you to be? Will you listen to the appeal of one who has deliberately shunned the method of war not without considerable success?

I must refuse to believe that the Germans contemplate with equanimity the evacuation of big cities like London for fear of destruction to be wrought by man's inhuman ingenuity. They cannot contemplate with equanimity such destruction of themselves and their own monuments.

Whatever Hitler may ultimately prove to be, we know what Hitlerism has come to mean. It means naked ruthless force reduced to an exact science and worked with scientific precision. In its effect it becomes almost irresistible. Hitlerism will never be defeated by counter-Hitlerism. It can only breed a superior-Hitlerism raised to the nth degree. What is going on before our eyes is a demonstration of the futility of violence as also of Hitlerism.

I do not think that the Germans as a nation are any worse than the English, or the Italians are any worse. We are all tarred with the same brush; we all are members of the vast human family. I decline to draw any distinctions.

WORLD WAR II

[To the Chinese people:] The Japanese cannot corrupt your soul. If the soul of China is injured, it will not be by Japan.

My personal reaction to this war is one of greater horror than ever before. . . . And yet, strange as it may appear, my sympathies are wholly with the Allies. Willy-nilly, this war is resolving itself into one between such democracy as the West has evolved and totalitarianism as it is typified in Herr Hitler.

Herr Hitler is fighting for the extension of German boundaries, although he was told that he should allow his claims to be submitted to an impartial tribunal for examination. He contemptuously rejected the way of peace and persuasion and chose that of the sword. Hence my sympathy for the cause of the Allies. But my sympathy must *not* be interpreted to mean endorsement in any shape or form of the doctrine of the sword for the defense of even proved right.

My prayer still is not only that Britain and France should win but also that Germany should not be ruined.

I think French statesmen have shown rare courage in bowing to the inevitable and refusing to be a party to senseless mutual slaughter. There can be no sense in France coming out victorious if the stake is, in truth, lost. The cause of liberty becomes a mockery if the price to be paid is the wholesale destruction of those who are to enjoy liberty. It then becomes an inglorious satiation of ambition.

I appeal [to every Briton] for the cessation of hostilities, not because you are too exhausted to fight, but because war is bad in essence. You want to kill Nazism. You will never kill it by its indifferent adoption. Your soldiers are doing the same work of destruction as the Germans. The only difference is that, perhaps, yours are not as thorough as the Germans. If that be so, yours will soon require the same thoroughness as theirs, if not much greater. On no other condition can you win the war. In other words you will have to be more ruthless than the Nazis.

I hold a new order to be impossible if the war is fought to a finish or if mutual exhaustion leads to a patched-up peace.

If the press accounts are to be relied upon, British skill and valor have wrought more havoc in Berlin than have the Germans in London. What wrong have the German people done to the British people? Their leaders have. Hang them by all means, but why destroy German homes and German civilian life?

The very thoroughness of the Nazi method makes people think that nothing but counter-violence can check the terror. I have suggested that counter-violence can only result in further brutalization of human nature. Drastic diseases require drastic remedies. In this instance nothing but non-violence can cure Nazi violence.

I am not yet certain that the democracies will make a better world when they defeat the Fascists. They may become very much like the Fascists themselves.

WAR

The frightful outrage that is just now going on in Europe [World War II] perhaps shows that the message of Jesus of Nazareth, the Son of Peace, has been little understood in Europe, and that light may have to be thrown upon it from the East.

It may be long before the law of love will be recognized in international affairs. The machineries of governments stand between and hide the hearts of one people from those of another.

We have been deceived by the temporary but brilliant results achieved by some wars.

All of us recognized the immorality of war. If I was not prepared to prosecute my assailant, much less should I be willing to participate in a war, especially when I knew nothing of the justice or otherwise of the cause of the combatants. . . . It was quite clear to me that participation in war could never be consistent with *ahimsa*.

War is wrong, is an unmitigated evil. . . . It has got to go. . . . Freedom won through bloodshed or fraud is no freedom.

The ever-growing militarism under which the nations of the West are groaning and are being almost crushed to death . . . promises to overwhelm even the nations of the East.

If the mad race for armaments continues, it is bound to result in a slaughter such as has never occurred in history. If there is a victor left the very victory will be a living death for the nation that emerges victorious.

Immediately the spirit of exploitation is gone, armaments will be felt as a positive unbearable burden. Real disarmament cannot come unless the nations of the world cease to exploit one another.

No cause, however just, can warrant the indiscriminate slaughter that is going on minute by minute. I suggest that a cause which demands the inhumanities that are being perpetrated today cannot be called just.

Peace has its victories more glorious than those of war.

I believe all war to be wholly wrong. But if we scrutinize the motives of two warring parties, we may find one to be in the right and the other in the wrong. . . . I do not believe in violent warfare, but all the same [the side] whose cause is just, deserves my moral help and blessings.

What difference does it make to the dead, the orphans and the homeless, whether the mad destruction is wrought under the name of totalitarianism or the holy name of liberty or democracy?

A warrior lives on his wars whether offensive or defensive. He suffers a collapse if he finds that his warring capacity is unwanted.

Can we contemplate with equanimity or feel a glow of bravery and sacrifice at the prospect of Indian earth being scorched and everything being destroyed in order that the enemy's march may be hampered? I see no bravery in destroying life or property for offense or defense. I would far rather leave crops and homesteads for the enemy to use than destroy them for the sake of preventing their use by him. There is reasonable sacrifice and even bravery in so leaving my homestead and crops, if I do so not out of fear but because I refuse to regard anyone as my enemy.

In war time there must be civilian control of the military, even though the civilians are not as well trained in strategy as the military. If the British in Burma wish to destroy the golden pagoda because it is a beacon to Japanese airplanes, then I say you cannot destroy it, because when you destroy it you destroy something in the Burmese soul.

I cannot look at this butchery going on in the world with indifference. I have an unchangeable faith that it is beneath the dignity of men to resort to mutual slaughter.

WAR RESISTANCE

When two nations are fighting, the duty of a votary of *ahimsa* is to stop the war. He who is not equal to that duty, he who has no power of resisting war, he who is not qualified to resist war, may take part in war, and yet whole-heartedly try to free himself, his nation and the world from war. . . . I make no distinction, from the point of view of *ahimsa*, between combatants and non-combatants.

I draw no distinction between those who wield the weapons of destruction and those who do red cross work. Both participate in war and advance its cause.

Every single subject of a state must not hope to enforce his private opinion in all cases. The authorities may not always be right, but so long as the subjects owe allegiance to a state, it is their clear duty generally to accommodate themselves, and to accord their support, to acts of the state. Again, if any class among the subjects considers that the action of a government is immoral from a religious standpoint, before they help or hinder it, they must endeavor fully and even at the risk of their lives to dissuade the government from pursuing such a course.

If we are to reach real peace in this world and if we are to carry on a real war against war, we shall have to begin with children; and if they will grow up in their natural innocence, we won't have to struggle; we won't have to pass fruitless idle resolutions, but we shall go from love to love and peace to peace, until at last all the corners of the world are covered with that peace and love for which consciously or unconsciously the whole world is hungering.

If society is not to be destroyed by insane wars of nations against nations, and still more insane wars on its moral foundations, the woman will have to play her part, not manfully, as some are trying to do, but womanfully. She won't better humanity by vying with man in his ability to destroy life, mostly without purpose. Let it be her privilege to wean the erring man from his error, which will envelop in his ruin that of woman also.

While you may not try to wean people from war, you will in your person live non-violence in all its completeness and refuse all participation in war. It is very difficult to judge when both sides are employing violence which side deserves to succeed. You will therefore pray only that the right may prevail. Whilst you will keep yourself aloof from all violence, you will not shirk danger.

It is open to a war-resister to judge between two combatants and wish success to the one who has justice on his side. By so judging he is more likely to bring peace between the two than by remaining a mere spectator.

A man is not necessarily non-violent because he lays down his arms.

My resistance to war does not carry me to the point of thwarting those who wish to take part in it. I reason with them. I put before them the better way and leave them to make the choice.

I [am] "anti-all-wars."

A soldier of peace unlike the one of the sword has to give all his spare time to the promotion of peace alike in war time as in peace time.

Those who confine themselves to attending to the wounded in battle cannot be absolved from the guilt of war.

WORLD GOVERNMENT

Someday we must extend the national law to the universe, even as we have extended the family law to form nations—a larger family.

Isolated independence is not the goal of the world states. It is voluntary interdependence. The better mind of the world desires not absolutely independent states warring one against another, but a federation of friendly interdependent states.

A world federation could only be established by mutual agreement.

The structure of a world federation can be raised only on a foundation of non-violence.

8. Political Affairs

DEMOCRACY

It is a superstition and an ungodly thing to believe that an act of a majority binds a minority. Many examples can be given in which acts of majorities will be found to have been wrong, and those of minorities to have been right. All reforms owe their origin to the initiation of minorities in opposition to majorities.

The truest test of democracy is in the ability of anyone to act as he likes, so long as he does not injure the life or property of anyone else.

The wise policy is to enact as little class legislation as possible; and it would be wiser still to avoid it altogether. Once a law is enacted, many difficulties must be encountered before it can be reversed. It is only when public opinion is highly educated that the laws in force in a country can be repealed. A constitution under which laws are modified or repealed every now and then cannot be said to be stable or well organized.

People are generally unaware that Governments often deliberately violate their own laws. In face of emergency there is no time for undertaking fresh legislation. Governments therefore break the laws and do what they please. Afterwards they either enact new laws or else make the people forget their breach of the law.

States amenable to public opinion get out of . . . awkward positions by appointing a commission which conducts only a nominal inquiry, as its recommendations are a foregone conclusion.

The democracy of my conception is wholly inconsistent with the use of physical force for enforcing its will.

Legislation in a free state always represents the will of the majority. All legislation in advance of general opinion argues bankruptcy of missionary effort. My reliance, therefore, always has been on missionary effort.

I look upon an increase of the power of the State with the greatest of fear, because, although while apparently doing good by minimizing exploitation, it does the greatest harm to mankind by destroying individuality which lies at the root of all progress.

Democracy cannot be evolved by forcible methods. The spirit of democracy cannot be imposed from without. It has to come from within.

Democracy and violence can ill go together. The states that are today nominally democratic have either to become frankly totalitarian or, if they are to become truly democratic, they must become courageously non-violent. It is a blasphemy to say that non-violence can only be practised by individuals and never by nations which are composed of individuals.

Democracy must in essence mean the art and science of mobilizing the entire physical, economic and spiritual resources of all the various sections of the people in the service of the common good of all.

A born democrat is a born disciplinarian. Democracy comes naturally to him who is habituated normally to yield willing obedience to all laws, human or divine. . . . A democrat must be utterly selfless. He must think and dream not in terms of self or party but only of democracy.

Liberty and democracy become unholy when their hands are dyed red with innocent blood.

Power resides in the people and it is entrusted for the time being to those whom they may choose as their representatives. Parliaments have no power or even existence independently of the people.

Democracy will break under the strain of apron strings. It can exist only on trust.

Parliamentary democracy is not immune to corruption, as you who remember Tammany Hall and the Mayor of Chicago should know.

My notion of democracy is that under it the weakest should have the same opportunity as the strongest.

The rule of majority has a narrow application, i.e., one should yield to the majority in matters of detail. But it is slavery to be amenable to the majority, no matter what its decisions are. Democracy is not a state in which people act like sheep. Under democracy, individual liberty of opinion and action is jealously guarded. I therefore believe that the minority has a perfect right to act differently from the majority.

Any secrecy hinders the real spirit of democracy.

FREEDOM

In matters of conscience, the law of majority has no place.

There will never be equality so long as one feels inferior or superior to the other. There is no room for patronage among equals.

There is no such thing as slow freedom. Freedom is like a birth. Till we are fully free, we are slaves. All birth takes place in a moment.

When a slave begins to take pride in his fetters and hugs them like precious ornaments, the triumph of the slave-owner is complete.

I value individual freedom but you must not forget that man is essentially a social being. He has risen to his present status by learning to adjust his individualism to the requirements of social progress. . . . Unrestricted individualism is the law of the beast of the jungle. We have learned to strike the mean between individual freedom and social restraint. Willing submission to social restraint for the sake of the well-being of the whole society enriches both the individual and the society of which one is a member.

The chains of a slave are broken the moment he considers himself a free man.

Liberty is a dame exacting heavy price from her wooers.

A slave-holder, who decides to abolish slavery, does not consult his slaves whether they desire freedom or not.

CIVIL LIBERTIES

The indispensable condition of success is that we encourage the greatest freedom of opinion.

Liberty of speech means that it is unassailed, even when the speech hurts; liberty of the press can be said to be truly respected only when the press can comment in the severest terms upon and even misrepresent matters, protection against misrepresentation or violence being secured not by an administrative gagging order, not by closing down the press but by punishing the real offender, leaving the press itself unrestricted. Freedom of association is truly respected when assemblies of people can discuss even revolutionary projects, the State relying upon the force of public opinion and the civil police, not the savage military at its disposal, to crush any actual outbreak of revolution that is designed to confound public opinion and the State representing it.

Evolution of democracy is not possible if we are not prepared to hear the other side. We shut the doors of reason when we refuse to listen to our opponents, or having listened, make fun of them. If intolerance becomes a habit, we run the risk of missing the truth. Whilst, with the limits that Nature has put upon our understanding, we must act fearlessly according to the light vouchsafed to us, we must always keep an open mind and be ever ready to find that what we believed to be truth was, after all, untruth. This openness of mind strengthens the truth in us and removes the dross from it, if there is any.

RACIAL DISCRIMINATION

See also the section on "Discrimination" in Chapter 13.

The theory of racial equality in the eyes of the law, once recognized, can never be departed from; and its principle must at all costs be maintained—the principle, that is to say, that in all the legal codes which bind the Empire together there shall be no racial taint, no racial distinction, no color disability.

There is no place on earth and no race, which is not capable of producing the finest types of humanity, given suitable opportunities and education.

Both Britain and America lack the moral basis for engaging in this war [World War II] unless they put their own houses in order by making it their fixed determination to withdraw their influence and power from Africa and Asia and remove the color bar. They have no right to talk of protecting democracy, civilization and human freedom until the canker of white superiority is destroyed in its entirety.

A civilization is to be judged by its treatment of minorities.

ECONOMIC JUSTICE

The test of orderliness in a country is not the number of millionaires it owns, but the absence of starvation among its masses.

The hungry millions ask for one poem—invigorating food. They cannot be given it. They must earn it. And they can earn only by the sweat of their brow.

Do not say you will maintain the poor on charity. ... The iniquitous system of giving doles to the able-bodied idle is going on to our eternal shame and humiliation.

For the poor, the economic is the spiritual.

No one ... should suffer from want of food and clothing. ... These should be freely available to all as God's air and water are or ought to be; they should not be made a vehicle of traffic for the exploitation of others. Their monopolization by any country, nation or group of persons would be unjust.

I do not draw a sharp distinction between economics and ethics. Economics that hurt the moral well-being of an individual or a nation are immoral, and therefore sinful.

I may as well place before the dog . . . the message of God as before those hungry millions who have no lustre in their eyes and whose only God is their bread. . . . To them God can only appear as bread and butter.

An economics that inculcates Mammon worship, and enables the strong to amass wealth at the expense of the weak, is a false and dismal science. It spells death. True economics, on the other hand, stands for social justice, it promotes the good of all equally including the weakest, and is indispensable for decent life.

We may not be deceived by the wealth to be seen in the cities of India. It does not come from England or America. It comes from the blood of the poorest.

Economic equality must never be supposed to mean possession of an equal amount of worldly goods by everyone. It does mean, however, that everyone will have a proper house to live in, sufficient and balanced food to eat, and sufficient *khadi* with which to cover himself. It also means that the cruel inequality that obtains today will be removed by purely nonviolent means.

LABOR

The laborers are dissatisfied with their lot. They have every reason for dissatisfaction. They are being taught, and justly, to regard themselves as being chiefly instrumental in enriching their employers.

Strikes, cessation of work and *hartal* are wonderful things no doubt, but it is not difficult to abuse them. Workmen ought to organize themselves into strong labor unions, and on no account shall they strike work without the consent of these unions. Strikes should not be risked without previous negotiations with the mill-owners.

A satisfactory solution of the condition of labor must include the following: (1) the hours of labor must leave the workmen some hours of leisure; (2) they must get facilities for their own education; (3) provision should be made for an adequate supply of milk, clothing and necessary education for their children; (4) there should be sanitary dwellings for the workmen; (5) they should be in a position to save enough to maintain themselves during their old age. None of these conditions is satisfied today. For this both the parties are responsible.

The [Ahmedabad] mill owners ... refused to recognize the principle of arbitration. I had therefore to advise the laborers to go on strike. Before I did so, I came in very close contact with them and their leaders, and explained to them the conditions of a successful strike: (1) never to resort to violence; (2) never to molest blacklegs; (3) never to depend upon alms; and (4) to remain firm, no matter how long the strike continued, and to earn bread, during the strike, by any other honest labor.

The working class will never feel secure or develop a sense of self-assurance and strength unless its members are armed with an unfailing subsidiary means of subsistence to serve as a second string to their bow in a crisis.

A working knowledge of a variety of occupations is to the working class what metal is to the capitalist. A laborer's skill is his capital. Just as the capitalist cannot make his capital fructify without the cooperation of labor, even so the working man cannot make his labor fructify without the cooperation of capital. And if both labor and capital have the gift of intelligence equally developed in them and have confidence in their capacity to secure a fair deal, each at the hands of the other, they would get to respect and appreciate each other as equal partners in a common enterprise. They need not regard each other as inherently irreconcilable antagonists. . . . The intelligence of the working man is cramped by his soulless, mechanical occupation which leaves him little scope or chance to develop his mind. . . . It is the grossest of superstitions for the working man to believe that he is helpless before the employers.

If someone blocks the passage to my house, his action is violence just as much as if he pushed me bodily from the doorstep. . . . They may not obstruct the passage, or use any coercion against those who do not want to strike.

When labor is intelligent enough to organize itself and learns to act as one man, it will have the same weight as money if not much greater.

CLASS STRUGGLE

It would be folly to assume that an Indian Rockefeller would be better than the American Rockefeller.

In the struggle between capital and labor, it may be generally said that more often than not the capitalists are in the wrong box. But when labor comes fully to realize its strength, I know it can become more tyrannical than capital.

I cannot picture to myself a time when no man shall be richer than another. But I do picture to myself a time when the rich will spurn to enrich themselves at the expense of the poor and the poor will cease to envy the rich. Even in a most perfect world, we shall fail to avoid inequalities, but we can and must avoid strife and bitterness.

I do not fight shy of capital. I fight capitalism.

The dream I want to realize is not the spoliation of the property of private owners, but to restrict its enjoyment so as to avoid all pauperism, consequent discontent and the hideously ugly contrast that exists today between the lives and surroundings of the rich and the poor.

The rich are discontented no less than the poor. The poor man would become a millionaire and the millionaire a multi-millionaire. The poor are often not satisfied when they get just enough to fill their stomachs; but they are clearly entitled to it and society should make it a point to see that they get it.

By the non-violent method, we seek not to destroy the capitalist, we seek to destroy capitalism. . . . If capital is power, so is work. Either power can be used destructively or creatively. Either is dependent on the other. Immediately the worker realizes his strength, he is in a position to become a co-sharer with the capitalist instead of remaining his slave. . . . It can be easily demonstrated that destruction of the capitalist must mean destruction in the end of the worker.

I do not teach the masses to regard the capitalists as their enemies, but I teach them that they are their own enemies. . . . The system must be destroyed and not the individual.

I shall throw the whole weight of my influence in preventing class war.

All exploitation is based on cooperation, willing or forced, of the exploited. . . . There would be no exploitation if people refuse to obey the exploiter. But self comes in and we hug the chains that bind us. . . . What is needed is not the extinction of landlords and capitalists, but a transformation of the existing relationship between them and the masses into something healthier and purer.

Exploitation of the poor can be extinguished not by effecting the destruction of a few millionaires, but by removing the ignorance of the poor and teaching them to non-cooperate with their exploiters. That will convert the exploiters also.

A violent and bloody revolution is a certainty one day unless there is a voluntary abdication of riches and the power that riches give, and sharing them for the common good.

It should not happen that a handful of rich people should live in jewelled palaces and the millions in miserable hovels devoid of sunlight or ventilation.

I do not grudge the prince his palace and the millionaire his mansion, but it is my earnest request to them to do something to bridge the gulf that separates them from the peasant. Let them construct a bridge that would bring them closer to the poor agriculturist. Let their lives bear some proportion to the lives of the poor around them.

A nation may do without its millionaires and without its capitalists, but a nation can never do without its labor.

MACHINES AND INDUSTRIALIZATION

I know that there are friends who laugh at this attempt to revive this great art [hand spinning]. They remind me that, in these days of mills, sewing machines or typewriters, only a lunatic can hope to succeed in reviving the rusticated spinning wheel. These friends forget that the needle has not yet given place to the sewing machine nor has the hand lost its cunning in spite of the typewriter. There is not the slightest reason why the spinning wheel may not co-exist with the spinning mill even as the domestic kitchen co-exists with the hotels. Indeed, typewriters and sewing machines may go, but the needle and the reed pen will survive.

Machinery has its place; it has come to stay. But it must not be allowed to displace necessary human labor.

I refuse to be dazzled by the seeming triumph of machinery. . . . Simple tools and instruments and such machinery as saves individual labor and lightens the burden of the millions . . . I should welcome.

Even the body is a most delicate piece of machinery. The spinning wheel itself is a machine. What I object to is the craze for machinery, not machinery as such. The craze is for what they call labor-saving machinery. Men go on "saving labor" till thousands are without work and thrown on the open streets to die of starvation. I want to save time and labor, not for a fraction of mankind, but for all. I want the concentration of wealth, not in the hands of a few, but in the hands of all. Today machinery merely helps a few to ride on the backs of millions. The impetus behind it all is not the philanthropy to save labor but greed.

Scientific truths and discoveries should first of all cease to be the mere instruments of greed. Then laborers will not be overworked, and machinery, instead of becoming a hindrance, will be a help. I am aiming, not at the eradication of all machinery, but its limitation. . . . The supreme consideration is man. The machine should not tend to make atrophied the limbs of men.

The Singer Sewing Machine is one of the few useful things ever invented.

It is an alteration in the conditions of labor that I want. This mad rush for wealth must cease; and the laborer must be assured, not only of a living wage, but of a daily task that is not a mere drudgery. The machine will, under these conditions, be as much a help to the man working it as to the State.

Machines will remain because, like the body, they are inevitable.

Industrialism is . . . going to be a curse for mankind. Industrialism depends entirely on your capacity to exploit, in foreign markets being open to you, and on the absence of competitors.

As I look to Russia where the apotheosis of industrialization has been reached, the life there does not appeal to me. To use the language of the Bible, "What shall it avail a man if he gain the whole world and lose his soul?" In modern terms, it is beneath human dignity to lose one's individuality and become a mere cog in the machine. I want every individual to become a full-blooded, full-developed member of the society.

Pandit Nehru wants industrialization because he thinks that, if it is socialized, it would be free from the evils of capitalism. My own view is that the evils are inherent in industrialism, and no amount of socialization can eradicate them.

America was the most industrialized country in the world and yet it had not banished poverty and degradation. That was because it neglected the universal man-power and concentrated power in the hands of the few who had amassed fortunes at the expense of the many. The result was that its industrialization had become a menace to its own poor and to the rest of the world.

I would not shed a tear if there were no railroads in India.

Mechanization is good when hands are too few for the work intended to be accomplished. It is an evil where there are more hands than required for the work as is the case in India. . . . Dead machinery should not be pitted against the living machines represented by the villagers scattered in the seven hundred thousand villages of India. Machinery to be well used has to help and ease human effort. The present use of machinery tends more and more to concentrate wealth in the hands of a few, in total disregard of millions of men and women whose bread is snatched by it out of their mouths.

SOCIALISM

I am socialist enough to say that . . . factories should be nationalized, or State-controlled. They ought only to be working under the most attractive and ideal conditions, not for profit, but for the benefit of humanity, love taking the place of greed as the motive.

What I would personally prefer would be, not a centralization of power in the hands of the State, but an extension of the sense of trusteeship; as in my opinion, the violence of private ownership is less injurious than the violence of the State. However, if it is unavoidable, I would support a minimum of State-ownership.

I desire to end capitalism almost, if not quite, as much as the most advanced socialist and even communist. But our methods differ, our languages differ.

I have claimed that I was a socialist long before those I know in India had avowed their creed. But my socialism was natural to me and not adopted from any books. It came out of my unshakable belief in non-violence. No man could be actively non-violent and not rise against social injustice, no matter where it occurred. Unfortunately, western socialists have, so far as I know, believed in the necessity of violence for enforcing socialistic doctrines.

There can be no rule of God in the present state of iniquitous inequalities in which a few roll in riches and the masses do not get enough to eat. I accepted the theory of socialism even while I was in South Africa.

Socialism is a beautiful word and so far as I am aware in socialism all the members of society are equal—none low, none high. In the individual body, the head is not high because it is the top of the body, nor are the soles of the feet low because they touch the earth. Even as members of the individual body are equal, so are the members of society. This is socialism.

PROHIBITION

People drink because of the conditions to which they are reduced. It is the factory laborers and others that drink. They are forlorn, uncared for and they take to drink. They are no more vicious by nature than teetotallers are saints by nature. The majority of people are controlled by their environment.

State prohibition is not the end of this great temperance reform, but it is the indispensable beginning of it.

India is not America. The American example [of prohibition] is a hindrance rather than a help to us. In America drinking carries no shame with it. It is the fashion there to drink. It reflects the greatest credit on the determined minority in America that by sheer force of its moral weight it was able to carry through the prohibition measure however short-lived it was. I do not regard that experiment to have been a failure.

Prohibition means a type of adult education of the nation and not merely a closing down of grog shops.

Drink is more a disease than a vice.

9. The Family

WOMEN

See also the section on "Family Affairs" in Chapter 12; and the section on "Family Relations" in Chapter 13.

Man and woman are of equal rank, but they are not identical.

Woman is the companion of man, gifted with equal mental capacities. She has the right to participate in very minutest detail in the activities of man, and she has an equal right of freedom and liberty with him. She is entitled to a supreme place in her own sphere of activity, as man is in his.

Chastity is not a hot-house growth. It cannot be superimposed. . . . It must grow from within, and to be worth anything, it must be capable of withstanding every unsought temptation.

I have regarded woman as an incarnation of tolerance. A servant wrongly suspected may throw up his job, a son in the same case may leave his father's roof, and a friend may put an end to the friendship. The wife, if she suspects her husband, will keep quiet.

Refuse to decorate yourselves, don't go in for scents and lavender waters; if you want to give out the proper scent, it must come out of your heart, and then you will captivate not man, but humanity.

Woman . . . should labor under no legal disability not suffered by man. . . . The root of the evil [of legal inequality] lies much deeper than most people realize. It lies in man's greed of power and fame, and, deeper still, in mutual lust. Man has always desired power.

Of all the evils for which man has made himself responsible, none is so degrading, so shocking, or so brutal as his abuse of the *better* half of humanity; to me—the female sex —*not* the weaker sex, for it is the nobler of the two. It is, even today, the embodiment of sacrifice, silent suffering, humility, faith, and knowledge.

A woman's intuition has often proved truer than man's arrogant assumption of superior knowledge.

The real ornament of woman is her character, her purity. Metal and stones can never be real ornaments. . . . Real ornamentation lies, not in loading the body with metal and stones, but in purifying the heart and developing the beauty of the soul.

I hold that the right education in this country is to teach woman the art of saying "no" even to her husband, to teach her that it is no part of her duty to become a mere tool or a doll in her husband's hands.

I believe in the proper education of women. But I do believe that woman will not make her contribution to the world by mimicking or running a race with man. She can run the race, but she will not rise to the great heights she is capable of, by mimicking man. She has to be the complement of man.

Equality of sexes does not mean equality of occupations. . . . Nature has created sexes as complements to each other.

Just as fundamentally man and woman are one, their problem must be one in essence. The soul in both is the same. The two live the same life, have the same feelings. Each is a complement of the other. The one cannot live without the other's active help.

It is given to [woman] to teach the art of peace to the warring world, thirsting for that nectar.

Let not women, who can count many . . . heroines among them, ever despise their sex or deplore that they were not born men. . . . There is as much reason for man to wish that he was born a woman, as for woman to do otherwise. But the wish is fruitless. Let us be happy in the state to which we are born, and do the duty for which nature has destined us.

The slavery of the kitchen is a remnant of barbarism mainly. It is high time that our womankind was freed from this incubus. Domestic work ought not to take the whole of a woman's time.

As long as the birth of a girl does not receive the same welcome as that of a boy, so long we should know that India is suffering from partial paralysis.

MARRIAGE

Marriage is a fence that protects religion. If the fence were to be destroyed, religion would go to pieces. The foundation of religion is restraint, and marriage is nothing but restraint.

A wife is not bound to be an accomplice in her husband's crimes. And when she holds anything to be wrong, she must dare to do the right.

The peace of the household is a most desirable thing. But it cannot be an end in itself.

The wife is not the husband's bondslave, but his companion and his helpmate, and an equal partner in all his joys and sorrows—as free as the husband to choose her own path.

When there is a heart union ... it is hardly right to postpone marriage merely for financial considerations. If poverty is a bar, poor men can never marry.

Spiritual relationship is far more precious than physical. Physical relationship divorced from spiritual is body without soul.

The only honorable terms in marriage are mutual love and mutual consent.

Marriage is a sacrament and ought not to carry any expenditure with it. If those who have money will not curb the desire to spend it on feasting and revelry, the poor people will want to copy them and incur debts in so doing. You will, if you are brave, rise in revolt against any extravagant expenditure when you are ready to be married.

If the wife has to prove her loyalty and undivided devotion to her husband, so has the husband to prove his allegiance and devotion to his wife. You cannot have one set of weights and measures for the one and a different one for the other.

Marriage outside one's religion stands on a different footing [than outside one's caste]. Even here, so long as each is free to observe his or her religion, I can see no moral objection to such unions.

Marriage, for the satisfaction of sexual appetite, is no marriage. It is concupiscence.

The very purpose of marriage is restraint and sublimation of the sexual passion. If there is any other purpose, marriage is no consecration.

Spiritual development ought to be given the first place in the choice for marriage. Service should come next, family considerations and the interest of the social order should have the third place, and mutual attraction or "love" the fourth and last place. This means that "love" alone, where the other four conditions are not fulfilled, should not be held as a valid reason for marriage. At the same time, marriage where there is no love should equally be ruled out even though all the other conditions are fully complied with.

It is no doubt an excellent thing for girls to remain unmarried for the sake of service, but the fact is that only one in a million is able to do so. Marriage is a natural thing in life, and to consider it derogatory in any sense is wholly wrong. . . . The ideal is to look upon marriage as a sacrament and therefore to lead a life of self-restraint in the married state.

BIRTH CONTROL

Is it right for us . . . to bring forth children in an atmosphere so debasing? We only multiply slaves and weaklings, if we continue the process of procreation whilst we feel and remain helpless, diseased and famine-striken. Not till India has become a free nation, able to withstand avoidable starvation, well able to feed herself in times of famine, possessing the knowledge to deal with malaria, cholera, influenza and other epidemics, have we the right to bring forth progeny. . . . I have contemplated with satisfaction the prospect of suspending procreation by voluntary self-denial. . . . Not by immoral and artificial checks that are resorted to in Europe, but by a life of discipline and self-control.

The [married] couple [should] never have sexual union for the fulfilment of their lust, but only when they desire issue. I think it is the height of ignorance to believe that the sexual act is an independent function necessary like sleeping or eating. The world depends for its existence on the act of generation, and as the world is the playground of God and a reflection of His glory, the act of generation should be controlled for the ordered growth of the world. He who realizes this will control his lust at any cost, equip himself with the knowledge necessary for the physical, mental and spiritual well-being of his progeny.

Birth control by contraceptives and the like is a profound error. . . . Birth control through self-control is no doubt difficult. But no one has yet been known seriously to dispute its efficacy, and even superiority over the use of contraceptives.

The introduction of contraceptives under the name of science and the imprimatur of known leaders of society has intensified complication and made the task of reformers, who work for purity of social life, well-nigh impossible for the moment. . . . It is impossible to confine their use to married women. Marriage loses its sanctity when its purpose and highest use is conceived to be the satisfaction of the animal passion, without contemplating the natural result of such satisfaction. . . . The greatest harm, however, . . . lies in its rejection of the old ideal and substitution in its place of one which, if carried out, must spell the moral and physical extinction of the race.

Sex urge is a fine and noble thing. There is nothing to be ashamed of in it. But it is meant only for the act of creation. Any other use of it is a sin against God and humanity.

Propagation of the race rabbit-wise must undoubtedly be stopped, but not so as to bring greater evils in its train. It should be stopped by methods which in themselves ennoble the race.

PROSTITUTION

All of us men must hang our heads in shame so long as there is a single woman whom we dedicate to our passion. I would far rather see the race of men extinct than that we should become less than beasts by making the noblest of God's creation the object of our lust.

It is a matter of bitter shame and sorrow, of deep humiliation, that a number of women have to sell their chastity for man's lust. Man, the law-giver, will have to pay a dreadful penalty for the degradation he has imposed upon the so-called weaker sex. . . . It is an evil which cannot last for a single day if we men of India realize our own dignity.

Before these unfortunate sisters could be weaned from their degradation two conditions have to be fulfilled. We men must learn to control our passions, and these women should be found a calling that would enable them to earn an honorable living.

PARENTHOOD

Every home is a university and the parents are the teachers.

Parents . . . should not tie a mill-stone round the necks of their sons by marrying them in their teens. They should look also to the welfare of their sons, and not only to their own interests.

Parents ... feel that their children should be educated only in order that they may earn wealth and position. Education and knowledge are thus prostituted and we look in vain for the peace, innocence and bliss that the life of students ought to be.

It is idle to expect one's children and wards necessarily to follow the same course of evolution as oneself.

What a terrible responsibility it is to be a parent.

In a well-regulated family, the relations are governed by the unitary method. Thus a father gives to his children not as a result of a pact. He gives out of love, a sense of justice without expecting any return therefor. Not that there is none. But everything is natural, nothing is forced. Nothing is done out of fear or distrust. What is true of a well-regulated family is equally true of a well-regulated society which is but an extended family.

There is no school equal to a decent home and no teachers equal to honest virtuous parents.

10. Education

THEORY

Education ... simply means a knowledge of letters. It is merely an instrument, and an instrument may be well used or abused.

Education to be universal must therefore be free.

An academic grasp without practice behind it is like an embalmed corpse, perhaps lovely to look at but nothing to inspire or ennoble.

The higher [the student] goes, the farther he is removed from his home, so that at the end of his education he becomes estranged from his surroundings. He feels no poetry about the home life. The village scenes are all a sealed book to him. His own civilization is presented to him as imbecile, barbarous, superstitious and useless. . . . His education is calculated to wean him from his traditional culture.

Knowledge without character is a power for evil only, as seen in the instances of so many "talented thieves" and "gentleman rascals" in the world.

No [educational] system will be even passable that does not lay stress on adult education equally with that of children.

There is something radically wrong in the system of education that fails to arm girls and boys to fight against social or other evils. That education alone is of value which draws out the faculties of a student, so as to enable him or her to solve correctly the problems of life in every department.

Man is neither mere intellect, nor the gross animal body, nor the heart or soul alone. A proper and harmonious combination of all the three is required for the making of the whole man and constitutes the true economics of education.

We have up to now concentrated on stuffing children's minds with all kinds of information, without ever thinking of stimulating and developing them.

It is not literacy or learning that make a man, but education for real life. What would it matter if [men] knew everything but did not know how to live in brotherliness with their neighbors?

THE CHILD

It is a sign of national degradation when little children are removed from schools and are employed in earning wages. No nation worthy of the name can possibly afford so to misuse her children. At least up to the age of sixteen they must be kept in schools.

The true education of the child begins from the very moment of its birth. The rudiments of knowledge are imbibed almost in the course of play.

Punishment does not purify; if anything it hardens children.

We labor under a sort of superstition that the child has nothing to learn during the first five years of its life. On the contrary the fact is that the child never learns in after life what it does in its first five years.

Under ideal conditions, true education could be imparted only by the parents, and there should be the minimum of outside help.

If good children are taught together with bad ones and thrown into their company, they will lose nothing, provided the experiment is conducted under the watchful care of their parents and guardians. Children wrapped up in cottonwool are not always proof against all temptation and contamination.

Passive resistance is the noblest and best education. . . . It will not be denied that a child, before it begins to write its alphabet and to gain worldly knowledge, should know what the soul is, what truth is, what love is, what powers are latent in the soul. It should be an essential of real education that a child should learn that, in the struggle of life, it can easily conquer hate by love, untruth by truth, violence by self-suffering.

Children are innocent, loving and benevolent by nature. Evil comes only when they become older.

THE STUDENT

Students must become pioneers in conservative reform, conserving all that is good in the nation and fearlessly ridding society of the innumerable abuses that have crept into it.

In the case of the vast majority of students, whilst they entertain noble impulses during their student days, these disappear when they finish their studies. The vast majority of them look out for loaves and fishes.

Scholastic education is not merely brick and mortar. It is true boys and true girls who build such institutions from day to day. I know some huge, architecturally perfect buildings going under the name of scholastic institutions, but they are nothing but whited sepulchres. Conversely, I know also some institutions which have to struggle from day to day for their material existence, but which, because of this very want, are spiritually making advance from day to day.

One might as well hope to restrain the winds as hope to curb the roused enthusiasm of students.

Vacations must be utilized for recreation, never for memorizing books.

I warn the youth of the country against always discounting whatever old men or women say, for the mere fact that it is said by such persons. Even as wisdom often comes from the mouths of babes, so does it often come from the mouths of old people.

[A student's] mental equipment is counterbalanced by false notions of dignity, inculcated during school and college days. And so students think that they can earn their living only at the desk.

A student cannot be an active politician and pursue his studies at the same time. . . . Students should have the greatest freedom of expression and of opinion. They may openly sympathize with any political party they like.

THE TEACHER

The education of the heart ... can [not] be imparted through books. It can only be done through the living touch of the teacher.

It is the duty of the teacher to teach his pupils discrimination. If we go on taking in indiscriminately, we would be no better than machines. We are thinking, knowing beings, and we must ... distinguish truth from untruth, sweet from bitter language, clean from unclean things, and so on.

On Tolstoy Farm we made it a rule that the youngsters should not be asked to do what the teachers did not do, and therefore, when they were asked to do any work, there was always a teacher co-operating and actually working with them.

Of text-books, about which we hear so much, I never felt the want. ... I did not find it at all necessary to load the boys with quantities of books. I have always felt that the true text-book for the pupil is his teacher. I remember very little that my teachers taught me from books, but I have even now a clear recollection of the things they taught me independently of books.

Religious instruction, I discovered, was imparted by teachers living the religion themselves. I have found that boys imbibe more from the teachers' own lives than they do from the books that they read to them, or the lectures that they deliver to them with their lips. I have discovered to my great joy that boys and girls have unconsciously a faculty of penetration whereby they read the thoughts of their teachers. Woe to the teacher who teaches one thing with his lips, and carries another in his breast.

The teachers' work lies more outside than inside the lecture room.

THE CURRICULUM

Literary training by itself adds not an inch to one's moral height and character-building is independent of literary training.

An appreciation of other cultures can fitly follow, never precede, an appreciation and assimilation of our own.

Physical education should have as much place in the curriculum as mental training.

Bad handwriting should be regarded as a sign of an imperfect education. . . . Good handwriting is a necessary part of education.

An intelligent approach to an industrial training is often a more valuable aid to the intellect than an indifferent reading of literature.

Literacy is not the end of education nor even the beginning. It is only one of the means whereby man and woman can be educated. Literacy in itself is no education.

The vast amount of the so-called education in arts, given in our colleges, is sheer waste and has resulted in unemployment among the educated classes. What is more, it has destroyed the health, both mental and physical, of the boys and girls who have the misfortune to go through the grind in our colleges.

RELIGIOUS EDUCATION

If India is not to declare spiritual bankruptcy, religious instruction of its youth must be held to be at least as necessary as secular instruction.

I had always given the first place to the culture of the heart or the building of character, and I felt confident that moral training could be given to all alike, no matter how different their ages and their upbringing.

I believed that every student should be acquainted with the elements of his own religion and have a general knowledge of his own scriptures. . . . The training of the spirit [is] a thing by itself. To develop the spirit is to build character and to enable one to work towards a knowledge of God and self-realization. . . . All training without culture of the spirit [is] of no use, and might even be harmful. . . . It [is] not through books that one could impart training of the spirit. Just as physical training [is] to be imparted through physical exercise, and intellectual through intellectual exercise, even so the training of the spirit [is] possible only through the exercise of the spirit. And the exercise of the spirit entirely depends on the life and character of the teacher. . . . I saw that I must be an eternal object-lesson to the boys and girls living with me. They thus became my teachers, and I learned I must be good and live straight, if only for their sakes.

A curriculum of religious instruction should include a study of the tenets of faith other than one's own. For this purpose, the students should be trained to cultivate the habit of understanding and appreciating the doctrines of various great religions of the world, in a spirit of reverence and broad-minded tolerance. This, if properly done, would help to give them a spiritual assurance and a better appreciation of their own religion.

The culture of the mind must be subservient to the culture of the heart.

I do not believe that the State can concern itself or cope with religious instruction. I believe that religious education must be the sole concern of religious associations. Do not mix up religion and ethics. I believe that fundamental ethics is common to all religions. Teaching of fundamental ethics is undoubtedly a function of the State. By religion I have not in mind fundamental ethics but what goes by the name of denominationalism. We have suffered enough from State-aided religion and a State Church. A society, or a group, which depends partly or wholly on State aid for the existence of its religion, does not deserve or, better still, does not have any religion worth the name.

CRIME

See also the section on "Imprisonment" in Chapter 6.

When vice becomes a fashion and even a virtue, it is a long process to deal with it.

The word criminal should be taboo from our dictionary. Or we are all criminals. . . . As a jailor once said, all are criminals in secret. There is profound truth in that saying, uttered in half jest.

It is the duty of society not to take up a heartless step-motherly attitude toward those who might disregard or break the established conventions.

I cannot in all conscience agree to any one being sent to the gallows. . . . Once a man is killed, the punishment is beyond recall or reparation. God alone can take life, because He alone gives it.

Personally I do not believe in imprisoning by way of punishment even those who commit violence.

If I had my way I would fling open doors of prisons and discharge even murderers.

All crimes are different kinds of diseases and they should be treated as such by the reformers. That does not mean that the police will suspend their function of regarding such cases as public crimes, but their measures are never intended to deal with causes of these social disturbances.

All criminals should be treated as patients, and the jails should be hospitals admitting this kind of patient for treatment and cure.

11. Culture and the Professions

EAST vs. WEST

See also the section on "Machines and Industrialization" in Chapter 8.

The tendency of the Indian civilization is to elevate the moral being, that of the Western civilization is to propagate immorality. The latter is godless, the former is based on belief in God.

Modern civilization is chiefly materialistic, as ours is chiefly spiritual. Modern civilization occupies itself in the investigation of the laws of matter, and employs the human ingenuity in inventing or discovering means of production and weapons of destruction; ours is chiefly occupied in exploring spiritual laws.

The pandemonium that is going on in Europe shows that modern civilization represents forces of evil and darkness, whereas the ancient, i.e., Indian civilization, represents in its essence the divine force.

Systematic study of Asiatic culture is no less essential than the study of Western sciences.

I wholeheartedly detest this mad desire to destroy distance and time, to increase animal appetites and go to the ends of the earth in search of satisfaction. If modern civilization stands for all this, and I have understood it to do so, I call it Satanic.

I do not hold that everything ancient is good, because it is ancient. I do not advocate surrender of God-given reasoning faculty in the face of ancient tradition. Any tradition, however ancient, if inconsistent with morality, is fit to be banished from the land.

Many who are professing to revive ancient culture do not hesitate under the name of that revival to revive old superstitions and prejudices.

I am no indiscriminate, superstitious worshipper of all that goes under the name of ancient! I never hesitate to endeavor to demolish all that is evil or immoral, no matter how ancient it may be, but with that reservation. I must confess to you that I am an adorer of ancient institutions and it hurts me to think that a people, in their rush for everything modern, despise all their ancient traditions and ignore them in their lives.

Whatever service I have been able to render to the nation has been *entirely* due to the retention by me of Eastern culture to the extent it has been possible. I should have been thoroughly useless to the masses as an anglicized, denationalized being, knowing little of, caring less for and perhaps even despising, their ways, habits, thoughts and aspirations.

No Eastern thinker fears that if Western nations came in free contact with Orientals, Oriental culture would be swept away like sand by the onrushing tide of Western civilization. . . . Oriental civilization not only does not fear but would positively welcome free contact with Western civilization.

Why should we be blotting sheets of Western civilization?

I want the cultures of all lands to be blown about my house as freely as possible. But I refuse to be blown off my feet by any.

WESTERN CULTURE

Civilization is like a mouse gnawing while it is soothing us. When its full effect is realized, we shall see that religious superstition is harmless compared to that of modern civilization.

I am and I have been a determined opponent of modern civilization.

Modern civilization as represented by the West of today in my opinion has given matter a place which by right belongs to spirit. It has therefore put violence upon the throne of triumph and held under bondage truth and innocence.

I do not like many Western ways, but there are certain things in them for which I cannot disguise my admiration. Their "hobby" is a thing full of meaning.

Western thinkers claim that the foundation of Western civilization is the predominance of might over right. Therefore the protagonists of that civilization devote most of their time to the conservation of brute force.

I wish to utter a word of caution against your believing that I am an indiscriminate despiser of everything that comes from the West. There are many things which I have myself assimilated from the West.

The West has always commanded my admiration for its surgical inventions and all-round progress in that direction.

I have been a sympathetic student of the Western social order and I have discovered that underlying the fever that fills the soul of the West there is a restless search for truth. I value that spirit.

There is nothing to prevent me from profiting by the light that may come from the West. Only I must take care that I am not overpowered by the glamor of the West. I must not mistake the glamor for true light.

Western nations are today groaning under the heel of the monster god of materialism. Their moral growth has become stunted. They measure their progress in pounds, shillings, and pence. American wealth has become the standard. She is the envy of other nations. I have heard many of our countrymen say that we will gain American wealth but avoid its methods. I venture to suggest that such an attempt, if it were made, is foredoomed to failure. We cannot be "wise, temperate and furious" in a moment.

LANGUAGES

See also the section on "Vernacular vs. English" in Chapter 12.

The world is full of many a gem of priceless beauty; but, then, these gems are not all of English setting.

No country can become a nation by producing a race of translators. Think of what would have happened to the English if they had not an authorized version of the Bible.

Children of the nation that receive instruction in a tongue other than their own commit suicide. It robs them of their birth right. A foreign medium means an undue strain upon the youngsters. It robs them of all originality. It stunts their growth and isolates them from their home.

There never was a greater superstition than that a particular language can be incapable of expansion or of expressing abstruse or scientific ideas. A language is an exact reflection of the character and growth of its speakers.

How dare we rub off from our memory all the years of our infancy? But that is precisely what we do when we commence our higher life through the medium of a foreign tongue.

Different scripts are an unnecessary hindrance to the learning by the people of one province the language of other provinces.

THE ARTS

Music means rhythm, order. Its effect is electrical. It immediately soothes. I have seen, in European countries, a resourceful superintendent of police by starting a popular song controlling the mischievous tendencies of mobs. Unfortunately . . . music has been the prerogative of the few, either the banter of prostitutes or high class religious devotees. It has never become nationalized in the modern sense.

True art takes note not merely of form but also of what lies behind. There is an art that kills and an art that gives life. . . . True art must be evidence of happiness, contentment and purity of its authors.

True beauty after all consists in purity of heart.

Music has given me peace. I can remember occasions when music instantly tranquillized my mind, when I was greatly agitated over something. Music has helped me to overcome anger.

All true art is the expression of the soul. The outward forms have value only in so far as they are the expression of the inner spirit of man. . . . I know that many call themselves artists in whose works there is absolutely no trace of the soul's upward urge and unrest. . . . All true art must help the soul to realize its inner self.

I see and find beauty through Truth. All Truths, not merely true ideas, but truthful faces, truthful pictures, truthful songs, are highly beautiful. Whenever men begin to see beauty in Truth, then art will arise. . . . There is . . . no beauty apart from Truth. On the other hand, Truth may manifest itself in forms which may not be outwardly beautiful at all. Socrates, we are told, was the most truthful man of his time, and yet his features are said to have been the ugliest in Greece. To my mind he was beautiful because all his life was a striving after Truth.

Purity of life is the highest and truest art. The art of producing good music from a cultivated voice can be achieved by many, but the art of producing that music from the harmony of a pure life is achieved very rarely.

My room may have blank walls, and I may even dispense with the roof, so that I may gaze out upon the starry heavens overhead that stretch in an unending expanse of beauty. What conscious art of man can give me the panoramic scenes that open out before me, when I look above with all its shining stars? Anything which is a hindrance to the flight of the soul, is a delusion and a snare.

Mankind cannot live by logic alone, but also needs poetry.

THE PRESS

One of the objects of a newspaper is to understand popular feeling and to give expression to it; another is to arouse among the people certain desirable sentiments; and the third is fearlessly to expose popular defects.

What a financial gain it would be to the country, if there was for each province only one advertising medium— not a newspaper—containing innocent, unvarnished notices of things useful for the public! But for our criminal indifference, we would decline to pay the huge indirect taxation by way of mischievous advertisements.

I do not believe in publishing newspapers indefinitely at a loss or by means of advertisements. If a paper supplies a felt want, it must pay its way.

Many amongst you [students] read newspapers. I do not think I can ask you to eschew them altogether; but I would ask you to eschew everything of ephemeral interest, and I can tell you that newspapers afford nothing of permanent interest. They offer nothing to help the formation of character, and yet I know the craze for newspapers.

I always aimed at establishing an intimate and clean bond between the editor and the readers. . . . The sole aim of journalism should be service. The newspaper press is a great power, but just as an unchained torrent of water submerges whole countrysides and devastates crops, even so an uncontrolled pen serves but to destroy. If the control is from without, it proves more poisonous than want of control. It can be profitable only when exercised from within. If this line of reasoning is correct, how many of the journals of the world would stand the test? But who would stop those that are useless? And who should be the judge? The useful and the useless must, like good and evil generally, go on together, and man must make his choice.

A subject which is considered worthy of being communicated by cablegram becomes invested with an importance it does not intrinsically possess.

The newspaperman has become a walking plague.

THE LAW AND LAWYERS

Railways, lawyers and doctors have impoverished the country so much that, if we do not wake up in time, we shall be ruined.

Lawyers are also men, and there is something good in every man. Whenever instances of lawyers having done good can be brought forward, it will be found that the good is due to them as men rather than as lawyers.

Lawyers will, as a rule, advance quarrels instead of repressing them. Moreover, men take up that profession, not in order to help others out of their miseries, but to enrich themselves. It is one of the avenues of becoming wealthy and their interest exists in multiplying disputes. It is within my knowledge that they are glad when men have disputes.

The true function of a lawyer [is] to unite parties riven asunder. The lesson was so indelibly burned into me that a large part of my time during the twenty years of my practice as a lawyer was occupied in bringing about private compromises of hundreds of cases. I lost nothing thereby—not even money, certainly not my soul. . . . I had learned the true practice of law. I had learned to find out the better side of human nature and to enter men's hearts.

It was not impossible to practice law without compromising truth. Even truthfulness in the practice of the profession cannot cure it of the fundamental defect that vitiates it.

If you would spiritualize the practice of law, [do not] make your profession subservient to the interests of your purse, as is unfortunately but too often the case at present, but use your profession for the service of your country. . . . The fees charged by lawyers are unconscionable everywhere. . . . In the practice of their profession, lawyers are consciously or unconsciously led into untruth for the sake of their clients. . . . The duty of a lawyer is always to place before the judges and to help them to arrive at the truth, never to prove the guilty as innocent.

Lawyers and English-educated persons do not by any means enjoy a monopoly of hair-splitting.

SCIENCE

I abhor vivisection with my whole soul. I detest the unpardonable slaughter of innocent life in the name of science and humanity so-called, and all the scientific discoveries stained with innocent blood I count as of no consequence. If the circulation of blood theory could not have been discovered without vivisection, the human kind could well have done without it.

I am not opposed to the progress of science as such. On the contrary, the scientific spirit of the West commands my admiration, and if that admiration is qualified, it is because the scientist of the West takes no note of God's lower creation.

All things in the universe, including the sun and the moon and the stars, obey certain laws. Without the restraining influence of these laws, the world will not go on for a single moment.

How little science knows. There is more in life than science, and there is more in God than in chemistry.

HISTORY

Hundreds of nations live in peace. History does not and cannot take note of this fact. History is really a record of every interruption of the even working of the force of love or of the soul. . . . History is a record of an interruption of the course of nature.

History, as we know it, is a record of the wars of the world. . . . How kings acted, how they became enemies of one another, and how they murdered one another—all this is found accurately recorded in history; and, if this were everything that had happened in the world, it would have been ended long ago.

The nations have progressed both by evolution and revolution. . . . History is more a record of wonderful revolution than of so-called ordered progress—no history more so than the English.

If we are to make progress, we must not repeat history but make new history. We must add to the inheritance left by our ancestors.

Indian history written from original sources by an Indian patriot will be different from that written by an English bureaucrat, though each may be quite honest. We have grievously erred in accepting English estimates of events in our national life.

It is my faith that what seems Utopian . . . today will be regarded as practical tomorrow. History is replete with such instances. . . . Is it not most tragic that things of the spirit, eternal verities, should be regarded as Utopian by our youth, and transitory make-shifts alone appeal to them as practical?

12. Indian Problems

INDIA

India must learn to live before she can aspire to die for humanity.

I do not subscribe to the superstition that everything is good because it is ancient. I do not believe either that anything is good because it is Indian.

Instead of being sullen and discontented, India free will be a mighty force for the good of mankind in general.

Indian culture is neither Hindu, Islamic nor any other, wholly. It is a fusion of all and essentially Eastern.

India's freedom must revolutionize the world's outlook upon peace and war. . . . An India awakened and free has a message of peace and goodwill to a groaning world.

[India] will only then be a truly spiritual nation when we shall show more truth than gold, greater fearlessness than pomp of power and wealth, greater charity than love of self. If we will but cleanse our houses, our palaces and temples of the attributes of wealth and show in them the attributes of morality, we can offer battle to any combinations of hostile forces without having to carry the burden of a heavy militia.

INDEPENDENCE (*SWARAJ*)

If man will only realize that it is unmanly to obey laws that are unjust, no man's tyranny will enslave him. This is the key to self- and home-rule.

Swaraj for India must be an impossible dream without an indissoluble union between the Hindus and the Muslims of India. It must not be a mere truce. It must be a partnership between equals, respecting the religion of the other.

Swaraj . . . means complete freedom of opinion and action without interference with another's right to equal freedom of opinion and action. Therefore it means India's complete control of sources of revenue and expenditure without interference from or with any other country.

Swaraj is freedom for everyone, the smallest among us, to do as he likes without any physical interference with his liberty.

Swaraj does not consist in the change of Government. . . . [It] is a real change of heart on the part of the people.

Swaraj can never be a free gift by one nation to another. It is a treasure to be purchased with a nation's best blood. *Swaraj* will be the fruit of incessant labor, suffering beyond measure.

By *Swaraj* I mean the government of India by the consent of the people as ascertained by the largest number of the adult population, male or female, native born or domiciled, who have contributed by manual labor to the service of the State and who have taken the trouble of having their names registered as voters. . . . *Swaraj* is to be attained by educating the masses to a sense of their capacity to regulate and control authority.

The pilgrimage to *Swaraj* is a painful climb. . . . It means national education, i.e., education of the masses. It means an awakening of national consciousness among the masses· It will not spring like the magician's mango. It will grow almost unperceived like the banian tree.

Self-government means continuous effort to be independent of government control whether it is foreign government or whether it is national.

To postpone social reform till after the attainment of *Swaraj* is not to know the meaning of *Swaraj*.

Insult offered to a single innocent member of a nation is tantamount to insulting the nation as a whole.

Mere withdrawal of the English is not independence. It means the consciousness in the average villager that he is the maker of his own destiny, he is his own legislator through his chosen representative.

Conversion of a nation that has consciously or unconsciously preyed upon another far more numerous, far more ancient, and no less cultured than itself is worth any amount of risk. I have deliberately used the word conversion, for my ambition is no less than to convert the British people through non-violence and thus make them see the wrong they have done to India.

HOME INDUSTRY (*SWADESHI*)

Swadeshi is that spirit within us which restricts us to the use and service of our immediate surroundings to the exclusion of the more remote.

If not a single article of commerce had been brought from outside India she would today be a land flowing with milk and honey. . . . She can live for herself only if she produces everything for her own requirements within her own borders.

Swadeshi . . . is not . . . merely confined to wearing on occasion a *swadeshi* cloth. . . . We commit a breach of the *swadeshi* spirit certainly if we wear foreign made cloth, but we do so also if we adopt the foreign cut.

India as a nation can live and die only for the spinning wheel. Every woman will tell the curious that with the disappearance of the spinning wheel, vanished India's happiness and prosperity.

We stint ourselves in the matter of food in order to be able to spend on clothing, and sink to greater misery day by day. We are bound to perish if the twin industries of agriculture and spinning as well as weaving disappear from our villages or our homes.

I would make the spinning wheel the foundation on which to build a sound village life; I would make the wheel the center round which all other activities will revolve.

The broad definition of *swadeshi* is the use of all home-made things to the exclusion of foreign things, in so far as such use is necessary for the protection of home-industry.

Hand-spinning . . . offers an immediate, practicable, and permanent solution of that problem of problems that confronts India, viz. the enforced idleness for nearly six months in the year of an overwhelming majority of India's population, owing to lack of a suitable supplementary occupation to agriculture and the chronic starvation of the masses that results therefrom.

Charkha . . . stands not for the greatest good of the greatest number, but for the greatest good of all.

I considered no price too high for securing home-spun yarn. . . . The wheel began merrily to hum in my room, and I may say without exaggeration that its hum had no small share in restoring me to health. I am prepared to admit that its effect was more psychological than physical. . . . I now grew impatient for the exclusive adoption of *khadi* for my dress. . . . My work . . . is to organize the production of homespun cloth, ·and to find means for the disposal of the *khadi* thus produced. . . . I swear by this form of *swadeshi* because, through it, I can provide work to the semi-starved, semi-employed women of India. My idea is to get these women to spin yarn, and to clothe the people of India with *khadi* woven out of it.

I have never been an advocate of prohibition of all things foreign because they are foreign. My economic creed is a complete taboo in respect of all foreign commodities, whose importation is likely to prove harmful to our indigenous interests. This means that we may not, in any circumstances, import a commodity that can be adequately supplied from our own country. . . . I would not countenance the boycott of a single foreign article out of ill-will or a feeling of hatred.

Hand-spinning does not compete with, in order to displace, any existing type of industry; it does not aim at withdrawing a single able-bodied person who can otherwise find a more remunerative occupation from his work.

Charkha is no new invention, like Ford's motor-car; it is rediscovery, like the discovery of its own mother by a strayed child.

It is sinful for me to wear the latest finery of Regent Street when I know that if I had but worn the things woven by the neighboring spinners and weavers, that would have clothed me, and fed and clothed them at the same time.

Every yard of foreign cloth brought into India is one bit of bread snatched out of the mouths of these starving poor.

I think of *swadeshi* not as a boycott movement undertaken by way of revenge. I conceive it as a religious principle to be followed by all.

VERNACULAR vs. ENGLISH

See also the section on "Languages" in Chapter 11.

English is a language of international commerce; it is the language of diplomacy, and it contains many a rich literary treasure, it gives us an introduction to Western thought and culture. For a few of us, therefore, a knowledge of English is necessary. They can carry on the departments of national commerce and international diplomacy, and for giving to the nation the best of Western literature, thought and science. That would be the legitimate use of English. Whereas today, English has usurped the dearest place in our hearts and dethroned our mother-tongues.

The highest development of the Indian mind must be possible without a knowledge of English. It is doing violence to the manhood, and especially the womanhood of India, to encourage our boys and girls to think that an entry into the best society is impossible without a knowledge of English. It is too humiliating a thought to be bearable. To get rid of the infatuation for English is one of the essentials of *Swaraj*.

Of all the superstitions that affect India, none is so great as that a knowledge of the English language is necessary for imbibing ideas of liberty and developing accuracy of thought.

It is unbearable to me that the vernaculars should be crushed and starved as they have been. I cannot tolerate the idea of parents writing to their children, or husbands writing to their wives, not in their own vernaculars but in English. . . . I would not have a single Indian to forget, neglect or be ashamed of his mother-tongue or to feel that he or she cannot think or express the best thought in his or her own vernacular.

Indian parents who train their children to think and talk in English from their infancy betray their children and their country. They deprive them of the spiritual and social heritage of the nation, and render them to that extent unfit for the service of the country.

The youth of a nation to remain a nation must receive all instruction, including the highest, in its own vernacular or vernaculars. . . . The youth of a nation cannot keep or establish a living contact with the masses unless their knowledge is received and assimilated through a medium understood by the people. Who can calculate the immeasurable loss sustained by the nation, owing to thousands of its young men having been obligated to waste years in mastering a foreign language and its idiom, of which in their daily life they have the least use and in learning which they had to neglect their own mother-tongue and their own literature?

VILLAGES AND AGRICULTURE

Whenever I hear of a great palace rising in any great city of India, be it in British India or be it in India which is ruled by our great Chiefs, I become jealous at once and I say, "Oh, it is the money that has come from the agriculturists."

Our salvation can only come through the farmer. Neither the lawyers, nor the doctors, nor the rich landlords are going to secure it.

Farmers and workers ... make India. Their poverty is India's curse and crime. Their prosperity alone can make India a country fit to live in.

The village movement is an attempt to establish healthy contact with the villages by inducing those who are fired with the spirit of service to settle in them and find self-expression in the service of villagers.

India is to be found not in its few cities but in its 700,000 villages.

The moment you talk to [the Indian peasants] and they begin to speak, you will find wisdom drops from their lips. Behind the crude exterior you will find a deep reservoir of spirituality.

Landlords would do well to take time by the forelock. Let them cease to be mere rent collectors. They should become trustees and trusted friends of their tenants.

UNTOUCHABILITY

We can never reach *Swaraj* with the poison of untouchability corroding the Hindu part of the national body. *Swaraj* is a meaningless term, if we desire to keep a fifth of India under perpetual subjection, and deliberately deny to them the fruits of national culture.

I have never been able to reconcile myself to untouchability. I have always regarded it as an excrescence. . . . Untouchability is repugnant to reason and to the instinct of mercy, pity, or love. A religion that establishes the worship of the cow cannot possibly countenance or warrant cruel and inhuman boycott of human beings, the suppressed classes. Hindus will certainly never deserve freedom or get it if they allow their noble religion to be disgraced by the retention of the taint of untouchability. . . . Let us not deny God by denying to a fifth of our race the right of association on an equal footing.

That there is untouchability even amongst "untouchables" merely demonstrates that evil cannot be confined and that its deadening effect is all-pervading. The existence of untouchability amongst the "untouchables" is an additional reason for cultured Hindu society to rid itself of the curse with the quickest dispatch.

It is painful to discover that even after five years of continuous propaganda against untouchability, there are learned people enough to support such an immoral and evil custom. That belief in untouchability can coexist with learning in the same person, adds no status to untouchability but makes one despair of mere learning being an aid to character or sanity.

If I have to be reborn I should wish to be born an "untouchable," so that I may share their sorrows, sufferings, and the affronts levelled against them, in order that I may endeavor to free myself and them from that miserable condition. Therefore I prayed that if I should be born again I should be so, not as a *Brahmin, Kshattriya, Vaishya,* or *Shudra,* but as an "untouchable."

Some think of removing physical untouchability, some talk of the removal of the so-called untouchables' disabilities in regards to the use of public wells, schools and temples. But you should go much further. You should love them even as yourselves, so that the moment they see you they might feel that you are one of them.

The "untouchable" to me is, compared to us, really a *Harijan*—a man of God, and we are "*Durijan*" [men of evil]. For whilst the "untouchable" has toiled and moiled and dirtied his hands so that we may live in comfort and "cleanliness," we have delighted in suppressing him. We are solely responsible for all the shortcomings and faults that we lay at the door of these "untouchables." It is still open to us to be *Harijans* ourselves, but we can only do so by heartily repenting of our sin against them.

We are too near the scene of tragedy to realize that this canker of untouchability has travelled far beyond its prescribed limits and has sapped the foundations of the whole nation. The touch-me-not spirit pervades the atmosphere. If, therefore, this white ant is touched at its source, I feel sure that we shall soon forget the differences with regard to caste and caste and religion and religion and begin to believe that even as all Hindus are one and indivisible, so are all Hindus, Mussalmans, Sikhs, Parsis, Jews and Christians, branches of the same parent tree. Though religions are many, Religion is one. That is the lesson I would have us learn from the campaign against untouchability. And we will learn it, if we prosecute it in the religious spirit with a determination that will not be resisted.

Temples and the like are the property not of orthodoxy but of all Hindus. Therefore, this idea of excluding a section of Hindus from the use of public utilities is, itself, a species of violence, and, therefore, the support of legislation has got to be invoked in order to protect this fundamental right.

In the eyes of God, who is the creator of all, His creatures are all equal. Had He made any distinctions of high and low between man and man, they would have been visible as are the distinctions between say, an elephant and an ant. But he has endowed all human beings impartially with the same shape and the same natural wants. . . . It can never be an act of merit to look down upon any human being as inferior to us.

There should be, not only no untouchability as between Hindus and Hindus, but there should be no untouchability whatsoever between Hindus, Christians, Mussalmans, Parsis, and the rest. . . . It is untouchability with all its subtle forms that separates us from one another, and makes life itself unlovely and difficult to live.

The "touch-me-not"-ism that disfigures the present day Hinduism is a morbid growth. It only betrays a woodenness of mind, a blind self-conceit. It is abhorrent alike to the spirit of religion and morality.

The message of anti-untouchability does not end in merely touching the so-called untouchables. It has a much deeper meaning.

I do not desire to be born again, but if I am really born again, I desire to be born amidst the untouchables, so as to share their difficulties and to work for their liberation.

CASTE (*VARNA*)

Varnashrama [caste-system] is, in my opinion, inherent in human nature, and Hinduism has simply reduced it to a science. It does not attach to birth. A man cannot change his *varna* [caste] by choice. Not to abide by one's *varna* is to disregard the law of heredity. The division, however, into innumerable castes is an unwarranted liberty taken with the doctrine. The four divisions are all-sufficing. . . . The four divisions define a man's calling, they do not restrict or regulate social intercourse. . . . All are born to serve God's creation, a *Brahmin* with his knowledge, a *Kshattriya* with his power of protection, a *Vaishya* with his commercial ability, and a *Shudra* with bodily labor. . . . *Varnashrama* is self-restraint and conservation and economy of energy.

Varna has nothing to do with caste. Caste is an excrescence, just like untouchability, upon Hinduism. . . . But don't you find similar ugly excrescences in Christianity and Islam also? Fight them as much as you like. Down with the monster of caste that masquerades in the guise of *varna*.

Assumption of superiority by any person over any other is a sin against God and man. Thus caste, in so far as it connotes distinctions in status, is an evil.

I do not believe in caste in the modern sense. It is an excrescence and a handicap on progress.

There are in reality no *varnas*, the *varna* principle has ceased to operate. The present state of Hindu society may be described as that of anarchy, the four *varnas* today exist in name only. If we must talk in terms of *varna*, there is only one *varna* today for all, whether men or women; we are all *Shudras*.

V_{arna} does not connote a set of rights or privileges; it prescribes duties or obligations only. And no one can divest us of our duty, unless we ourselves choose to shirk it.

I believe that every man is born in the world with certain natural tendencies. Every person is born with certain definite limitations which he cannot overcome. From a careful observation of those limitations, the law of *varna* was deduced. It establishes certain spheres of action for certain people with certain tendencies.

Caste has nothing to do with religion. It is harmful both to spiritual and national growth.

FAMILY AFFAIRS

See also Chapter 9, "The Family"; and the section on "Family Relations" in Chapter 13.

Hinduism does not regard the married state as by any means essential for salvation. Marriage is a fall even as birth is a fall.

The maintenance of one's aged and infirm parents is a first charge upon grown-up sons. They may not marry if they are not in a position to support their parents. . . . Young men are not expected to . . . comply with the demand of thoughtless or ignorant parents. Parents have been known to demand money for things not required for sustenance but for false show, or for uncalled-for marriage expenses of daughters.

We may not contribute a single *pice* towards the expenses of conforming to meaningless and superstitious customs, such as caste-dinners or towards forming expensive marriage connections. Every marriage and every death bring an unnecessary cruel burden upon the head of the family. We must refuse to regard such acts of self-denial as self-sacrifice. They are evils to be counteracted with courage and resolution.

The custom of child-marriage is both a moral as well as a physical evil. For it undermines our morals and induces physical degeneration.

The God of the Hindus will pardon that boy who has preferred to marry out of his caste, rather than ravish a girl of twelve.

Any young man who makes dowry a condition of marriage, discredits his education and his country and dishonors womanhood. . . . A strong public opinion should be created in condemnation of the degrading practice of dowry, and young men, who soil their fingers with such ill-gotten gold, should be ex-communicated from society. Parents of girls should cease to be dazzled by English degrees, and should not hesitate to travel outside their little castes and provinces to secure true gallant young men for their daughters.

Hindu culture has erred on the side of excessive subordination of the wife to the husband, and has insisted on the complete merging of the wife in the husband. This has resulted in the husband, sometimes, usurping and exercising authority that reduces him to the level of the brute.

I passionately desire the utmost freedom for our women. I detest child marriages. I shudder to see a child-widow, and shiver with rage when a husband, just widowed, with brutal indifference contracts another marriage. I deplore the criminal indifference of parents who keep their daughters utterly ignorant and illiterate, and bring them up only for the purpose of marrying them off to some young man of means.

A child of ten or fifteen years old, who was no consenting party to the so-called marriage; who, having married, having never lived with the so-called husband, is suddenly declared to be a widow, is not a widow. It is an abuse of the term, abuse of language, and a sacrilege. . . . There is no warrant for this kind of widowhood in Hinduism.

Every widow has as much right to remarry as every widower. Voluntary widowhood is a priceless boon in Hinduism; enforced widowhood is a curse.

Girls are taught English as a passport to marriage.

GURU

I believe in the institution of *gurus*, but in this age millions must go without a *guru*, because it is a rare thing to find a combination of perfect purity and perfect learning.

It is better to grope in the dark and wade through a million errors to Truth than to entrust oneself to one who "knows not that he knows not."

I believe in the Hindu theory of *Guru* and his importance in spiritual realization. I think there is a great deal of truth in the doctrine that true knowledge is impossible without a *Guru*. An imperfect teacher may be tolerable in mundane matters, but not in spiritual matters. Only a perfect [seer] deserves to be enthroned as *Guru*. There must, therefore, be ceaseless striving after perfection. For one gets the *Guru* that one deserves. Infinite striving after perfection is one's right. It is its own reward. The rest is in the hands of God.

Think of God Himself as one's *guru*.

COMMUNAL UNITY

If the Hindus believe that India should be peopled only by Hindus, they are living in dream-land. The Hindus, the Mussalmans, the Parsis and the Christians who have made India their country are fellow countrymen, and they will have to live in unity, if only for their own interest. In no part of the world are one nationality and one religion synonymous terms; nor has it ever been so in India.

I see no way of achieving anything in this afflicted country without a lasting heart unity between Hindus and Mussalmans of India. I believe in the immediate possibility of achieving it because it is so natural, so necessary for both and because I believe in human nature.

True Hindu-Muslim unity requires Mussalmans to tolerate, not as a virtue of necessity, not as a policy, but as part of their religion, the religion of others so long as they, the latter, believe it to be true. Even so is it expected of Hindus to extend the same tolerance as a matter of faith and religion to the religions of others; no matter how repugnant they may appear to their, the Hindus', sense of religion.

I was seeking the friendship of good Mussalmans, and was eager to understand the Mussalman mind through contact with their purest and most patriotic representatives. . . . In South Africa there was no genuine friendship between the Hindus and the Mussalmans. I never missed a single opportunity to remove obstacles in the way of unity. It was not in my nature to placate anyone by adulation, or at the cost of self-respect. But my South African experiences had convinced me that it would be on the question of Hindu-Muslim unity that my *ahimsa* would be put to its severest test, and that the question presented the widest field for my experiments in *ahimsa*. The conviction is still there.

That interdining and intermarrying [between Hindus and Muslims] are necessary for national growth is a superstition borrowed from the West. . . . If brothers and sisters can live on the friendliest footing without ever thinking of marrying each other, I can see no difficulty in my daughter regarding every Mussalman as a brother and vice versa. . . . I should despair of ever cultivating amicable relations with the world if I had to recognize the right or propriety of any young man offering his hand in marriage to my daughter. . . . I hold it to be utterly impossible for Hindus and Mussalmans to intermarry and yet retain intact each other's religion.

The true beauty of Hindu-Muslim unity lies in each remaining true to his own religion and yet being true to each other. . . . Hindu-Muslim unity . . . consists in our having a common purpose, a common goal, and common sorrows. It is best promoted by cooperating in order to reach the common goal, by sharing one another's sorrows and by mutual toleration.

To revile one another's religion, to make reckless statements, to utter untruth, to break the head of innocent men, to desecrate temples or mosques, is a denial of God. . . . It is true penance for a Mussalman to harbor no ill for his Hindu brother, and an equally true penance for a Hindu to harbor none for his Mussalman brother. I ask of no Hindu or Mussalman to surrender an iota of his religious principle. Only let him be sure that it is religion.

PAKISTAN

See also the section on "Tolerance" in Chapter 1, and the section on "Communal Unity" in this chapter.

The "two-nation" theory is an untruth.

As a man of non-violence, I cannot forcibly resent the proposed partition if the Muslims of India really insist upon it. But I can never be a willing party to the vivisection. I would employ every non-violent means to prevent it. For it means the undoing of centuries of work done by number-less Hindus and Muslims to live together as one nation. Partition means a patent untruth. My whole soul rebels against the idea that Hinduism and Islam represent two antagonistic cultures and doctrines.

Pakistan cannot be worse than foreign domination.

To divide [India] into two is worse than anarchy. It is vivisection which cannot be tolerated—not because I am a Hindu. . . . Vivisect me before you vivisect India.

I hold it to be utterly wrong . . . to divide man from man by reason of religion which is liable to change.

If one can divide a living body into two parts, you may divide India into two parts.

[To Jinnah:] You can cut me in two, but don't cut India in two.

MISSIONARIES

See also the sections on "Conversion" and "Christianity" in Chapter 1.

I miss receptiveness, humility and willingness on the part of the missionaries to identify themselves with the masses of India.

Christian missionaries come to India under the shadow or, if you like, under the protection of a temporal power, and it creates an impassable bar.

One missionary friend of mine in South Africa still writes to me and asks me, "How is it with you?" I have always told this friend that so far as I know it is all well with me.

You, the missionaries, come to India thinking that you come to a land of heathen, of idolators, of men who do not know God. . . . You are here to find out the distress of the people of India and remove it. But I hope you are here also in a

receptive mood; and if there is anything that India has to give
you, you will not stop your ears, you will not close your eyes
and steel your hearts, to receive all that may be good in this
land.

[The missionaries] have to alter their attitude.
Today they tell people there is no salvation for them except
through the Bible and through Christianity. It is customary to
decry other religions and to offer their own as the only one that
can bring deliverance. That attitude should be radically changed.
Let them appear before the people as they are, and try to rejoice
in seeing Hindus become better Hindus, and Mussalmans better
Mussalmans. Let them start work at the bottom, let them enter
into what is best in their life and offer nothing inconsistent with
it. That will make their work far more efficacious, and what
they will say and offer to the people will be appreciated without suspicion and hostility. . . . Let them go to the people, not
as patrons, but as one of them, not to oblige them, but to serve
them and to work among them.

Let my missionary friends remember that it
was none but that most Christlike of all Christians, Albert
Schweitzer, who gave Christianity a unique interpretation when
he himself resolved "not to preach any more, not to lecture any
more," but to bury himself in Equatorial Africa simply with a
view to fulfill somewhat the debt that Europe owes to Africa.

Christian missions are not beyond reproach. If
I had power and could legislate, I should stop all proselytizing.
It is the cause of much avoidable conflict between classes and
unnecessary heart-burning amongst missionaries. But I should
welcome people of any nationality if they came to serve here for
the sake of service. In Hindu households the advent of a missionary has meant the disruption of the family, coming in the
wake of change of dress, manners, languages, food and drink.

The great and rich Christian missions will render true service to India if they can persuade themselves to confine their activities to humanitarian service without the ulterior motive of converting India or at least her unsophisticated villagers to Christianity, and destroying their social superstructure, which notwithstanding its many defects has stood now from time immemorial the onslaughts upon it from within and from without. Whether they—the missionaries—and we wish it or not, what is true in the Hindu faith will abide, what is untrue will fall to pieces. Every living faith must have within itself the power of rejuvenation if it is to live.

To the missionary I would say: Just forget that you have come to a country of heathens, and think that they are as much in search of God as you are; just feel that you are not attempting to give your spiritual goods to the people, but share your worldly goods, of which you have a good stock.

Missionaries in India are laboring under a double fallacy: that what they think best for another person is really so; and that what they regard as the best for themselves is the best for the whole world. I am pleading for a little humility.

There is certainly plenty of good work for American missionaries to do in America.

American and British money which has been voted for Missionary Societies has done more harm than good. You cannot serve God and Mammon both. And my fear is that Mammon has been sent to serve India and God has remained behind, with the result that He will one day have His vengeance.

The gift of healing is commercialized, because at the back of the mind is the feeling that because of this service, some day the recipient of the gift will accept Christ. Why should not the service be its own reward?

Proselytization under the cloak of humanitarian work is, to say the least, unhealthy. It is most certainly resented by the people here. Religion after all is a deeply personal matter; it touches the heart. Why should I change my religion because a doctor who professes Christianity as his religion has cured me of some disease or why should the doctor expect or suggest such a change while I am under his influence? Is not medical relief its own reward and satisfaction? Or why should I whilst I am in a missionary educational institution have Christian teaching thrust upon me? In my opinion these practices are not uplifting and give rise to suspicion if not even secret hostility. The methods of conversion must be, like Caesar's wife, above suspicion. Faith is not imparted like secular subjects. It is given through the language of the heart.

I am not against conversion. But I am against the modern methods of it. Conversion nowadays has become a matter of business, like any other.

First, I would suggest that all you Christians, missionaries and all, must begin to live more like Jesus Christ. Second, practice your religion without adulterating it or toning it down. Third, emphasize love and make it your working force, for love is central in Christianity. Fourth, study the non-Christian religions more sympathetically to find the good that is within them, in order to have a more sympathetic approach to the people.

Don't talk about it [Christianity]. The rose doesn't have to propagate its perfume. It just gives it forth, and people are drawn to it. Don't talk about it. Live it. And people will come to see the source of your power.

13. About Himself

RELIGIOUS FAITH

See Chapter 1, Chapter 2, and several sections of Chapter 12.

I yield to no Christian in the strength of devotion with which I sing "Lead, Kindly Light" and several other inspired hymns of a similar nature.

I can describe my feeling for Hinduism no more than for my own wife. She moves me as no other woman in the world can. Not that she has no faults. I dare say she has many more than I see myself. But the feeling of an indissoluble bond is there. Even so, do I feel for and about Hinduism, with all its faults and limitations.

I love Hinduism more dearly than life itself.

I must tell you in all humility that Hinduism, as I know it, entirely satisfies my soul, fills my whole being, and I find a solace in the *Bhagavad Gita* and *Upanishads* that I miss even in the Sermon on the Mount. Not that I do not prize the ideal presented therein, not that some of the precious teachings in the Sermon on the Mount have not left a deep impression upon me, but I must confess to you that when doubt haunts me, when disappointments stare me in the face, and when I see not one ray of light on the horizon I turn to the *Bhagavad Gita* and find a verse to comfort me; and I immediately begin to smile in the midst of overwhelming sorrow. My life has been full of external tragedies and, if they have not left any visible and indelible effect on me, I owe it to the teaching of the *Bhagavad Gita*.

I read the book of Genesis, and the chapters that followed invariably sent me to sleep. But just for the sake of being able to say that I read it, I plodded through the other books with much difficulty and without the least interest or understanding. I disliked reading the book of Numbers. But the New Testament produced a different impression, especially the Sermon on the Mount which went straight to my heart. I compared it with the *Gita*. . . . My young mind tried to unify the teaching of the *Gita* . . . and the Sermon on the Mount.

I attended the Wesleyan Church every Sunday. . . . The church did not make a favorable impression on me. The sermons seemed to be uninspiring. The congregation did not strike me as being particularly religious. They were not an assembly of devout souls; they appeared rather to be worldly-minded people, going to church for recreation and in conformity to custom.

During my first sojourn in South Africa it was Christian influence that had kept alive in me the religious sense.

If I had to face only the Sermon on the Mount and my own interpretation of it, I should not hesitate to say, "Oh yes, I am a Christian." But I know that at the present moment if I said any such thing I would lay myself open to the gravest misinterpretation. . . . Much of that which passes for Christianity is a negation of the Sermon on the Mount.

Believing as I do in the influence of heredity and being born in a Hindu family, I have remained a Hindu. I should reject Hinduism if I found it inconsistent with my moral sense or my spiritual growth. But on examination I have found it to be the most tolerant of all religions known to me, because it gives the Hindu the largest scope for self-expression. Not being an exclusive religion, it enables its followers not merely to respect all the other religions, but also to admire and assimilate whatever may be good in them.

Today the *Gita* is not only my Bible or my Koran, it is more than that—it is my mother. I lost my earthly mother who gave me birth long ago; but this eternal mother has completely filled her place by my side. She has never changed, she has never failed me. When I am in difficulty or distress I seek refuge in her bosom.

My patriotism is subservient to my religion.

The Sermon on the Mount went straight to my heart. The verses, "But I say unto you, That ye resist not evil; but whosoever shall smite thee on thy right cheek, turn to him the other also. And if any man . . . take away thy coat, let him have thy cloke also" delighted me beyond measure. . . . That renunciation was the highest form of religion appealed to me greatly.

FAMILY RELATIONS

See Chapter 9; and the section on "Family Affairs" in Chapter 12.

I have led a fairly happy married life for the past forty years in spite of occasional jars.

It is my painful duty to have to record here my marriage at the age of thirteen. . . . I do not think it meant to me anything more than the prospect of good clothes to wear, drum beating, marriage processions, rich dinners and a strange girl to play with.

I was a cruelly kind husband. I regarded myself as [my wife's] teacher, and so harassed her out of my blind love for her. . . . [Once] I forgot myself, and the spring of compassion dried up in me. I caught her by the hand, dragged the helpless woman to the gate, which was just opposite the ladder, and proceeded to open it with the intention of pushing her out. . . . We have had numerous bickerings, but the end has always been peace between us. The wife, with her matchless powers of endurance, has always been the victor. Today I am in a position to narrate the incident with some detachment, as it belongs to a period out of which I have fortunately emerged. I am no longer a blind, infatuated husband.

She is blessed with one great quality to a very considerable degree, a quality which most Hindu wives possess in some measure. And it is this: willingly or unwillingly, consciously or unconsciously, she has considered herself blessed in following in my footsteps, and has never stood in the way of my endeavor to lead a life of restraint. Though, therefore, there is a wide difference between us intellectually, I have always had the feeling that ours is a life of contentment, happiness and progress.

I really came to enjoy my married life after I ceased to look at [my wife] sexually. . . . I saw in a flash that I was born, as we all are, for a sacred mission. I did not know this when I was married. But on coming to my senses, I felt that I must see that the marriage subserved the mission for which I was born.

I cannot imagine life without Ba [my wife] . . . Her passing has left a vacuum which never will be filled . . . We lived together for sixty-two years.

WESTERN WAYS

I directed my attention to other details that were supposed to go towards the making of an English gentleman. I was told it was necessary for me to take lessons in dancing, French and elocution. I decided to take dancing lessons at a class and paid down three pounds as fees for a term. I must have taken about six lessons in three weeks. But it was beyond me to achieve anything like rhythmic motion. I could not follow the piano and hence found it impossible to keep time.

I believed . . . that in order to look civilized, our
dress and manners had as far as possible to approximate to the
European standard. Because, I thought, only thus could we have
some influence, and without influence it would not be possible to
serve the community.

About the time I took up chambers in Bombay,
an American insurance agent had come there—a man with a
pleasing countenance and a sweet tongue. . . . I succumbed to
the temptation of the American agent. . . . I persuaded myself
to take out a policy of 10,000 rupees. . . . But when my mode of
life changed in South Africa . . . [I] deplored the life policy and
felt ashamed of having been caught in the net of the insurance
agent. If, I said to myself, my brother is really in the position of
my father, surely he would not consider it too much of a burden
to support my widow, if it came to that. And what reason had I
to assume that death would claim me earlier than the others?
After all the real protector was neither I nor my brother, but the
Almighty. In getting my life insured I had robbed my wife and
children of their self-reliance. Why should they not be expected
to take care of themselves? What happened to the families of the
numberless poor in the world? Why should I not count myself as
one of them?

HEALTH HABITS

See also the sections on "Health" and "Diet" in Chapter 3.

We went in search of a lonely spot by the river,
and there I saw, for the first time in my life—meat. . . . The goat's
meat was as tough as leather. I simply could not eat it. I was
sick and had to leave off eating. I had a very bad night afterwards. A horrible nightmare haunted me. Every time I dropped
off to sleep it would seem as though a live goat were bleating
inside me, and I would jump up full of remorse. But then I would
remind myself that meat-eating was a duty and so became more
cheerful.

I abjured meat out of the purity of my desire not to lie to my parents. . . . I have never since gone back to meat.

Ever since I have been grown up, I have never desired to smoke and have always regarded the habit of smoking as barbarous, dirty, and harmful. I have never understood why there is such a rage for smoking throughout the world. I cannot bear to travel in a compartment full of people smoking. I become choked.

My dislike for medicines steadily increased. . . . I believe that man has little need to drug himself. Nine hundred and ninety-nine cases out of a thousand can be brought round by means of a well-regulated diet, water and earth treatment and similar household remedies. He who runs to the doctor . . . for every little ailment, and swallows all kinds of vegetable and mineral drugs, not only curtails his life, but, by becoming the slave of his body instead of remaining its master, loses self-control, and ceases to be a man.

I held my views on vegetarianism independently of religious texts.

Milk stimulated animal passion. . . . Milk was not necessary for supporting the body. . . . I decided to live on a pure fruit diet, and that, too, composed of the cheapest fruit possible. Our ambition was to live the life of the poorest people. The fruit diet turned out to be convenient also. Cooking was practically done away with. Raw groundnuts [peanuts], bananas, dates, lemons, and olive oil composed our usual diet.

Religious considerations had been predominant in the giving up of milk. I had before me a picture of the wicked processes the *govals* in Calcutta adopted to extract the last drop of milk from their cows and buffaloes. I also had the feeling that, just as meat was not man's food, even so animal's milk could not be man's food. . . . I will not take milk, milk-products or meat. If not to take these things should mean my death, I feel I had better face it.

I was convinced that, if I did not impose . . . restrictions on myself, I should put my future hosts to considerable inconvenience and should engage them in serving me rather than engage myself in service. So I pledged myself never whilst in India to take more than five articles [of food] in twenty-four hours, and never to eat after dark. . . . I have been under these vows for now thirteen years. They have subjected me to a severe test, but I am able to testify that they have also served as my shield. I am of opinion that they have added a few years to my life and saved me from many an illness.

Lord Sankey once told me to take care of myself and I said to him, "Do you think I would have reached this green old age if I hadn't taken care of myself?" This is one of my faults.

JAIL EXPERIENCES

See also the section on "Imprisonment" in Chapter 6.

My friends need not be at all anxious about me. I am as happy as a bird. And I do not feel that I am accomplishing less here than outside the prison. My stay here is a good school for me, and my separation from my fellow workers should prove whether our movement is an independently evolving organism or merely the work of one individual and, therefore, something very transient.

Most of my reading since 1893 has been done in jail.

I would not expect you [C. F. Andrews] to come to see me in jail. I am as happy as a bird! My ideal of a jail life —especially that of a civil resister—is to be cut off entirely from all connection with the outside world. To be allowed a visitor is a privilege—a civil resister may neither seek nor receive a privilege. The religious value of jail discipline is enhanced by renouncing privilege. The forthcoming imprisonment will be to me more than a political advantage. If it is a sacrifice, I want it to be the purest.

Non-violence implies voluntary submission to the penalty for non-cooperation with evil. I am here, therefore, to invite and submit cheerfully to the highest penalty that can be inflicted upon me for what in law is a deliberate crime, and what appears to me to be the highest duty of a citizen.

Jail is jail for thieves and bandits. For me it is a palace.

UNDER DISCRIMINATION

See also the section on "Racial Discrimination" in Chapter 8.

I lived in South Africa for twenty years, but never once thought of going to see the diamond mines there, partly because I was afraid lest as an "untouchable" I should be refused admission and insulted.

The train reached Maritzburg, the capital of Natal [South Africa], at about 9 P.M. . . . A passenger came next and looked me up and down. He saw that I was a "colored" man. . . . Another official came to me and said, "Come along, you must go to the van compartment." "But I have a first class ticket," said I. "That doesn't matter," rejoined the other. . . . "You must leave this compartment, or else I shall have to call a police constable to push you out." "Yes, you may. I refuse to get out voluntarily." The constable came. He took me by the hand and pushed me out. . . . I refused to go to the other compartment and the train steamed away.

I reached Johannesburg quite safely that night. . . . Taking a cab I asked to be driven to the Grand National Hotel. I saw the manager and asked for a room. He eyed me for a moment, and politely saying, "I am very sorry, we are full up," bade me good-bye.

I applied for admission as an advocate of the Supreme Court [of Natal]. . . . The Law Society now sprang a surprise on me by serving me with a notice opposing my application for admission. . . . The main objection was that, when the regulations regarding admission of advocates were made, the possibility of a colored man applying could not have been contemplated.

Mr. Ellerthorpe . . . invited me to the Bengal Club [of Calcutta] where he was staying. He did not then realize that an Indian could not be taken to the drawing-room of the Club. . . . He expressed his sorrow regarding this prejudice of the local Englishmen and apologized to me for not having been able to take me to the drawing-room.

I once went to an English hair-cutter in Pretoria. He contemptuously refused to cut my hair. I certainly felt hurt, but immediately purchased a pair of clippers and cut my hair before the mirror. I succeeded more or less in cutting the front hair, but I spoiled the back. The friends in the court shook with laughter. "What's wrong with your hair, Gandhi? Rats have been at it?" "No, the white barber would not condescend to touch my black hair."

TITLES

The word "saint" should be ruled out of present life. It is too sacred a word to be lightly applied to anybody, much less to one like myself who claims only to be a humble searcher after Truth, knows his limitations, makes mistakes, never hesitates to admit them and frankly confesses that he, like a scientist, is making experiments about some "of the eternal verities" of life, but cannot even claim to be a scientist because he can show no tangible proof of scientific accuracy in his methods or such tangible results of his experiments as modern science demands.

I assure all my admirers and friends that they will please me better if they will forget the *Mahatma* and remember Gandhiji . . . or think of me simply as Gandhi.

Often the title [*Mahatma*] has deeply pained me; and there is not a moment I can recall when it may be said to have tickled me.

The woes of *Mahatmas* are known to *Mahatmas* alone.

Abdulla Sheth hit upon a fine appellation— "*bhai*," i.e., brother. Others followed him and continued to address me as "*bhai*" until the moment I left South Africa. There was a sweet flavor about the name when it was used by the ex-indentured Indians.

Immediately the crowd surrounded me and yelled, "*Mahatma Gandhi ki jai*" [Victory to Mahatma Gandhi]. That sound usually grates on my ears.

CONSISTENCY

My aim is not to be consistent with my previous statements on a given question, but to be consistent with truth as it may present itself to me at a given moment. The result has been that I have grown from truth to truth; I have saved my memory an undue strain, and what is more, whenever I have been obligated to compare my writing even of fifty years ago with the latest, I have discovered no inconsistency between the two. But friends who observe inconsistency will do well to take the meaning that my latest writing may yield unless, of course, they prefer the old. But before making the choice, they should try to see if there is not an underlying abiding consistency between the two seeming inconsistencies.

I must admit my many inconsistencies. Since I am called "*Mahatma*," I might well endorse Emerson's saying that "foolish consistency is the hobgoblin of little minds."

I have never made a fetish of consistency. I am a votary of Truth and I must say what I feel and think at a given moment on the question, without regard to what I may have said before on it. . . . As my vision gets clearer, my views must grow clearer with daily practice. Where I have deliberately altered an opinion, the change should be obvious. Only a careful eye would notice a gradual and imperceptible evolution. I am not at all concerned with appearing to be consistent. In my pursuit after Truth I have discarded many ideas and learned many new things.

There is a consistency running through my seeming inconsistencies, as in nature there is unity running through seeming diversity.

LIMITATIONS

Experience has made me wiser.

It is not possible for me, a weak, frail, miserable being, to mend every wrong or to hold myself free of blame for all the wrong I see.

I am still myself too full of passion and other frailties of human nature. . . . I am incessantly trying to overcome every one of my weaknesses. I have attained great capacity, I believe, for suppressing and curbing my senses, but I have not become incapable of sin, i.e., of being acted upon by my senses.

I am far from claiming any finality or infallibility about my conclusions.

Let us not reduce the standard of truth even by a hair's breadth for judging erring mortals like myself.

My shyness has been in reality my shield and buckler. It has allowed me to grow. It has helped me in my discernment of truth.

My hesitancy in speech, which was once an annoyance, is now a pleasure. Its greatest benefit has been that it has taught me the economy of words. I have naturally formed the habit of restraining my thoughts. And I can now give myself the certificate that a thoughtless word hardly ever escapes my tongue or pen. I do not recollect ever having had to regret anything in my speech or writing. I have thus been spared many a mishap and waste of time.

I had long since taught myself to follow the inner voice. I delighted in submitting to it. To act against it would be difficult and painful to me.

All my life through, the very insistence on truth has taught me to appreciate the beauty of compromise. . . . It has often meant endangering my life and incurring the displeasure of friends. But truth is hard as adamant and tender as a blossom.

I never attempted to disguise my ignorance from my pupils.

I claim no infallibility. I am conscious of having made Himalayan blunders, but I am not conscious of having made them intentionally or having ever harbored enmity towards any person or nation, or any life, human or subhuman.

I claim to be no more than an average man with less than average ability. . . . I have not the shadow of a doubt that any man or woman can achieve what I have, if he or she would make the same effort and cultivate the same hope and faith.

My writings should be cremated with my body. What I have done will endure, not what I have said and written.

I have no university education worth the name. My high school career was never above average. I was thankful if I could pass my examinations. Distinction in the school was beyond my aspiration.

There is always a saving clause about all my advice. No one need follow it unless it appeals to his head and heart. No one who has honestly the inner call need be deterred from obeying it because of my advice. In other words, it applies only to those who are not conscious of any inner call and who have faith in my riper experience and soundness of judgment.

My life is made up of compromises, but they have been compromises that have brought me nearer the goal.

I am made by nature to side with weak parties.

My influence, great as it may appear to outsiders, is strictly limited. I may have considerable influence to conduct a campaign for redress of popular grievance because people are ready and need a helper. But I have no influence to direct people's energy in a channel in which they have no interest.

I am essentially a man of compromise because I am never sure that I am right.

Life for me would be a burden, if I were to make it a point of controverting every false report about me or distortion of my writings.

I am painfully conscious of my imperfections, and therein lies all the strength I possess. . . . It is a million times better that I should be the laughingstock of the world than that I should act with insincerity toward myself. . . . I lay claim to no superhuman powers. I wear the same corruptible flesh as the weakest of my fellow beings wear, and am, therefore, as liable to err as any.

Every one of my failures has been a stepping-stone.

Never take anything for gospel truth even if it comes from a *Mahatma* unless it appeals to both . . . head and heart.

MISSION

I am not a visionary. I claim to be a practical idealist.

I live for India's freedom and would die for it, because it is part of Truth.

I lay claim to nothing exclusively divine in me. I do not claim prophetship. I am but a humble seeker after Truth and bent upon finding It. I count no sacrifice too great for the sake of seeing God face to face. The whole of my activity whether it may be called social, political, humanitarian or ethical is directed to that end. As I know that God is found more often in the lowliest of His creatures than in the high and mighty, I am struggling to reach the status of these. I cannot do so without their service. Hence my passion for the service of the suppressed classes. As I cannot render this service without entering politics, I find myself in them. Thus I am no master, I am but a struggling, erring, humble servant of India and there-through, of humanity.

A persistent correspondent from Simla asks me whether I intend to found a sect or claim divinity. . . . He would have me make a public declaration for the sake of posterity. I should have thought that I had in the strongest terms repudiated all claim to divinity. I claim to be a humble servant of India and humanity and would like to die in the discharge of such service. I have no desire to found a sect. I am really too ambitious to be satisfied with a sect for a following.

My conclusions from my current experiments can hardly as yet be regarded as decisive . . . I set a high value on my experiments. I do not know whether I have been able to do justice to them.

To describe truth, as it appeared to me, and in the exact manner in which I have arrived at it, has been my ceaseless effort.

I am a humble servant of India, and in trying to serve India, I serve humanity at large. I discovered, in my early days, that the service of India is not inconsistent with the service to humanity. . . . The service of one's nation is not inconsistent with the service of the world.

I am, indeed, a practical dreamer. My dreams are not airy nothings. I want to convert my dreams into realities, as far as possible.

I am an impatient reformer. I am all for thorough-going, radical, social reordering; but it must be an organic growth, not a violent super-imposition.

To dismiss my evidence as useless, because I am popularly regarded as a *Mahatma*, is not proper in a serious inquiry.

It is wrong to call me an ascetic. The ideals that regulate my life are presented for acceptance by mankind in general. I have arrived at them by gradual evolution. Every step was thought out, well considered, and taken with greatest deliberation.

If Gandhism is another name for sectarianism, it deserves to be destroyed. If I were to know, after my death, that what I stood for had degenerated into sectarianism, I should be deeply pained. . . . Let no one say that he is a follower of Gandhi. . . . You are no followers but fellow students, fellow pilgrims, fellow seekers, fellow workers.

Sometimes a man lives in his day dreams. I live in mine and picture the world as full of good human beings— not goody-goody human beings. . . . If you try to dream these day dreams, you will also feel exalted as I do.

I have not conceived my mission to be that of a knight-errant wandering everywhere to deliver people from difficult situations. My humble occupation has been to show people how they can solve their own difficulties.

I am but a poor struggling soul yearning to be wholly good—wholly truthful and wholly non-violent in thought, word and deed, but ever failing to reach the ideal which I know to be true. I admit . . . that it is a painful climb, but the pain of it is a positive pleasure for me. Each step upward makes me feel stronger and fit for the next.

I have made the frankest admission of my many sins. But I do not carry their burden on my shoulders. If I am journeying Godward, as I feel I am, it is safe with me. I feel the warmth and sunshine of His presence. My austerities, fastings and prayers are I know of no value if I rely upon them for reforming me. But they have an inestimable value if they represent, as I hope they do, the yearnings of a soul striving to lay his weary head in the lap of his Maker.

Truth and beauty I crave for, live for, and would die for.

Most religious men I have met are politicians in disguise; I, however, who wear the guise of a politician, am at heart a religious man.

I am taking good care of my body. I feel as responsible as a pregnant woman. God in his infinite mercy has chosen, it seems to me, that I be instrumental in bringing forth India's freedom. I, therefore, cannot afford to die as yet.

I am a born fighter who does not know failure.

ASSASSINATION

One may not swear to kill another in the name of the Most High. . . . Death is the appointed end of all life. To die by the hand of a brother, rather than by disease or in such other way, cannot be for me a matter of sorrow. And if even in such a case I am free from the thoughts of anger or hatred against my assailant, I know that that will redound to my eternal welfare, and even the assailant will later on realize my perfect innocence.

Just suppose that Mir Alam and his friends, instead of only wounding, had actually destroyed my body. And suppose also that the community had deliberately remained calm and unperturbed, and forgiven the offenders perceiving that according to their lights they could not behave otherwise than they did. Far from injuring the community, such a noble attitude would have greatly benefited them. All misunderstanding would have disappeared, and Mir Alam and party would have had their eyes opened to the error of their ways. As for me, nothing better can happen to a *satyagrahi* than meeting death all unsought in the very act of *satyagraha.* . . . The death of a fighter, however eminent, makes not for slackness but on the other hand intensifies the struggle.

Truth is that God saves me so long as He wants me in this body. The moment His wants are satisfied, no precautions on my part will save me.

Thousands like myself may die in trying to vindicate the idea, but *ahimsa* will never die.

Let us all be brave enough to die the death of a martyr, but let no one lust for martyrdom.

If I am to die by the bullet of a madman, I must do so smiling. There must be no anger within me. God must be in my heart and on my lips. And you [Rajkumari Amrit Kaur] promise me one thing. Should such a thing happen, you are not to shed one tear.

I keep no bodyguard to protect me. My chest is literally bare.

If I were to die among a shower of bullets, with a smile on my lips, that would be a hero's death.

Last words upon assassination:

He, Ram! He, Ram! [Ah, God! Ah, God!]

Biographical Chronology

1869: Oct. 2. Born at Porbandar, Kathiawad, India, son of Karamchand (Kaba) and Putlibai Gandhi.
1876: Attended primary school in Rajkot, where family moved when father became a judge.
Betrothed to Kasturbai (called Kasturba in her old age), daughter of Gokuldas Makanji, a merchant.
1881: Entered high school in Rajkot.
1883: Married to Kasturbai.
1885: Father died at age of 63.
1887: Passed matriculation examination at Ahmedabad and entered Samaldas College, Bhavnagar, Kathiawad, but found studies difficult and remained only one term.
First of four sons born.
1888: Sept. Sailed from Bombay for England to study law.

His Twentieth Year

1891: Summer. Returned to India after being called to bar. Began practice of law in Bombay and Rajkot.
1893: April. Sailed for South Africa to become lawyer for an Indian firm.
Found himself subjected to all kinds of color discrimination.
1894: Prepared to return to India after completing law case, but was persuaded by Indian colony to remain in South Africa and do public work and earn a living as a lawyer.
Drafted first petition sent by the Indians to a South African legislature.
May. Organized the Natal Indian Congress.
1896: Returned to India for six months to bring back his wife and two children to Natal.
Dec. Sailed for South Africa with family. Was mobbed when he disembarked at Durban for what Europeans thought he wrote about South Africa when he was in India.

His Thirtieth Year

1899: Organized Indian Ambulance Corps for British in Boer War.
1901: Embarked with family for India, promising to return to South Africa if Indian community there needed his services again.

1901–02: Traveled extensively in India, attended Indian National Congress meeting in Calcutta, and opened law office in Bombay.

1902: Returned to South Africa after urgent request from Indian community.

1903: Summer. Opened law office in Johannesburg.

1904: Established the weekly journal, *Indian Opinion*.
Organized Phoenix Farm near Durban, after reading Ruskin's *Unto This Last*.

1906: March. Organized Indian Ambulance Corps for Zulu "Rebellion." Took vow of continence for life.

Sept. First *satyagraha* campaign began with meeting in Johannesburg in protest against proposed Asiatic ordinance directed against Indian immigrants in Transvaal.

Oct. Sailed for England to present Indians' case to Colonial Secretary and started back to South Africa in December.

1907: June. Organized *satyagraha* against compulsory registration of Asiatics ("The Black Act").

1908: Jan. Stood trial for instigating *satyagraha* and was sentenced to two months' imprisonment in Johannesburg jail (his first imprisonment).

Jan. Was summoned to consult General Smuts at Pretoria; compromise reached; was released from jail.

Feb. Attacked and wounded by Indian extremist, Mir Alam, for reaching settlement with Smuts.

Aug. After Smuts broke agreement, second *satyagraha* campaign began with bonfire of registration certificates.

HIS FORTIETH YEAR

Oct. Arrested for not having certificate, and sentenced to two months' imprisonment in Volksrust jail.

1909: Feb. Sentenced to three months' imprisonment in Volksrust and Pretoria jails.

June. Sailed for England again to present Indians' case. Stayed until November, observing organization of women's suffrage movement in England.

1910: May. Established Tolstoy Farm near Johannesburg.

1913: Began penitential fast (one meal a day for more than four months) because of moral lapse of two members of Phoenix settlement.

Sept. Helped campaign against nullification of marriages not celebrated according to Christian rites, with Kasturbai and other women being sentenced for crossing the Transvaal border without permits.

Nov. Third *satyagraha* campaign begun by leading "great march" of 2,000 Indian miners from Newcastle across Transvaal border.

Nov. Arrested for third time in four days (at Palmford, Standerton, and Teakworth) and sentenced at Dundee to nine months' imprisonment; tried at Volksrust in second trial and sentenced to three months' imprisonment with his European co-workers, Polak and Kallenbach. Imprisoned in Volksrust jail for a few days and then taken to Bloemfontein in Orange Free State.

Dec. Released unconditionally in expectation of a compromise settlement, C. F. Andrews and W. W. Pearson having been sent by Indians in India to negotiate.

1914: Jan. Underwent fourteen days' fast for moral lapse of members of Phoenix Farm.

1914: Jan. *Satyagraha* campaign suspended, with pending agreement between Smuts, C. F. Andrews, and Gandhi, and with ultimate passage of Indian Relief Act.

July. Left South Africa forever, sailing from Capetown for London with Kasturbai and Kallenbach, arriving just at beginning of World War I.

Organized Indian Ambulance Corps in England, but was obliged to sail for India because of pleurisy.

1915: Secured removal of customs harassment of passengers at Viramgam; first incipient *satyagraha* campaign in India.

May. Established *Satyagraha Ashram* at Kochrab, near Ahmedabad, and soon admitted an untouchable family; in 1917 moved ashram to new site on Sabarmati River.

1917: Helped secure removal of recruiting of South African indenture workers in India.

Led successful *satyagraha* campaign for rights of peasants on indigo plantations in Champaran. Defied order to leave area in April, was arrested at Motihari and tried, but case was withdrawn. Mahadev Desai joined him at Champaran.

1918: Feb. Led strike of millworkers at Ahmedabad. Millowners agreed to arbitration after his three-day fast (his first fast in India).

March. Led *satyagraha* campaign for peasants in Kheda.

Attended Viceroy's War Conference at Delhi and agreed that Indians should be recruited for World War I.

Began recruiting campaign, but was taken ill and came near death; agreed to drink goat's milk and learned spinning during convalescence.

1919: Spring. Rowlatt Bills (perpetuating withdrawal of civil liberties for seditious crimes) passed, and first all-India *satyagraha* campaign conceived.

April. Organized nation-wide *hartal*—suspension of activity for a day—against Rowlatt Bills.

April. Arrested at Kosi near Delhi on way to Punjab and escorted back to Bombay, but never tried.

April. Fasted at Sabarmati for three days in penitence for violence and suspended *satyagraha* campaign, which he called a "Himalayan miscalculation" because people were not disciplined enough.

Assumed editorship of English weekly, *Young India*, and Gujarati weekly, *Navajivan*.

His Fiftieth Year

Oct. After five months' refusal, authorities allowed him to visit scene of April disorders in Punjab. Worked closely with Motilal Nehru. Conducted extensive inquiry into violence in many Punjab villages.

1920: April. Elected president of All-India Home Rule League.

June. Successfully urged resolution for a *satyagraha* campaign of non-cooperation at Muslim Conference at Allahabad and at Congress sessions at Calcutta (Sept.) and Nagpur (Dec.).

Aug. Second all-India *satyagraha* campaign began when he gave up Kaiser-i-Hind medal.

1921: Presided at openings of first shop selling homespun (*khadi*) in Bombay.

Aug. Presided at bonfire of foreign cloth in Bombay.

1921: Sept. Gave up wearing shirt and cap and resolved to wear only a loin-cloth in devotion to homespun cotton and simplicity.

Nov. Fasted at Bombay for five days because of communal rioting following visit of Prince of Wales (later Edward VIII and Duke of Windsor).

Dec. Mass civil disobedience, with thousands in jail. Gandhi invested with "sole executive authority" on behalf of Congress.

1922: Feb. Suspended mass disobedience because of violence at Chauri Chaura and undertook five-day fast of penance at Bardoli.

March. Arrested at Sabarmati on charge of sedition for articles in *Young India*. Pleaded guilty in famous statement at the "great trial" in Ahmedabad before Judge Broomfield. Sentenced to six years' imprisonment in Yeravda jail.

1923: Wrote *Satyagraha in South Africa* and part of his autobiography in prison.

1924: Jan. Was operated on for appendicitis and unconditionally released from prison in February.

Sept. Began 21-day "great fast" at Mohamed Ali's home near Delhi as penance for communal rioting (between Hindus and Muslims), especially at Kohat.

Dec. Presided over Congress session at Belgaum as president.

1925: Nov. Fasted at Sabarmati for seven days because of misbehavior of members of ashram.

Dec. Announced one-year political silence and immobility at Congress session at Cawnpore.

1927: No-tax *satyagraha* campaign launched at Bardoli, led by Sardar Patel.

1928: Dec. Moved compromise resolution at Congress session at Calcutta, calling for complete independence within one year, or else the beginning of another all-Indian *satyagraha* campaign.

1929: March. Arrested for burning foreign cloth in Calcutta and fined one rupee.

His Sixtieth Year

Dec. Congress session at Lahore declared complete independence and a boycott of the legislature and fixed January 26 as National Independence Day. Third all-Indian *satyagraha* campaign began.

1930: March 12. Set out from Sabarmati with 79 volunteers on historic salt march 200 miles to sea at Dandi.

April 6. Broke salt law by picking salt up at seashore as whole world watched.

May. Arrested by armed policemen at Karadi and imprisoned in Yeravda jail without trial.

One hundred thousand persons arrested. There was no session of Congress in December because all leaders were in jail.

1931: Jan. Released unconditionally with 30 other Congress leaders.

March. Gandhi-Irwin (Viceroy) Pact signed, which ended civil disobedience.

Aug. Sailed from Bombay accompanied by Desai, Naidu, Mira, etc., for the second Round Table Conference, arriving in London via Marseilles, where he was met by C. F. Andrews.

Autumn. Resided at Kingsley Hall in London slums, broadcast to America, visited universities, met celebrities, and attended Round Table Conference sessions.

1931: Dec. Left England for Switzerland where he met Romain Rolland, and Italy where he met Mussolini.

Dec. Arrived in India. Was authorized by Congress to renew *satyagraha* campaign (fourth nationwide effort).

1932: Jan. Arrested in Bombay with Sardar Patel and detained without trial at Yeravda prison.

Sept. 20. Began "perpetual fast unto death" while in prison in protest of British action giving separate electorate to untouchables.

Sept. 26. Concluded "epic fast" with historic cell scene in presence of Tagore after British accepted "Yeravda Pact."

Dec. Joined fast initiated by another prisoner, Appasaheb Patwardhan, against untouchability; but fast ended in two days.

1933: Began weekly publication of *Harijan* in place of *Young India*.

May 8. Began self-purification fast of 21 days against untouchability and was released from prison by government on first day. Fast concluded after 21 days at Poona.

July. Disbanded Sabarmati Ashram which became center for removal of untouchability.

Aug. Arrested and imprisoned at Yeravda for four days with 34 members of his ashram. When he refused to leave Yeravda village for Poona, he was sentenced to one year's imprisonment at Yeravda.

Aug. 16. Began fast against refusal of government to grant him permission to work against untouchability while in prison; on fifth day of fast he was removed to Sassoon Hospital; his health was precarious; he was unconditionally released on eighth day.

Nov. Began ten-month tour of every province in India to help end untouchability.

Nov. Kasturba arrested and imprisoned for sixth time in two years.

1934: Summer. Three separate attempts made on his life.

July. Fasted at Wardha ashram for seven days in penance against intolerance of opponents of the movement against untouchability.

Oct. Launched All-India Village Industries Association.

1935: Health declined; moved to Bombay to recover.

1936: Visited Segaon, a village near Wardha in the Central Provinces, and decided to settle there. (This was renamed Sevagram in 1940 and eventually became an ashram for his disciples.)

1937: Jan. Visited Travancore for removal of untouchability.

1939: March. Began fast unto death as part of *satyagraha* campaign in Rajkot; fast ended four days later when Viceroy appointed an arbitrator.

His Seventieth Year

1940: Oct. Launched limited, individual civil-disobedience campaign against Britain's refusal to allow Indians to express their opinions regarding World War II— 23,000 persons imprisoned within a year.

1942: *Harijan* resumed publication after being suspended for 15 months.

March. Met Sir Stafford Cripps in New Delhi but called his proposals "a post-dated check"; they were ultimately rejected by Congress.

Aug. Congress passed "Quit India" resolution—the final nation-wide *satyagraha* campaign—with Gandhi as leader.

1942: Aug. 9. Arrested with other Congress leaders and Kasturba and imprisoned in Aga Khan Palace near Poona, with populace revolting in many parts of India.

Aug. Mahadev Desai, Gandhi's secretary and intimate, died in Palace.

1943: Feb. 10. Began 21-day fast at Aga Khan Palace to end deadlock of negotiations between Viceroy and Indian leaders.

1944: Feb. 22. Kasturba died in detention at Aga Khan Palace at age of seventy-four.

May 6. After decline in health, was released unconditionally from detention (this was his last imprisonment; he had spent 2,338 days in jail during his lifetime).

Sept. Important talks with Jinnah of Muslim League in Bombay on Hindu-Moslem unity.

1946: March. Conferred with British Cabinet Mission in New Delhi.

Nov. Began four-month tour of 49 villages in East Bengal to quell communal rioting over Moslem representation in provisional government.

1947: March. Began tour of Bihar to lessen Hindu-Moslem tensions.

March. Began conferences in New Delhi with Lord Mountbatten and Jinnah.

May. Opposed Congress decision to accept division of country into India and Pakistan.

Aug. 15. Fasted and prayed to combat riots in Calcutta as India was partitioned and granted independence.

Sept. Fasted for three days to stop communal violence in Calcutta.

Sept. Visited Delhi and environs to stop rioting and to visit camps of refugees (Hindus and Sikhs from the Punjab).

1948: Jan. 13. Fasted for five days in Delhi for communal unity.

Jan. 20. Bomb exploded in midst of his prayer meeting at Birla House, Delhi.

Jan. 30. Assassinated in 78th year at Birla House by Vinayak N. Godse.

Bibliographies[1]

A. THE MAJOR WORKS BY GANDHI IN ENGLISH

1909: *Hind Swaraj, or Indian Home Rule*. 1938, rev. ed., 80 p., Ahmedabad: Navajivan.
    This was written on a voyage from London to South Africa and was first published serially in *Indian Opinion*. It consists of a dialogue between the "reader" and the "editor"—Mr. Gandhi.

1917a: *Mahatma Gandhi: His Life, Writings, and Speeches*. (Foreword by Sarojini Naidu.) Madras: Ganesh. 1921, 3rd ed., 444 p.

1917b: *Speeches and Writings of Mahatma Gandhi*. (Intro. by C. F. Andrews.) Madras: Natesan. 1934, 4th ed., 1072 p.

1920: *A Guide to Health*. (Trans. by A. Rama Iyer.) Madras: Ganesan. 1923, 114 p.
    This first appeared serially in *Indian Opinion* in Gujarati and consists of advice on food and simple treatments for disease.

1921a: *Freedom's Battle*. Madras: Ganesh. 341 p.

1921b: *Swaraj in One Year*. Madras: Ganesh. 2nd ed., 121 p.

1922a: *Ethical Religion, or Dithi Dharma*. (Trans. from Hindi by A. Rama Iyer with an appreciation of the author by John Haynes Holmes.) 2nd ed., 64 p. Madras: Ganesan.
    This is not an entirely original work by Gandhi. He read William MacKintire Salter's *Ethical Religion* (Boston: Little, Brown, 1899) and published an abridged Gujarati translation in *Indian Opinion*. This now passes as an original work of Gandhi and has been re-translated into English and other Indian languages!

1922b: *Gaol Experiences*. Madras: Tagore & Co.

1922c: *The Wheel of Fortune*. Madras: Ganesh. 160 p. Collected essays on home industry and spinning—bound in *khadar!*

1923: *Young India, 1919–22*. Madras: Ganesan. 1199 p. 1924, 2nd ed., 1471 p. 1923, New York: Viking. 1924, 2nd ed., New York: B. W. Huebsch.

1924: *Hindu-Muslim Tension: Its Cause and Cure*. Ahmedabad: Navijivan.

1927a: *An Autobiography, or The Story of My Experiments with Truth*. Vol. I, 1927, 602 p.; Vol. II, 1929, 608 p. Ahmedabad: Navajivan. 1948, 1st American edition in one volume, Washington: Public Affairs Press, 840 p.
    This was begun while Gandhi was in prison in 1922 and first appeared serially in *Young India* in December 1925 and thereafter. It was written in Gujarati and translated into English by Mahadev Desai.

1927b: *Young India, 1924–26*. Madras: Ganesan. New York: Viking. 984 p.

[1] For a remarkably complete bibliography of Gandhi literature to 1949, see Deshpande, 1948.

1928: *Satyagraha in South Africa.* (Trans. by Valji G. Desai.) Madras: Ganesan. 511 p.

1930: *Self-Restraint versus Self-Indulgence.* Ahmedabad: Navajivan. Part I, 1930, 130 p.; Part II, 1939, 147 p. 1947, 1 vol., 232 p.

1932: *My Soul's Agony: Statements Issued from Yeravda Prison on the Removal of Untouchability among Hindus.* Bombay: Servants of Untouchables Society.

1933: *From Yeravda Mandir.* (Trans. by Valji G. Desai.) Ahmedabad: Navajivan. 1947, 3rd ed., 68 p.

This consists of weekly letters written in 1930 from prison to members of his ashram.

1934: *Songs from Prison.* (Adapted by John Boyland.) London: George Allen. New York: Macmillan. 160 p.

These are translations from the *Upanishads* and other Indian lyrics made in Yeravda prison in 1930.

1935: *Young India, 1927–28.* Madras: Ganesan. 1104 p.

1938: *Cent Per Cent Swadeshi or The Economics of Village Industries.* Ahmedabad: Navajivan. 1948, 3rd ed., 132 p.

1941a. *Economics of Khadi.* Ahmedabad: Navajivan. 627 p.

1941b: *Christian Missions and Their Place in India.* Ahmedabad: Navajivan. 311 p.

1941c: *Constructive Programme: Its Meaning and Place.* Ahmedabad: Navajivan. 1948, 2nd ed., 31 p.

1941d: *The Indian States' Problem.* Ahmedabad: Navajivan. 687 p.

1942a: *Non-Violence in Peace and War.* Ahmedabad: Navajivan. Vol. I, 1944, 2nd ed., 589 p. Vol. II, 1950, 1st ed., 403 p.

1942b: *Women and Social Injustice.* Ahmedabad: Navajivan. 1947, 3rd ed., 216 p.

1945: *Gandhi's Correspondence with the Government, 1942–44.* Ahmedabad: Navajivan. 2nd ed., 360 p.

1946: *The Gospel of Selfless Action, or The Gita According to Gandhi.* (Trans. by Mahadev Desai.) Ahmedabad: Navajivan. 390 p.

1948a. *Key to Health.* (Trans. by Sushila Nayyar.) Ahmedabad: Navajivan. 83 p.

1948b: *Why the Constructive Programme.* New Delhi: A. J. Kishore.

1948c: *Delhi Diary.* Ahmedabad: Navajivan. 406 p.

Prayers and speeches from September 10, 1947, to his death on January 30, 1948.

1948d: *Communal Unity.* Ahmedabad: Navajivan. 1006 p.

1949a: *Bapu's Letters to Mira.* Ahmedabad: Navajivan. 387 p. 1950, *Gandhi's Letters to a Disciple* (intro. by John Haynes Holmes), New York: Harper. 234 p. 351 letters from Gandhi to Madeleine Slade (Mirabehn) from 1924 to 1948.

1949b: *For Pacifists.* Ahmedabad: Navajivan. 106 p.

1950: *Selected Letters—I.* (Chosen and trans. by V. G. Desai.) Ahmedabad: Navajivan. 56 p.

B. COLLECTIONS OF GANDHI'S WRITINGS IN ENGLISH

Bose, Nirmal K., ed. *Selections from Gandhi.* Ahmedabad: Navajivan. 311 p. 1948.

Chander, Jag P., ed. *Ethics of Fasting.* Lahore: Indian Printing Works. 123 p. 1944.

Chander, Jag P., ed. *Gita, the Mother.* Lahore: Indian Printing Works. 4th ed., 157 p. 1947.

Chander, Jag P., ed. *Gandhi Against Fascism*. Lahore: Free India Publications. 102 p. 1943.

Chander, Jag P., ed. *Teachings of Mahatma Gandhi*. Lahore: Indian Printing Works. 620 p. 1947.

Desai, Mahadev, ed. *My Early Life (1869–1914)*. London: Oxford. 112 p. 1947.

Deshpande, M. S. *Light of India*. Sangli: M. S. Deshpande. 293 p. 1950.

Duncan, Ronald, ed. *Selected Writings of Mahatma Gandhi*. Boston: Beacon Press. 253 p. 1951.

Hingorani, Anand T., ed. *To the Students*. Karachi: Hingorani. 1935. 1945, 5th ed., 343 p.

Hingorani, Anand T., ed. *To the Women*. Karachi: Hingorani. 1941. 1946, 3rd ed., 247 p.

Hingorani, Anand T., ed. *My Appeal to the British*. Karachi: Hingorani. New York: John Day. 72 p. 1942a.

Hingorani, Anand T., ed. *To the Hindus and Muslims*. Karachi: Hingorani. 504 p. 1942b.

Hingorani, Anand T., ed. *To the Princes and Their People*. Karachi: Hingorani. 464 p. 1942c.

Hingorani, Anand T., ed. *To the Protagonists of Pakistan*. Karachi: Hingorani. 268 p. 1947.

Khipple, R. L., ed. *Famous Letters of Mahatma Gandhi*. Lahore: Indian Printing Works. 148 p. 1947.

Manshardt, Clifford, ed. *Mahatma and the Missionary*. Chicago: Regnery. 140 p. 1949.

Mira, ed. *Gleanings Gathered at Bapu's Feet*. Ahmedabad: Navajivan. 26 p. 1949.

Prabhu, R. K., and Rao, U. R., eds. *The Mind of Mahatma Gandhi*. Bombay: Oxford University Press. 191 p. 1945a.

Prabhu, R. K., and Rao, U. R., eds. *Conquest of Self: Being Gleanings from His Writings and Speeches*. Bombay: Thacker. 286 p. 1945b.

Prabhu, R. K., ed. *The India of My Dreams*. Bombay: Hind Kitabs. 129 p. 1947.

Prabhu, R. K., ed. *Mohanmala: A Gandhian Rosary*. Bombay: Hind Kitabs. 132 p. 1949.

Rajogopalachari, C., and Kumarappa, J. C., eds. *The Nation's Voice*. Ahmedabad: Navajivan. 1932. 1947, 2nd ed., 256 p.

This contains an account by M. Desai of Gandhi's trip to England for the Round Table Conference in 1931, as well as Gandhi's speeches while in England.

Sarma, D. S., ed. *The Gandhi Sutras*. New York: Devin-Adair. 174 p. 1949.

Suman, Ramnath, ed. *The Bleeding Wound*. Benares City: Shyam Lal. 226 p. 1932.

Tikekar, S. R., ed. *Gandhigrams*. Bombay: Hind Kitabs. 92 p. 1947.

Walker, Roy, ed. *The Wisdom of Gandhi*. London: Andrew Dakers. 65 p. 1943.

C. SELECTED WRITINGS ABOUT GANDHI'S LIFE AND TEACHINGS

All India Congress Committee. *Congress Handbook*. Allahabad: Congress. 294 p. 1946.

Ambedkar, B. R. *What Congress and Gandhi Have Done to the Untouchables*. Bombay: Thacker. 1946, 2nd ed., 399 p.

Andrews, C. F., ed. *His Own Story*. London: Allen and Unwin. 350 p. 1930. 1930, New York: Macmillan.

This is an abridgment of his Autobiography.

Andrews, C. F. *Mahatma Gandhi's Ideas*. London: Allen and Unwin. 382 p. 1929. 1930, New York: Macmillan.

Andrews, C. F., ed. *Mahatma Gandhi at Work; His Own Story Continued*. London: G. Allen. 1931. 1931, New York: Macmillan, 407 p.
    This recounts Gandhi's experiences in South Africa, abridged from his works.

Baros, Jan, ed. *Mahatma Gandhi; Pictorial History of a Great Life*. Calcutta: Gossain. 1949, 2nd ed., 233 p.

Barr, F. Mary. *Bapu: Conversations and Correspondence with Mahatma Gandhi*. Bombay: Int. Book House. 214 p. 1949.

Bernays, Robert. *Naked Fakir*. London: Gollancz. 351 p. 1931. 1932, New York: Holt.

Bourke-White, Margaret. *Halfway to Freedom*. New York: Simon and Schuster. 245 p. 1949.

Catlin, George. *In the Path of Mahatma Gandhi*. London: Macdonald. 332 p. 1948. 1950, Chicago: Regnery.

Chander, Jag P., ed. *Tagore and Gandhi Argue*. Lahore: Indian Printing Works. 181 p. 1945.

Chaturvedi, Benarsidas, and Sykes, Marjorie. *Charles Freer Andrews: A Narrative*. London: George Allen and Unwin. 334 p. 1949.

Chitambar, Jashwant Rao. *Mahatma Gandhi: His Life, Work and Influence*. Philadelphia: Winston. 266 p. 1933.

Desai, Mahadev H. *Gandhiji in Indian Villages*. Madras: Ganesan. 349 p. 1927.

Desai, Mahadev H. *With Gandhiji in Ceylon*. Madras: Ganesan. 159 p. 1928.

Desai, Mahadev H. *The Story of Bardoli*. Ahmedabad: Navajivan. 363 p. 1929.

Desai, Mahadev H. *The Epic of Travancore*. Ahmedabad: Navajivan. 251 p. 1937.

Deshpande, P. G., ed. *Gandhiana: A Bibliography of Gandhian Literature*. Ahmedabad: Navajivan. 240 p. 1948.
    A splendid bibliography containing 1400 titles in English and an equal number in several Indian languages.

Dhawan, Gopi N. *The Political Philosophy of Mahatma Gandhi*. Bombay: Popular Book Depot. 354 p. 1946.

Diwakar, R. R. *Satyagraha: The Power of Truth*. Hinsdale: Regnery. 108 p. 1948. 1946, Bombay: Hind Kitabs, 202 p.

Diwakar, R. R. *Glimpses of Gandhiji*. Bombay: Hind Kitabs. 90 p. 1949.

Doke, Joseph J. *An Indian Patriot in South Africa*. London: London Indian Chronicle. 97 p. 1909. 1919, Madras: Natesan, 103 p.

Eaton, Jeanette. *Gandhi: Fighter Without a Sword*. New York: Morrow. 253 p. 1950.
    A biography written especially for high-school students.

Fischer, Louis. *A Week with Gandhi*. New York: Duell, Sloan and Pearce. 122 p. 1942.

Fischer, Louis. *Gandhi and Stalin*. New York: Harper. 183 p. 1947.

Fischer, Louis, *The Life of Mahatma Gandhi*. New York: Harper. 558 p. 1950.
    This is probably the best biography of Gandhi published.

Fisher, Frederick B. *The Strange Little Brown Man*. New York: R. Long and R. R. Smith. 239 p. 1932.

Gandhi, Devadas, ed. *India Unreconciled*. New Delhi: The Hindustan Times. 528 p. 1943.
    A documented history of Indian political events from the crisis of August 1942 to February 1944.

Gandhi, Devadas, ed. *Memories of Bapu*. New Delhi: The Hindustan Times. 96 p. 1948.

George, S. K. *Gandhi's Challenge to Christianity*. London: Allen and Unwin. 112 p. 1939.

Gregg, Richard B. *Economics of Khaddar.* 1938. 1946, 2nd ed., 212 p., Ahmedabad: Navajivan.

Gregg, Richard B. *The Power of Non-Violence.* Philadelphia: Lippincott. 359 p. 1934. 1944, New York: Fellowship Publications, 253 p.

Hindustani Talimi Sangh. *Educational Reconstruction.* Sevagram: Hindustani Talimi Sangh. 1939, 2nd ed., 296 p.

Holmes, John Haynes. *The Christ of Today.* Madras: Tagore and Co. 1922.

India Ministry of Information and Broadcasting. *Homage to Gandhi.* New Delhi: India Ministry of Information. 112 p. 1948a.

India Ministry of Information and Broadcasting. *Homage.* New Delhi: India Ministry of Information. 65 p. 1948b.

Jain, Jagdishchandra. *I Could Not Save Bapu.* Benares: Jagran S. Mandir. 242 p. 1950.

Jones, E. Stanley. *Mahatma Gandhi: An Interpretation.* New York: Abingdon-Cokesbury. 160 p. 1948.

Jones, Marc E. *Gandhi Lives.* Philadelphia: D. McKay. 184 p. 1948.

Kalelkar, Kaka. *Stray Glimpses of Bapu.* Ahmedabad: Navajivan. 153 p. 1950.

Khosla, Kanshi Ram. *Mahatma Gandhi's Life Through Pictures.* Delhi. 259 p. 1948.

Kripalani, Acharya J. B. *The Gandhian Way.* Bombay: Vora. 1945, 3rd ed., 184 p.

Krishnadas. *Seven Months with Mahatma Gandhi.* Vol. I, 1928, Madras: Ganesan, 449 p. Vol. II, 1928, Bihar: Rambinode Sinha, 471 p.

Lester, Muriel. *Entertaining Gandhi.* London: Nicholson and Watson. 246 p. 1932.

Masani, Shakuntala. *Gandhi's Story.* New York: Oxford. 101 p. 1950.
    A biography for young people.

Maurer, H. *Great Soul: The Growth of Gandhi.* New York: Doubleday. 128 p. 1948.

Nayyar, Sushila. *Kasturba, Wife of Gandhi.* Wallingford, Penn.: Pendle Hill. 71 p. 1948.

Nehru, Jawaharlal. *Towards Freedom.* New York: John Day. 445 p. 1941. 1936, London, 618 p.
    An autobiography.

Nehru, Jawaharlal. *Nehru on Gandhi.* New York: John Day. 150 p. 1948.

Nehru, Krishna. *The Story of Gandhi.* New York: Didier. 64 p. 1950.
    A short illustrated biography for young people.

Peare, Catherine O. *Mahatma Gandhi.* New York: Henry Holt. 229 p. 1950.
    An excellent biography for high-school students.

Polak, H. S. L., ed. *Souvenir of the Passive Resistance Movement in South Africa (1906–14).* Golden Number, *Indian Opinion.* Natal: Phoenix Farm. 54 p. 1914.

Polak, H. S. L., H. N. Brailsford, and Lord Pethick-Lawrence. *Mahatma Gandhi.* London: Odhams. 320 p. 1949.

Polak, Millie Graham. *Mr. Gandhi: The Man.* London: G. Allen. 186 p. 1931.

Prabhu, R. K., ed. *Sati Kasturba.* Bombay: Hind Kitabs. 87 p. 1944.

Prasad, Rajendra. *Mahatma Gandhi and Bihar.* Bombay: Hind Kitabs. 132 p. 1949.

Pyarelal, Nair. *The Epic Fast.* Ahmedabad: M. M. Bhatt. 325 p. 1932.

Pyarelal, Nair. *A Pilgrimage for Peace: Gandhi and Frontier Gandhi Among N.W.F. Pathans.* Ahmedabad: Navajivan. 208 p. 1950.

Radhakrishnan, Sarvepalli, ed. *Mahatma Gandhi: Essays and Reflections on His Life and Work.* London: G. Allen and Unwin. 1939, 1st ed., 382 p. 1949, 2nd ed., 557 p.
    This was presented to Gandhi on his seventieth birthday in 1939 and contains contributions from well-known persons. The second edition includes memorials on his death.

Ramachandran, G. *A Sheaf of Gandhi Anecdotes.* Bombay: Hind Kitabs. 56 p. 1945.

Raman, T. A. *What Does Gandhi Want?* London: Oxford. 117 p. 1943.

Rolland, Romain. *Mahatma Gandhi; The Man Who Became One with the Universal Being.* New York: Century. 250 p. 1924.

Sheean, Vincent. *Lead, Kindly Light.* New York: Random House. 374 p. 1949.

Shridharani, Krishnalal J. *War Without Violence.* New York: Harcourt. 351 p. 1939.

Shridharani, Krishnalal J. *The Mahatma and the World.* New York: Duell, Sloan and Pearce. 247 p. 1946.

Shukla, Chandrashanker, ed. *Gandhiji as We Know Him.* Bombay: Vora. 145 p. 1945.

Shukla, Chandrashanker, ed. *Incidents in Gandhiji's Life.* Bombay: Vora. 344 p. 1949.

Sitaramayya, B. Pattabhi. *The History of the Indian National Congress, 1885–1935.* Vol. I, 1935, Allahabad: All India Congress Committee, 1038 p. Vol. II, 1947, Bombay: Padina Pub., 827 p.

Tendulkar, D. G., and others. *Gandhiji: His Life and Work.* Bombay: Karnatak Pub. House. 501 p. 1944.

This was presented to Gandhi on his seventy-fifth birthday in 1944 and contains contributions from Albert Einstein, Pearl Buck, and others. In addition, this contains a remarkably complete chronology of his life and many photographs, paintings, and designs. The edition on hand-made paper limited to 250 numbered copies is a landmark in printing.

Thomas, K. P. *Kasturba Gandhi: A Biographical Study.* Calcutta: Orient Illustrated Weekly. 96 p. 1944.

Walker, Roy. *Sword of Gold: A Life of Mahatma Gandhi.* London: Indian Independence Union. 200 p. 1945.

Watson, Blanche. *Gandhi and Non-Violent Resistance: Gleanings from the American Press.* Madras: Ganesh. 549 p. 1923.

SOURCES

INTRODUCTION

1. Gandhi, 1928, p. 473.
2. Gandhi, 1923, p. xviii.
3. Gandhi; 1949, p. 6.
4. Gandhi, 1927a, p. 298 (1948).
5. Quoted by Fischer, 1942, p. 42.
6. Andrews, 1929, p. 10 (1949).
7. Quoted by Jones, 1948, p. 7.
8. Quoted by Tendulkar, 1944.
9. Fischer, 1942, pp. 116–19.
10. Quoted by Tendulkar, 1944, pp. 362–63.

11. *Harijan*, 9/30/39.
12. Gandhi, 1927a, p. 615 (1948).
13. *Young India*, 12/31/31.
14. Andrews, 1929, p. 4 (1949).
15. *Harijan*, 3/2/40.
16. *Harijan*, 5/1/37.
17. *Harijan*, 10/3/36.
18. *Harijan*, 5/30/36.
19. Quoted by Fischer, 1950, p. 414.

RELIGION
Page 15
Religions: Gandhi, 1909, pp. 23–24 (1944).
Humbug: Gandhi, 1909, p. 30 (1946).
It is not: Young India, 5/12/20.
Religion which: Young India, 5/7/25.
I came: 7/26/25, quoted by Andrews, 1929, pp. 73–74.
A man: Gandhi: 1927a, p. 615 (1948).
Page 16
The test: 5/28/27, Gandhi, 1949, p. 37.
The study: Young India, 12/6/28.
After long study: Gandhi, 1928, pp. 17–19.
One's own: Quoted by Andrews, 1929, p. 93.
If we are: Gandhi, 1933, p. 55.
For me: Quoted by Pyarelal, 1932, p. 133.
A religion: Harijan, 7/18/36.
Page 17
Religion deals: Harijan, 8/22/36.
The most: Harijan, 7/1/39.
I cannot: Harijan, 2/10/40.
Religions are: Harijan, 6/8/40.
His own: Quoted by Tikekar, 1947, p. 60.

[God] is: Young India, 3/5/25.
There are some: Young India, 1/23/30.
Page 18
It is the fashion: Harijan, 4/25/36.
I tolerate: Young India, 7/21/20.
Intolerance: Young India, 1/19/21.
Intolerance betrays: Young India, 2/2/22.
The golden rule: Young India, 9/23/26.
If you: Young India, 8/11/27.
So long: Gandhi, 1927a, p. 480 (1948).
Just as: Young India, 12/12/28.
Page 19
Even: Gandhi, 1933, p. 55 (1935).
I do not: Gandhi, 1933, p. 55 (1935).
If all faiths: Gandhi, 1933, p. 55 (1935).
Many: 2/14/16, quoted by Andrews, 1929, p. 122.
Page 20
Converts: Young India, 3/4/26.
I do not: Young India, 10/20/27.
A convert's: Gandhi, 1927a, p. 79 (1948).
I should not: Gandhi, 1927a, p. 152 (1948).
My own: Gandhi, 1928, pp. 17–19.
We do not: Quoted by Andrews, 1929, p. 95.

NOTE: For complete reference, consult the Bibliography (pages 211–216). Dates in parentheses indicate editions used. For example, "Gandhi, 1927a, p. 100 (1948)" refers to page 100 of the 1948 edition of the book originally published by Gandhi in 1927—his *Autobiography*.

If a person: Harijan, 9/25/37.
Scriptures: Young India: 1/19/21.
Spirituality: Young India, 10/13/21.
Page 21
  Divine knowledge: Young India,
    7/17/24.
  Error: Young India, 2/26/25.
  Knowledge: Young India, 8/25/27.
  Nothing can: Harijan, 7/18/36.
  Truth is: Quoted by Tikekar, 1947,
    p. 77.
  Hinduism: 2/14/16, quoted by
    Andrews, 1929, pp. 120–21.
  Unfortunately: Young India, 10/6/21.
Page 22
  Hinduism is: Young India, 10/6/21.
  A man: Young India, 2/24/24.
  Hinduism is like: Young India, 4/8/26.
  The Gita *is: Young India,* 8/25/27.
  Brahmanism: Young India, 9/15/27.
Page 23
  The Gita: *Young India,* 8/24/34.
  Hinduism is not: Quoted by Fischer,
    1942, p. 71.
  God: Young India, 8/11/27.
  I have not: Young India, 12/22/27.
Page 24
  My difficulties: Gandhi, 1927a, pp. 170–
    71 (1948).
  For many: Quoted by Andrews, 1929,
    p. 92.
Page 25
  Do not: Quoted by Andrews, 1929,
    p. 96.
  If Jesus: Harijan, 5/11/35.
  He: Quoted by Tendulkar, 1944,
    p. 154.
  Christianity: Quoted by Fischer, 1950,
    p. 424.

THEOLOGY

Page 26
  There can: Young India, 3/23/21.
  God is: Young India, 2/2/22.
  God is that: Young India, 3/5/25.
  The contents: Young India, 8/11/27.
  Mankind: Young India, 8/25/27.
Page 27
  I see: Young India, 9/22/27.
  God: Young India, 9/22/27.
  He: Gandhi, 1927a, p. 32 (1948).
  The voice: Gandhi, 1927a, p. 269
    (1948).
  I have not: Gandhi, 1927a, p. 341
    (1948).
  Let: Gandhi, 1927a, pp. 524–25(1948).

Page 28
  There is: Young India, 10/11/28.
  I do: Young India, 10/11/28.
  God seems: Gandhi, 1928, p. 325.
  We may: Quoted by Andrews, 1929,
    p. 95.
  I would: Young India, 12/31/31.
  God keeps: Harijan, 9/21/34.
Page 29
  Perfection: Harijan, 11/14/36.
  God is not: Private correspondence,
    Sevagram, 6/1/42.
  God may: Quoted by Tikekar, 1944,
    p. 23.
  There is: Quoted by Tendulkar, 1944,
    p. 321.
  I believe: Quoted by Fischer, 1950,
    p. 442.
  I refuse: Young India, 8/4/20.
  No matter: Gandhi, 1928, p. 126.
Page 30
  No human: Young India, 3/26/31.
  On God's Earth: Harijan, 1/5/34.
  Man: Modern Review, 1935, p. 412.
  I positively: Harijan, 7/12/42.
  I have: Harijan, 7/26/42.
  I have discovered: Quoted by Tikekar,
    1947, p. 30.
  Man's upward: Quoted by Tikekar,
    1947, p. 30.
  I have been: Quoted by Fischer, 1950,
    p. 298.
  Mankind: Quoted by Fischer, 1950,
    p. 445.
  You must: Quoted by Fischer, 1950,
    p. 474.
Page 31
  Virtue: Young India, 5/29/24.
  Prayer: Young India, 6/10/26.
  There can: Young India, 6/10/26.
  For those: Young India, 6/10/26.
  Prayer needs: Gandhi, 1927a, p. 96
    (1948).
  God never: Young India, 4/4/29.
Page 32
  Prayer is: Young India, 1/23/30.
  We should: Young India, 1/23/30.
  Do not worry: Young India, 1/23/30.
  But why pray: Harijan, 6/8/35.
  My faith: Harijan, 11/5/38.
Page 33
  I feel: Quoted by Tendulkar, 1944,
    p. 254
  Prayer is the key: Quoted by Tikekar,
    1947, p. 55.
  It is: Quoted by Tikekar, 1947, p. 56.

I do not: Young India: 10/6/21.
A congregational: Young India, 9/23/26.
Page 34
Worshipping: Quoted by Andrews, 1929, pp. 47–48.
It depends: Harijan, 1/23/37.
Idolatry: Harijan, 3/9/40.
Page 35
Churches: Harijan, 3/5/42.
Man alone: Gandhi, 1920, p. 129 (1930).
God: Gandhi, 1927a, p. 24 (1948).
Of the thing: Gandhi, 1927a, p. 94 (1948).
I do not: Gandhi, 1927a, p. 156 (1948).
Page 36
I know that: Gandhi, 1927a, p. 616 (1948).
If one: Quoted by Jones, 1948, p. 61.
Confession: Young India, 2/16/22.
There [is]: Gandhi, 1927a, p. 41 (1948).
A clean: Gandhi, 1927a, p. 42 (1948).
There is no discredit: Harijan, 10/8/38.
There is no defeat: Quoted by Jones, 1948, p. 114.
The brave: Young India, 10/13/21.
Page 37
Death: Young India, 2/2/22.
We are living: Young India, 9/23/26.
Death is no fiend: Young India, 12/20/26.
We really: 4/27/27, Gandhi, 1949, p. 31.
Whom: Gandhi, 1928, p. 190.
For many: Gandhi, 1928, p. 286.
Page 38
It is better: 7/6/31, Gandhi, 1949, p. 89.
Both: 5/18/36, Gandhi, 1949, p. 173.
[Death] is: Quoted by Fischer, 1950, p. 339.
Why should: Young India, 10/13/21.
Page 39
Transmigration: Young India, 10/6/27.
Man hankers: Young India, 10/17/29.
It is: 1/25/31, Gandhi, 1949, p. 87.
Our existence: Gandhi, 1933, p. 68.
Nothing: 5/8/38, Gandhi, 1949, p. 186.
I have: Quoted by Fischer, 1942, p. 70.
Page 40
One's faith: Young India, 4/3/24.
It is poor: Young India, 11/20/24.
Learning: Young India, 1/22/25.
Someone: Young India, 9/3/25.
Faith: Young India, 6/24/26.
A man: Gandhi, 1928, p. 371.

The man: Gandhi, 1928, p. 442.
Faith is: 2/4/29, Gandhi, 1949, p. 50.
It is faith: Quoted by Andrews, 1929, p. 48.
Those: 6/5/33. Gandhi, 1949, p. 152.
Page 41
God is: Gandhi, 1917b, p. 1069 (1934).
The fullest life: Harijan, 4/25/36.
Faith can: Harijan, 10/9/37.
Meetings: Harijan, 1/28/39.
Faith is a function: Harijan, 4/6/40.
Every: Young India, 2/26/25.
Ultimately: Young India, 11/12/25.
Page 42
Experience: Young India, 10/14/26.
I plead: Young India, 10/14/26.
Knowledge: Gandhi, 1928, p. 286.
If you: Young India, 11/5/31.
To renounce: Harijan, 11/21/36.
There are: Harijan, 3/6/37.
I cannot: Quoted by Jones, 1948, p. 60.
Page 43
He is: Young India, 3/5/25.
One's life: Young India, 11/5/25.
Man is higher: Young India, 6/3/26.
Fatalism: Young India, 11/18/26.
As we: Gandhi, 1927a, p. 37.
I had: Gandhi, 1927a, p. 308.
Page 44
Man can: Gandhi, 1928, p. 219.
Manliness: Young India, 8/29/29.
Accidents: 1/26/33, Gandhi, 1949, p. 136.
We cannot: Harijan, 5/6/39.
The free will: Harijan, 3/23/40.
We shall: Quoted by Maurer, 1948, p. 124.
Man: Quoted by Fischer, 1950, p. 303.
In order: Young India, 2/23/21.
Evil in itself: Young India, 2/23/21.
Page 45
Evil does: Young India, 12/4/24.
He is: Young India, 3/5/25.
I cannot: Quoted by Andrews, 1929, p. 45.
Vice pays: Young India, 1/16/30.
There is: Young India, 1/23/30.
Man must choose: Harijan, 2/1/35.
Man's estate: Harijan, 4/4/36.
Page 46
There is: Quoted by Tendulkar, 1944, p. 368.
In God's world: Quoted by Fischer, 1950, p. 433.
It is: Quoted by Fischer, 1950, p. 474.

PERSONAL ETHICS

Page 47
Good: Gandhi, 1909, p. 21 (1944).
Immorality: Gandhi, 1909, p. 26 (1946).
Civilization: Gandhi, 1909, p. 44 (1946).
There is no: Young India, 11/24/21.
To say: Young India, 4/24/24.
The most: Young India, 12/26/24.
A negative: Young India, 6/17/26.
Trivialities: 1/10/27, Gandhi, 1949, p. 23.
Page 48
Any tradition: Young India, 9/22/27.
One thing: Gandhi, 1927a, p. 51 (1948.)
It has: Gandhi, 1927a, p. 192 (1948).
Hypocrisy: Gandhi, 1928, p. 142.
The world: Gandhi, 1928, p. 413.
Duty: Young India, 10/10/29.
Life: Quoted by Andrews, 1929, p. 140.
Satan's: Quoted by Andrews, 1929, p. 273.
Page 49
There are: Young India, 1/23/30.
For the: Harijan, 10/3/36.
To err: Harijan, 2/6/37.
The motive: Quoted by Prabhu, 1947, p. 46.
If I: Young India, 3/2/22.
Ultimately: Gandhi, 1927a, p. 431.
Cunning: Gandhi, 1928, p. 318.
A cause: Quoted by Andrews, 1929, p. 322.
Any: Gandhi, 1949, p. 143, 3/11/33.
Page 50
I feared: Gandhi, 1927a, p. 483 (1948).
It is: Gandhi, 1927a, p. 575 (1948).
Truth: Young India, 12/31/31.
To cultivate: Gandhi, 1933, p. 67.
A life: Gandhi, 1933, p. 68.
Experience: Gandhi, 1927a, p. 84 (1948).
Page 51
Silence: Harijan, 12/10/38.
I wanted: Quoted by Fischer, 1942, p. 42.
It is: Young India, 4/24/24.
Real: Gandhi, 1949, p. 31.
One earns: 7/17/27, Gandhi, 1949, p. 40.
True: Gandhi, 1927a, p. 31 (1948).
Page 52
Even: Gandhi, 1928, p. 256.
When: Gandhi, 1928, p. 307.

There: 9/15/32, Gandhi, 1949, p. 118.
Friendship: Harijan, 1/27/40.
A friendship: Harijan, 3/9/40.
Cooperation: Quoted by Tikekar, 1947, p. 19.
Adversity: Quoted by Tikekar, 1947, p. 19.
Page 53
Those: Gandhi, 1909, p. 48 (1944).
If we: Gandhi, 1917b, p. 317.
Let us: Gandhi, 1917b, p. 329.
Fearlessness: Gandhi, 1917b, p. 329.
Fearlessness is: Young India, 10/13/21.
Courteousness: Young India, 6/22/24.
A man: Young India, 8/12/26.
When: Quoted by Andrews, 1929, p. 108 (1930).
Page 54
Passive: Gandhi, 1909, p. 62 (1946).
Fearlessness connotes: Gandhi, 1933, p. 41 (1935).
Fear: Gandhi, 1933, p. 43 (1935).
Strength: Young India, 8/11/20.
The best: Young India, 3/2/22.
Strength in: Young India, 6/17/26.
If a single: Gandhi, 1928, p. 5.
In every: Young India, 10/10/29.
Page 55
Performance: Quoted by Andrews, 1929, p. 135.
The example: Amrita Bazar Patrika, 8/3/34.
A small body: Harijan, 11/19/38.
In: Harijan, 3/25/39.
Interpretation: Gandhi, 1927a, p. 79 (1948).
Page 56
A vow: Gandhi, 1927a, pp. 254–55 (1948).
The ideal: Gandhi, 1927a, p. 557 (1948).
Failure: Gandhi, 1928, pp. 162–63.
Pledges: Gandhi, 1928, p. 166.
The taking: Gandhi, 1933, p. 25 (1935).
Page 57
A life: Quoted by Tendulkar, 1944, p. 365.
One: Quoted by Tendulkar, 1944, p. 366.
Moderation: Quoted by Tendulkar, 1944, p. 366.
A vow: Quoted by Tendulkar, 1944, p. 367.
He who: Gandhi, 1909, p. 131 (1930).
Restraint: Young India, 3/9/20.
Morally: Gandhi, 1927a, p. 400 (1948).

Page 58
Identification: Gandhi, 1927a, pp. 615–16 (1948).
To conquer: Gandhi, 1927a, p. 616 (1948).
Never: 1929, Gandhi, 1949, p. 49.
It is discipline: Young India, 1/23/30.
India's: 1909, Quoted by Andrews, 1929, p. 187.

Page 59
I preach: Young India, 7/21/21.
Europeans: Young India, 4/30/31.
In this: Harijan, 12/22/33.
A certain: Harijan, 8/29/36, p. 226.
Speed: Harijan, 9/25/39.
There is: Quoted by Tendulkar, 1944, p. 67.
It is far: Gandhi, 1920, p. 11.
Illness: Gandhi, 1920, p. 11.

Page 60
There is: Gandhi, 1920, p. 12.
[It is a]: Gandhi, 1920, p. 13.
When: Gandhi, 1920, p. 14.
Disease: Gandhi, 1920, p. 15.
The relation: Gandhi, 1920, p. 8 (1930).
Our aim: Gandhi, 1920, p. 14.
Our passion: Gandhi, 1920, p. 46.
Our body: Gandhi, 1920, p. 111.

Page 61
If we: 7/9/27, Gandhi, 1949, p. 39.
Cigars: Young India, 9/15/27.
If it is: Young India, 9/15/27.
No matter: Gandhi, 1927a, p. 287 (1948).
In trying: Gandhi, 1927a, p. 393 (1948).

Page 62
Abstemiousness: Young India,10/6/21.
It is: Gandhi, 1920, p. 18.
Man is: Gandhi, 1920, p. 19.
A calm: Gandhi, 1920, p. 20.
If we: Gandhi, 1920, pp. 27–28.
There is: Gandhi, 1920, p. 40.
True: Gandhi, 1920, p. 113.

Page 63
To sum: Young India, 10/7/26.
Many: Gandhi, 1927a, p. 77 (1948).
It is part: Gandhi, 1927a, pp. 302–03 (1948).
It is not: Gandhi, 1927a, p. 334 (1948).
All food: Gandhi, 1949, p. 125,11/3/32.
A "full": 1/26/33, Gandhi, 1949, p. 137.

Page 64
More people: 3/11/33, Gandhi, 1949, p. 144.

I do not: Tendulkar, 1944, p. 372.
The choice: Tendulkar, 1944, p. 372.
There is a great: Tendulkar, 1944, p. 373.
The mental: Young India, 2/16/22.
For me: Quoted by Rolland, 1924, p. 205.
The public: Young India, 12/3/25.

Page 65
Fasting: 1/26/33, Gandhi, 1949, p. 136.
Under: 5/8/33, Gandhi, 1949, p. 149.
Fasting is not: Quoted by Tendulkar, 1944, p. 368.
Evolution: Gandhi, 1917b, p. 245.
If we: Young India, 5/6/26, p. 164.
He who: Gandhi, 1927a, p. 376.

Page 66
Whether: Quoted by Andrews, 1929, p. 305.
We have: Amrita Bazar Patrika, 8/2/34.
As I have: Quoted by Fischer, 1950, p. 337.
Chastity: Gandhi, 1909, p. 61 (1946).
Continence: Young India, 10/13/20.
Incontinence: Gandhi, 1920, p. 53.
Realization: Young India, 6/24/26.
When: Young India, 9/15/27.

Page 67
In: Gandhi, 1927a, p. 257 (1948).
A mind: Gandhi, 1927a, p. 403 (1948).
The aim: Young India, 11/13/24.
Protestantism: Young India, 11/13/24.
It is: Young India, 11/13/24.
How: 4/27/33, Gandhi, 1949, p. 147.

Page 68
Observance: Harijan, 4/25/36.
Brahmacharya: Harijan, 6/13/36.
We cannot: Harijan, 11/21/36.

SOCIAL ETHICS

Page 69
Love never: Young India, 7/9/25.
Love is: Young India, 8/6/25.
If we: Young India, 10/7/26.
I know: Gandhi, 1927a, p. 24 (1948).
Where love: Gandhi, 1928, p. 360.
A love: Quoted by Andrews, 1929, p. 247.
Blind: Quoted by Andrews, 1929, p. 261.
The sword: Quoted by Jones, 1948, p. 99.
There is: Young India, 9/17/25.

Page 70
Truth is: Young India, 5/27/26.
Truth is the: Gandhi, 1927a, p. 6 (1948).
The instruments: Gandhi, 1927a, p. 7 (1948).
Truth is like: Gandhi, 1927a, p. 268 (1948).
A devotee: Gandhi, 1927a, p. 429 (1948).
My uniform: Gandhi, 1927a, p. 615 (1948).
Page 71
Truth . . . is: Young India, 12/31/31.
Devotion to: Gandhi, 1933, p. 2.
Truth is not: Harijan, 3/14/36.
In violence: Hindusthan Standard, 10/28/44.
When: Quoted by Fischer, 1950, p. 486.
We who: Gandhi, 1909, p. 16 (1946).
Justice: Young India, 7/9/25.
We win: Gandhi, 1927a, p. 225 (1948).
No tyrant: 11/20/29, Gandhi, 1949, p. 61.
Justice without: Harijan, 1/27/40.
Page 72
Even: Harijan, 2/24/40.
Even as: Quoted by Tikekar, 1947, p. 36.
Complete: Young India: 3/9/20.
The central: Young India, 10/6/21.
It is a: Young India, 9/24/25.
Page 73
Spiritual: Young India, 10/7/26.
To my mind: Gandhi, 1927a, p. 290 (1948).
By unnecessarily: Young India, 9/6/28.
I know: Young India, 12/31/31.
We have: 8/31/32. Gandhi, 1949, p. 117.
Page 74
Happiness: Gandhi, 1909, p. 44 (1946).
We are: Gandhi, 1917b, p. 384 (1934).
The greater: Gandhi, 1917b, p. 350 (1934).
The golden: Young India, 6/24/26.
I had: Gandhi, 1927a, p. 187 (1948).
Page 75
I understood: Gandhi, 1927a, p. 324 (1948).
Increase: Quoted by Andrews, 1929, p. 187.
The richest: Quoted by Andrews, 1929, p. 273.
I am: Associated Press Dispatch, Marseilles, 9/11/31.

It is: 5/13/32, Gandhi, 1949, p. 105.
Perfect: Gandhi, 1933, p. 34 (1935).
Non-possession: Gandhi, 1933, p. 38 (1935).
Page 76
The use: Harijan, 7/21/40.
It is more: Quoted by Fischer, 1950, p. 92.
Monotony: Young India, 8/18/21.
I can: Young India, 10/20/21.
Ruskin's: Gandhi, 1927a, pp. 364–65 (1948).
Page 77
It is: Young India, 9/20/28.
The divine: Gandhi, 1933, p. 50 (1935).
If all: Harijan, 6/29/35.

SERVICE

Page 78
Discontent: Gandhi, 1909, p. 19 (1946).
It is: 1909, Quoted by Andrews, 1929, pp. 186–87.
A movement: Young India, 8/11/20.
Power: Young India, 9/11/24.
It is not: Young India, 8/26/26.
To give: 11/29/27, Desai, 1928, p. 145.
I could not: Gandhi, 1927a, p. 267 (1948).
Page 79
I have: Gandhi, 1927a, p. 267 (1948).
Even: Gandhi, 1927a, p. 508 (1948).
I have noticed: Gandhi, 1927a, p. 567 (1948).
A chronic: Young India, 3/1/28.
Put: Young India, 11/5/31.
Service: Harijan, 5/25/35.
We won't: Harijan, 5/30/36.
Man's: Harijan, 8/29/36.
Page 80
Reform: Harijan, 4/20/40.
All reforms: Quoted by Tikekar, 1947, p. 58.
No cause: Quoted by Fischer, 1950, p. 474.
Those: Gandhi, 1909, p. 33 (1946).
Courage: Young India, 9/29/21.
A reformer's: Young India, 2/5/25.
I am: Young India, 5/27/26.
More: Young India, 6/9/27.
Service: Gandhi, 1927a, p. 215 (1948).
Page 81
Without: Gandhi, 1927a, p. 268 (1948).
A public: Gandhi, 1927a, p. 272 (1948).
Even: Gandhi, 1927a, p. 328 (1948).

A public worker: Gandhi, 1927a, p. 364 (1948).

[In] service: Gandhi, 1927a, p. 449 (1948).

An aspirant: Gandhi, 1928, p. 155.

It is always: Gandhi, 1928, p. 227.

It is in: Young India, 10/3/29.

The reformer's: Young India, 11/28/29.

Page 82

I regard: 9/28/30, Gandhi, 1949, p. 74.

It is the: Young India, 4/2/31.

One: Gandhi, 1933, p. 39 (1935).

No matter: Harijan, 7/27/35.

No reform: Harijan, 7/25/36.

A voice: Harijan, 3/27/37

In every: Harijan, 4/24/37.

Page 83

There is: Harijan, 1/28/39.

Where is: Quoted by Tikekar, 1947, p. 58.

We should: Young India, 10/6/21.

Whenever: Young India, 2/10/27.

Service: Gandhi, 1927a, p. 190 (1948).

Educated: Gandhi, 1927a, p. 295 (1948).

Page 84

I had: Gandhi, 1927a, p. 460 (1948).

If I am: Quoted by Jones, 1948, pp. 112–13.

I myself: Gandhi, 1917b, p. 317.

Every: Young India, 3/9/21.

I share: Young India, 12/11/24.

Page 85

In: Gandhi, 1928, p. 188.

The greater: Harijan, 6/29/40.

I have: Quoted by Fischer, 1942, p. 104.

I have: Young India, 1/20/27.

Though: Gandhi, 1927a, p. 72 (1948).

I had: Gandhi, 1927a, p. 186 (1948).

Economy: Gandhi, 1927a, p. 188 (1948).

Page 86

It is not: Gandhi, 1927a, pp. 243–44 (1948).

I do not: Young India, 4/16/31.

No movement: Harijan, 11/28/36.

I have always: Harijan, 12/10/38.

If we: Hindusthan Standard, 12/6/44.

SATYAGRAHA

Page 87

The: Gandhi, 1927a, p. 389 (1948).

Satyagraha: Gandhi, 1928, p. 180.

When: Quoted by Andrews, 1929, p. 192.

Page 88

Passive: Harijan, 7/21/40.

The statement: Quoted by Jones, 1948, p. 84.

That: Gandhi, 1909, p. 51 (1946).

They say: Young India, 7/17/24.

Means: Young India, 12/26/24.

Page 89

There is: Gandhi, 1928, p. 509.

Our: Amrita Bazar Patrika, 8/17/33.

Means to: Gandhi, 1933, p. 13.

If one: Harijan, 2/11/39.

Means are: 1/27/48, quoted by Sheean, 1949, pp. 184–85.

Fairest: Quoted by Tikekar, 1947, p. 45.

I am: Quoted by Fischer, 1950, p. 330.

Gift: Gandhi, 1917b, p. 346 (1934).

Forced: Young India, 8/11/20.

Page 90

A nation: Young India, 8/25/20.

Self-sacrifice: Young India, 2/12/25.

The willing: Young India, 2/12/25.

No sacrifice: Young India, 6/25/25.

There: Young India, 7/15/26.

The mice: Quoted by Andrews, 1929, p. 265.

In true: Young India, 5/8/30.

A satyagrahi: Quoted by Jones, 1948, p. 99.

Page 91

The mother: Young India, 8/11/20.

The secret: Young India, 9/29/21.

Suffering: Young India, 10/13/21.

The salvation: Gandhi, 1927a, p. 538 (1948).

Real: Gandhi, 1928, p. 32.

Suffering has: Young India: 3/12/31.

People: Young India, 10/29/31.

Page 92

Things: Young India, 11/5/31.

Whenever: Young India, 9/25/24.

Fasting: Quoted by Tendulkar, 1944, p. 370

In the: Quoted by Jones, 1948, p. 110.

It is: Quoted by Fischer, 1950, p. 221.

If one: Young India, 12/3/19.

Page 93

We are: Young India, 6/1/21.

Not all: 4/14/22, Gandhi, 1933.

The shame: Gandhi, 1927a, p. 451 (1948).

Jail-going: Gandhi, 1927a, p. 523 (1948).

When: Gandhi, 1927a, p. 536 (1948).

It is: Gandhi, 1928, p. 422.

Prison: 7/14/32, Gandhi, 1949, p. 113.
Over: 8/23/32, Gandhi, 1949, p. 116.
Page 94
A satyagrahi: Harijan, 11/5/38.
We must: Quoted by Fischer, 1950,
  p. 204.
Passive: Gandhi, 1909, p. 48 (1944).
Whilst: Young India, 5/25/21.
We: Young India, 9/29/21.
Immediately: Young India, 3/19/25.
Page 95
Let us: Young India, 6/4/25.
Man: Gandhi, 1927a, p. 337 (1948).
A satyagrahi bids: Gandhi, 1928, p. 246.
A satyagrahi must: Young India,
  8/8/29.
I am: Quoted by Andrews, 1929,
  p. 273.
Page 96
As no: Young India, 3/26/31.
The idea: Harijan, 12/10/38.
It is: Harijan, 3/25/39.
One: Harijan, 2/22/42.
When: Harijan, 2/9/47.
Whenever: Quoted by Tikekar, 1947,
  p. 41.
In the: Quoted by Tikekar, 1947, p. 65.
Every: Young India, 7/28/20.
Page 97
Non-cooperation is not: Young India,
  8/25/20.
Non-cooperation is an: Young India,
  12/1/20.
A non-cooperationist: Young India,
  1/12/21.
The sole: Young India, 2/23/21.
Non-cooperation does: Young India,
  2/23/21.
Page 98
The primary: Young India, 4/6/21.
Non-cooperation, when: Young India,
  12/29/21.
Non-cooperation with: 3/18/22, Quoted
  by Jones, 1948, p. 94.
My non-cooperation has: Young India,
  8/6/25.
Non-cooperation in: Quoted by
  Andrews, 1929, p. 305.
My non-cooperation is: Quoted by
  Tikekar, 1947, p. 48.
When: Gandhi, 1909, p. 58 (1946).
Page 99
If our: Gandhi, 1917b, p. 311.
Only: Young India, 11/5/19.
Those: Young India, 11/3/21.
Complete: Young India, 11/10/21.

Page 100
If I am: Gandhi, 1917b, p. 346(1934).
Ahimsa: Gandhi, 1917b, p. 348 (1934).
Non-violence: Young India, 8/11/20.
Non-violence . . . is a: Young India,
  8/12/26.
It is no: Young India, 10/21/26.
Ahimsa is: Young India, 11/4/26.
Participation: Gandhi, 1927a, p. 427–
  28 (1948).
Page 101
Ahimsa is: Young India, 9/6/28.
There is no: Gandhi, 1928, pp. 464–65.
Ahimsa means: Quoted by Andrews,
  1929, pp. 103–04.
Those who: 12/4/32, Quoted by Jones,
  1948, p. 89.
Page 102
Non-violence in: Amrita Bazar Patrika
  8/3/34.
They must: Harijan, 7/9/38.
Non-violence is: Harijan, 11/12/38.
Non-violence is never: Harijan, 7/8/39.
Prolonged: Harijan, 7/21/40.
We are: Harijan, 8/25/40.
Non-violence does: Harijan, 6/28/42.
Page 103
The votary: Quoted by Tikekar, 1947,
  p. 1.
He who: Quoted by Tikekar, 1947, p. 4.
Non-violence begins: Quoted by Tike-
  kar, 1947, p. 49.
A non-violent: Quoted by Tikekar,
  1947, p. 49.
Passive: Quoted by Jones, 1948, pp.
  104–05.
We shall: Young India, 11/10/19.
I do: Young India, 8/11/20.
Terrorism: Young India, 9/22/20.
The end: Young India, 1/5/21.
Page 104
Violence: Young India, 3/9/21.
Violence flourishes: Young India,
  3/30/21.
I object: Young India, 5/21/25.
History: Young India, 5/6/26.
The sin: Young India, 11/4/26.
Those: Young India, 3/17/27.
In satyagraha: Gandhi, 1928, p. 179.
Not only: Gandhi, 1928, p. 179.
If light: Gandhi, 1928, p. 289.
Page 105
We can: Harijan, 8/17/34.
A satyagrahi is: 3/12/40, Gandhi,
  1949, p. 196.
Hatred: Harijan, 5/31/42.

The religion: Young India, 8/11/20.
The danger: Young India, 7/28/21.
There is: Young India, 2/19/25.
Every: Young India, 3/19/25.
You need: Young India, 4/30/25.
Since: Young India, 10/20/27.
Page 106
Satyagraha: Gandhi, 1927a, p. 534
  (1948).
Civility: Gandhi, 1927a, pp. 534–35
  (1948).
The beauty: Gandhi, 1928, p. 5.
It is only: Gandhi, 1928, p. 5.
A satyagraha: Gandhi, 1928, p. 200.
The satyagrahis: Gandhi, 1928, p. 201.
Secrecy: Gandhi, 1928, p. 225.
In satyagraha: Gandhi, 1928, p. 319.
Page 107
Satyagraha against: Gandhi, 1928,
  p. 321.
A satyagraha: Gandhi, 1928, p. 355.
In a pure: Gandhi, 1928, p. 412.
The humility: Gandhi, 1928, p. 442.
A satyagrahi: Gandhi, 1928, p. 497.
No matter: Gandhi, 1928, p. 502.
Satyagraha is: Gandhi, 1928, p. 511.
I do not: Young India, 11/14/29.
Page 108
The end: Harijan, 3/23/40.
Truth-Force: Harijan, 7/21/40.

INTERNATIONAL AFFAIRS
Page 109
The English: Gandhi, 1909, p. 50
  (1946).
I bear: Gandhi, 1909, p. 76 (1946).
Look: Gandhi, 1917b, p. 317.
Superiority: Young India, 6/8/21.
I did not: Young India, 11/17/21.
The color: Gandhi, 1927a, p. 212 (1948).
As the: Gandhi, 1927a, p. 301 (1948).
Page 110
I knew: Gandhi, 1927a, p. 425 (1948).
Under: Gandhi, 1928, p. 136.
I discovered: Quoted by Andrews, 1929,
  p. 220.
An Englishman: Quoted by Andrews,
  1929, p. 250.
In a free: Young India, 11/12/31.
In the matter: Harijan, 9/24/38.
Page 111
The news: 5/22/41, Gandhi, 1949,
  p. 205.
Though: Harijan, 5/24/42.
The British: Quoted by Fischer, 1942,
  p. 25.

Britain: Quoted by Fischer, 1942,
  p. 33.
When: Harijan, 12/12/36.
American: 12/20/41, Raman, 1943,
  p. 45.
Americans: Harijan, 5/18/42.
Page 112
It was: Harijan, 5/24/42.
America and: Quoted by Fischer, 1942,
  p. 63.
America is: 1942, Quoted by Hingo-
  rani, 1942a, p. 30.
I have not: Quoted by Jones, 1948,
  p. 152.
Bolshevism: 1919, Quoted by Fischer,
  1950, p. 178.
I am yet: Young India, 12/11/24.
Page 113
From what: Young India, 11/15/28.
All: 1/26/41, Quoted by Fischer, 1950,
  p. 330.
What does: Quoted by Prabhu, 1947,
  p. 99.
Communism: Quoted by Prabhu, 1947,
  p. 99.
I do not: Young India, 2/23/21.
Page 114
The Jews: Harijan, 11/11/38.
You are: 7/23/39, Raman, 1943, p. 10.
I must: 9/39, Raman, 1943, p. 13.
Whatever: Harijan, 6/18/40.
I do not: 1940, Raman, 1943, p. 36.
Page 115
The Japanese: 1/39, Raman, 1943, p. 6.
My personal: Harijan, 9/25/39.
Herr Hitler: Harijan, 10/14/39.
My prayer: 10/28/39, Raman, 1943,
  p. 19.
I think: Harijan, 6/18/40.
Page 116
I appeal: Harijan, 7/6/40.
I hold: Harijan, 7/21/40.
If the press: Harijan, 9/29/40.
The very: Harijan, 10/20/40.
I am not: Quoted by Fischer, 1942, p. 58.
Page 117
The frightful: 2/14/16, Quoted by
  Andrews, 1929, p. 122 (1930).
It may: Young India, 6/23/19.
We have: Young India, 9/8/20.
All: Gandhi, 1927a, p. 427 (1948).
War is: Quoted by Andrews, 1929,
  pp. 142–43.
The ever-growing: 1914, Quoted by
  Andrews, 1929, p. 200.
If the mad: Harijan, 11/12/38.

226

Sources

Page 118
Immediately: Harijan, 11/12/38.
No cause: Harijan, 7/6/40.
Peace: Harijan, 7/21/40.
I believe: Harijan, 8/18/40.
What: Harijan, 9/29/40.
A warrior: Harijan, 1940, Quoted by
Raman, 1943, p. 27.
Can we: Harijan, 3/22/42.
Page 119
In war: Quoted by Fischer, 1942, p. 17.
I cannot: Hindusthan Standard,
7/20/44.
When: Gandhi, 1927a, p. 428 (1948).
I draw: Young India, 9/13/28.
Every: Gandhi, 1928, p. 115.
Page 120
If we are: Young India, 11/19/31.
If society: Harijan, 11/14/36.
While: 1/1/39, Quoted by Raman,
1943, p. 7.
It is open: Harijan, 11/4/39.
A man: The Times of India, 2/16/41.
My resistance: Harijan, 1/18/42.
Page 121
I [am]: Harijan, 7/5/42.
A soldier: Quoted by Tikekar, 1947,
p. 71.
Those: Quoted by Fischer, 1950, p. 123.
Someday: Young India, 3/2/22.
Isolated: Young India, 7/17/24.
A world: Press Message, 8/8/42.
The structure: Gandhi, 1945, p. 175.

POLITICAL AFFAIRS

Page 122
It is a: Gandhi, 1909, p. 59 (1946).
The truest: Young India, 12/18/20.
The wise: Gandhi, 1928, p. 140.
People: Gandhi, 1928, p. 342.
States: Gandhi, 1928, pp. 485–86.
Page 123
The democracy: Quoted by Pyarelal,
1932, p. 102.
Legislation: Quoted by Pyarelal, 1932,
p. 166.
I look: Gandhi, 1933, p. 413 (1935).
Democracy: Quoted by Sitaramaiyya,
1935, p. 982.
Democracy and: Harijan, 11/12/38.
Democracy must: Harijan, 5/27/39.
A born democrat: Harijan, 5/27/39.
Page 124
Liberty: Harijan, 9/29/40.
Power: Gandhi, 1941c, p. 4.

Democracy will: Gandhi, 1948c, p. 136.
Parliamentary: Quoted by Fischer,
1942, pp. 56–57.
My notion: Quoted by Tikekar, 1947,
p. 12.
The rule: Quoted by Prabhu, 1947,
p. 114.
Any: Quoted by Fischer, 1950, p. 242.
In matters: Young India, 8/4/20.
Page 125
There will: Young India, 7/28/21.
There is no: Young India, 3/9/22.
When: Harijan, 11/21/36.
I value: Harijan, 5/27/39.
The chains: Gandhi, 1945, p. 83.
Liberty: Quoted by Tikekar, 1947,
p. 18.
A slave-holder: Quoted by Tikekar,
1947, p. 70.
The indispensable: Young India,
10/27/21.
Page 126
Liberty: Young India, 1/12/22.
Evolution: Harijan, 5/31/42.
The theory: 1914, Quoted by Andrews,
1929, p. 233 (1930).
Page 127
There is: Gandhi, 1928, p. 61.
Both: Harijan, 5/18/42.
A civilization: Quoted by Fischer,
1950, p. 425.
The test: Gandhi, 1917b, p. 350 (1934).
The hungry: Young India, 10/13/21.
Do not: Young India, 2/24/27.
For the poor: Young India, 5/5/27.
No one: Young India, 11/15/28.
Page 128
I do not: Quoted by Andrews, 1929,
p. 263.
I may: Young India, 10/15/31.
An economics: Harijan, 10/9/37.
We may: Amrita Bazar Patrika,
6/30/44.
Economic: Quoted by Prabhu, 1947,
p. 21.
The laborers: Young India, 2/16/21.
Page 129
Strikes: Young India, 6/1/21.
A satisfactory: Young India, 6/1/21.
The . . . mill: Gandhi, 1927a, pp. 521–
22 (1948).
The working: Harijan, 7/3/37.
Page 130
A working: Harijan, 7/3/37.
If: Harijan, 3/4/39.
When: Harijan, 10/16/45.

It would: Gandhi, 1909, p. 68 (1946).
In the struggle: Young India, 6/1/21.
Page 131
I cannot: Young India, 10/7/26.
I do not: Young India, 10/7/26.
The dream: Young India, 11/21/29.
The rich: Young India, 9/4/30.
By: Young India, 3/26/31.
I do not teach: Young India, 11/26/31.
I shall throw: Amrita Bazar Patrika, 8/2/34.
Page 132
All exploitation: Amrita Bazar Patrika, 8/3/34.
Exploitation: Harijan, 7/28/40.
A violent: 1941, Quoted by Fischer, 1950, p. 327.
It should: Quoted by Prabhu, 1947, pp. 12–13.
I do not: Quoted by Prabhu, 1947, p. 49.
A nation: Quoted by Prabhu, 1947, p. 105.
Page 133
I know: Young India, 7/21/20.
Machinery: Young India, 11/5/25.
I refuse: Young India, 6/17/26.
Even: Young India, 11/13/24.
Page 134
Scientific: Young India, 11/13/24.
The Singer: Young India, 11/13/24.
It is: Young India, 11/13/24.
Machines: Young India, 11/13/24.
Industrialism: Young India, 11/12/31.
As I look: Harijan, 1/28/39.
Pandit Nehru: Harijan, 9/29/40.
Page 135
America: Harijan, 3/9/47.
I would: Quoted by Tendulkar, 1944, p. 42.
Mechanization: Quoted by Prabhu, 1947, p. 109.
I am: Young India, 11/13/24.
What: Modern Review, 1935, p. 412.
Page 136
I desire: Harijan, 12/16/39.
I have: Harijan, 4/20/40.
There can: Harijan, 6/1/47.
Socialism: Quoted by Prabhu, 1947, p. 96.
People: Young India, 9/8/27.
State: Quoted by Tendulkar, 1944, p. 377.
Page 137
India: Quoted by Tendulkar, 1944, p. 377.

Prohibition: Quoted by Tendulkar, 1944, p. 378.
Drink: Quoted by Prabhu, 1947, p. 69.

THE FAMILY
Page 138
Man: 2/20/18, Gandhi, 1917b, p. 423 (1934).
Woman: Gandhi, 1917b, p. 423 (1934).
Chastity: Young India, 2/3/27.
I have: Gandhi 1927a, p. 38 (1948).
Refuse: Desai, 1928, p. 18.
Page 139
Woman: Young India, 10/17/29.
Of all: Quoted by Andrews, 1929, p. 326.
A woman's: Quoted by Andrews, 1929, p. 326.
The real: Harijan, 1/12/34.
I hold: Harijan, 5/2/36.
I believe: Quoted by Hingorani, 1941, 2/37, p. 27.
Equality: Harijan, 12/2/39.
Page 140
Just as: Harijan, 2/24/40.
It is: Harijan, 2/24/40.
Let not: Harijan, 2/24/40.
The slavery: Harijan, 6/8/40.
As long: Quoted by Prabhu, 1947, p. 20.
Marriage: Young India, 6/3/26.
A wife: Young India, 10/21/26.
The peace: Young India, 10/21/26.
Page 141
The wife: Gandhi, 1927a, p. 38 (1948).
When: Gandhi, 1927a, p. 376 (1948).
Spiritual: Gandhi, 1927a, p. 472 (1948).
The only: Young India, 12/27/28.
Marriage: Young India, 9/19/29.
If the: Young India, 5/21/31.
Marriage outside: Young India, 6/4/31.
Marriage, for: Harijan, 4/24/37.
Page 142
The very: Harijan, 4/24/37.
Spiritual: Harijan, 6/5/37.
It is no doubt: Harijan, 3/22/42.
Is it right: Young India, 10/13/20.
Page 143
The [married]: Gandhi, 1927a, p. 251 (1948).
Birth: Harijan, 3/14/36.
The introduction: Harijan, 3/28/36.
Sex: Harijan, 3/28/36.
Page 144
Propagation: Quoted by Fischer, 1950, p. 415.

All: Quoted by Andrews, 1929, p. 322.
It is: Quoted by Andrews, 1929, p. 324.
Before: Quoted by Andrews, 1929, p. 327.
Every: Gandhi, 1917b, p. 510 (1934).
Parents: Gandhi, 1920, p. 57.
Page 145
Parents . . . feel: Young India, 1/29/25.
It is: Gandhi, 1927a, p. 325 (1948).
What: Gandhi, 1927a, p. 325 (1948).
In a: Harijan, 2/1/42.
There is: Quoted by Prabhu, 1947, p. 39.

EDUCATION

Page 146
Education: Gandhi, 1909, p. 63 (1946).
Education to be: Young India, 9/1/21.
An academic: Young India, 9/1/21.
The higher: Young India, 9/1/21.
Knowledge: Young India, 2/21/29.
No: Young India, 5/23/29.
Page 147
There is: Harijan, 5/23/36.
Man: Harijan, 5/8/37.
We have: Harijan, 9/18/37.
It is not: Quoted by Fischer, 1950, pp. 453–54.
It is a: Young India, 10/6/20.
The true: Gandhi, 1920, p. 97.
Punishment: Young India, 12/3/25.
Page 148
We labor: Gandhi, 1927a, p. 251(1948).
Under: Gandhi, 1927a, p. 407 (1948).
If good: Gandhi, 1927a, p. 417 (1948).
Passive: Harijan, 7/21/40.
Children: Quoted by Fischer, 1950, p. 212.
Students: Young India, 6/9/27.
Page 149
In the case: Young India, 9/8/27.
Scholastic: 11/24/27, Desai, 1928, p. 105.
One might: Young India, 1/24/29.
Vacations: Young India, 11/17/29.
I warn: Harijan, 3/28/36.
[A student's]: Harijan, 1/9/37.
A student: Young India, 10/2/37.
Page 150
The education: Young India, 9/1/21.
It is: Young India, 1/28/25.
On Tolstoy: Gandhi, 1927a, p. 409 (1948).
Of text-books: Gandhi, 1927a, pp. 411–12 (1948).

Religious: 11/24/27, Desai, 1928, p. 105.
Page 151
The teachers': Young India, 4/4/29.
Literary: Young India, 6/1/21.
An appreciation: Young India, 9/1/21.
Physical: Gandhi, 1927a, p. 27 (1948).
Bad: Gandhi, 1927a, p. 28 (1948).
An intelligent: Young India, 6/21/28.
Literacy: Harijan, 7/31/37.
The vast: Harijan, 7/9/38.
Page 152
If India: Young India, 8/25/27.
I had: Gandhi, 1927a, p. 408 (1948).
I believed: Gandhi, 1927a, pp. 413–14 (1948).
A curriculum: Young India, 12/12/28.
Page 153
The culture: Quoted by Andrews, 1929, p. 94.
I do not: Harijan, 3/23/47.
When: Young India, 4/27/21.
The word: 10/19/32, Gandhi, 1949, p. 124.
It is: Harijan, 5/29/37.
I cannot: Quoted by Tendulkar, 1944, p. 381.
Page 154
Personally: Quoted by Tendulkar, 1944, p. 381.
If I had: Quoted by Tendulkar, 1944, p. 381.
All crimes: Quoted by Tendulkar, 1944, p. 381.
All criminals: Quoted by Fischer, 1950, p. 484.

CULTURE AND THE PROFESSIONS

Page 155
The tendency: Gandhi, 1909, p. 46 (1946).
Modern: Gandhi, 1917b, p. 329.
The pandemonium: Gandhi, 1917b, p. 329.
Systematic: Quoted by Rolland, 1924, p. 112.
I wholeheartedly: Young India, 3/17/27.
Page 156
I do not: Young India, 9/22/27.
Many: 11/26/27, Desai, 1928, p. 128.
I am no: 11/24/27, Desai, 1928, p. 105.
Whatever: Young India, 7/5/28.

No Eastern: Gandhi, 1928, p. 144.
Why: Young India, 10/15/31.
I want: Quoted by Tendulkar, 1944,
    p. 64.
Page 157
    Civilization: Gandhi, 1909, p. 31(1946).
    I am: Gandhi, 1917b, p. 311.
    Modern: 3/5/22, Watson, 1923, p. 11.
    I do not: Young India, 1/28/25.
    Western: Gandhi, 1928, p. 145.
    I wish: Desai, 1928, p. 108.
    The West: 7/7/30, Gandhi, 1949, p. 69.
    I have: Amrita Bazar Patrika, 8/3/34.
Page 158
    There: Harijan, 1/13/40.
    Western: Quoted by Prabhu, 1947,
        p. 90.
    The world: 2/20/18, Gandhi, 1917b,
        p. 423.
    No country: Young India, 4/27/21.
    Children: 11/24/27, Desai, 1928,
        p. 105.
    There: Young India, 7/5/28.
Page 159
    How: Quoted by Andrews, 1929, p. 109.
    Different: Harijan, 5/16/36.
    Music: Young India, 9/8/20.
    True: Young India, 8/11/21.
    True beauty: Gandhi, 1927a, p. 378.
    Music has: Young India, 6/10/29.
    All true: Young India, 11/13/24.
Page 160
    I see: Young India, 11/13/24.
    Purity: Harijan, 2/19/38.
    My room: Quoted by Tendulkar, 1944,
        p. 69.
    Mankind: Quoted by Fischer, 1950,
        p. 424.
    One: Gandhi, 1909, p. 13 (1946).
Page 161
    What: Young India, 10/8/19.
    I do not: Young India, 4/3/24.
    Many: Young India, 1/28/25.
    I always: Gandhi, 1927a, p. 349 (1948).
    A subject: Gandhi, 1928, p. 86.
    The: Quoted by Tikekar, 1947, p. 36.
Page 162
    Railways: Gandhi, 1909, p. 32 (1946).
    Lawyers are: Gandhi, 1909, p. 39
        (1946).
    Lawyers will: Gandhi, 1909, p. 40
        (1946).
    The true: Gandhi, 1927a, p. 168
        (1948).
    It was not: Gandhi, 1927a, p. 447
        (1948).

Page 163
    If you: 11/15/27, Desai, 1928, p. 36.
    Lawyers: Gandhi, 1928, p. 202.
    I abhor: Young India, 12/17/25.
    I am not: Young India, 12/17/25.
    All things: Young India, 1/23/30.
    How: Quoted by Fischer, 1950, p. 496.
Page 164
    Hundreds: Gandhi, 1909, p. 45 (1944).
    History: Gandhi, 1909, p. 56 (1946).
    The nations: Young India, 2/2/22.
    If we: Young India, 5/6/26.
    Indian: Young India, 6/21/28.
    It is my: Young India, 11/14/29.

INDIAN PROBLEMS

Page 165
    India: Young India, 10/13/21.
    I do not: Young India: 1/8/25.
    Instead: Harijan, 6/7/42.
    Indian: Quoted by Tendulkar, 1944,
        p. 63.
    India's: Quoted by Prabhu, 1947, p. 2.
    [India]: Quoted by Prabhu, 1947, p. 93.
Page 166
    If man: Gandhi, 1909, p. 58 (1946).
    Swaraj for: Young India, 10/6/20.
    Swaraj . . . means: Young India,
        10/27/21.
    Swaraj is: Young India, 11/24/21.
    Swaraj does: 1921, Quoted by An-
        drews, 1929, p. 366.
    Swaraj can: Young India, 1/5/22.
    By Swaraj: Young India, 1/29/25.
Page 167
    The pilgrimage: Young India, 5/21/25.
    Self-government: Young India, 8/6/25.
    To: Young India, 6/28/28.
    Insult: Gandhi, 1928, p. 159.
    Mere: Young India, 2/13/30.
    Conversion: 3/30, Quoted by Jones,
        1948, p. 65.
    Swadeshi: 2/14/16, Quoted by
        Andrews, 1929, p. 120.
Page 168
    If not: 2/14/16, Quoted by Andrews,
        1929, p. 124.
    Swadeshi . . . is not: Gandhi, 1917b,
        p. 329.
    India: Young India, 4/13/21.
    We stint: Young India, 1/8/25.
    I would: Young India, 5/21/25.
    The broad: Young India, 6/17/26.
    Hand-spinning: Young India,
        10/21/26.

Page 169
  Charkha: Young India, 2/10/27.
  I considered: Gandhi, 1927a, pp. 603–
    04, 607 (1948).
  I have: Young India, 11/15/28.
  Hand-spinning: Quoted by Andrews,
    1929, p. 147.
  Charkha is: Quoted by Andrews, 1929,
    p. 151.
Page 170
  It is: Quoted by Andrews, 1929, p. 264.
  Every: Young India, 11/13/24.
  I think: Quoted by Tendulkar, 1944,
    p. 335.
  English: Young India, 2/2/21.
  The highest: Young India, 2/2/21.
Page 171
  Of all: Young India, 4/27/21.
  It is: Young India, 6/1/21.
  Indian: Gandhi, 1927a, p. 381 (1948).
  The youth: Young India, 7/5/28.
  Whenever: Gandhi, 1917b, p. 317.
Page 172
  Our: Gandhi, 1917b, p. 317.
  Farmers: Young India, 10/8/19.
  The village: Quoted by Tendulkar,
    1944, p. 383.
  India: Quoted by Prabhu, 1947, p. 22.
  The moment: Quoted by Prabhu, 1947,
    p. 39.
  Landlords: Quoted by Fischer, 1950,
    p. 326.
  We can: Young India, 5/25/21.
Page 173
  I have: Young India, 10/6/21.
  That: Young India, 7/29/26.
  It is: Young India, 7/29/26.
  If I have: Quoted by Andrews, 1929,
    p. 167.
Page 174
  Some: Young India, 1/23/30.
  The: 8/2/31, Pyarelal, 1932, p. 306.
  We are: 11/5/32, Gandhi, 1933.
  Temples: Pyarelal, 1932, p. 165.
Page 175
  In the: Harijan, 12/22/33.
  There: Harijan, 1/26/34.
  The "touch-me-not" -ism: Harijan,
    4/20/34.
  The message: Harijan, 6/1/40.
  I do not: Quoted by Tendulkar, 1944,
    p. 266.
Page 176
  Varnashrama: Young India, 10/6/21.
  Varna: Quoted by Andrews, 1929,
    p. 352.

Assumption: Young India, 6/4/31.
I do not: Young India, 6/4/31.
There: Harijan, 10/12/34.
Page 177
  Varna: Harijan, 10/12/34.
  I believe: Modern Review, 10/35, p. 413.
  Caste: Quoted by Bose, 1948, p. 234.
  Hinduism: Young India, 10/6/21.
  The maintenance: Young India,
    6/25/25.
  We.may: Young India, 6/24/26.
Page 178
  The custom: Young India, 8/26/26.
  The God: Young India, 9/15/27.
  Any: Young India, 6/21/28.
  Hindu: Young India, 10/3/29.
  I passionately: Quoted by Andrews,
    1929, p. 322.
  A child: Quoted by Andrews, 1929,
    pp. 328–29.
Page 179
  Every: Harijan, 6/22/35.
  Girls: Quoted by Tikekar, 1947, p. 44.
  I believe: Young India, 10/6/21.
  It is better: Young India, 12/3/25.
  I believe in the Hindu: Gandhi, 1927a,
    pp. 113–14 (1948).
  Think: 1/25/31, Gandhi, 1949, p. 86.
  If the: Gandhi, 1909, p. 35 (1946).
Page 180
  I see: Young India, 5/29/24.
  True: Young India, 8/28/24.
  I was: Gandhi, 1927a, pp. 539–40
    (1948).
  That: Quoted by Andrews, 1929,
    pp. 57–59.
Page 181
  The true: Quoted by Andrews, 1929,
    p. 59.
  To revile: Quoted by Andrews, 1929,
    p. 307.
  The "two-nation": Harijan, 4/6/40.
  As a man: Harijan, 4/13/40.
  Pakistan: Harijan, 5/4/40.
Page 182
  To divide: Harijan, 9/22/40.
  I hold: Harijan, 1/25/42.
  If one: Quoted by Tikekar, 1947, p.
    32.
  You can: Quoted by Sheean, 1949,
    p. 150.
  I miss: Young India, 8/6/25.
  Christian: Young India, 8/6/25.
  One: Young India, 8/6/25.
  You: 7/28/25, quoted by Andrews,
    1929, pp. 74–77.

Page 183
[*The missionaries*]: Quoted by Andrews, 1929, pp. 356–57.
Let my: Harijan, 1/25/35.
Christian: Harijan, 5/11/35.
Page 184
The great: Harijan, 9/28/35.
To the: Harijan, 7/18/36.
Missionaries: Harijan, 7/18/36.
There is: Harijan, 7/18/36.
American: Harijan, 12/26/36.
The gift: Harijan, 4/17/37.
Page 185
Proselytization: Gandhi, 1941b, pp. 7–10.
I am not: Gandhi, 1941b, pp. 7–10.
First: Quoted by Jones, 1948, pp. 51–52.
Don't: Quoted by Jones, 1948, p. 62.

ABOUT HIMSELF

Page 186
I yield: 2/14/16, Quoted by Andrews, 1929, p. 121.
I can: Young India, 10/6/21.
I love: Young India, 10/6/21.
I must: Young India, 8/6/25.
Page 187
I read: Gandhi, 1927a, pp. 91–92 (1948).
I attended: Gandhi, 1927a, p. 199 (1948).
During: Gandhi, 1927a, p. 321 (1948).
If I: Quoted by Andrews, 1929, pp. 93–94.
Believing: Quoted by Andrews, 1929, pp. 358–59.
Page 188
Today: Harijan, 8/24/39.
My: Quoted by Prabhu, 1947, p. 5.
The Sermon: Quoted by Jones, 1948, p. 83.
I have: Young India, 10/21/26.
It is: Gandhi, 1927a, pp. 18–19 (1948).
I was: Gandhi, 1927a, pp. 339–40 (1948).
Page 189
She is: Gandhi, 1927a, p. 340 (1948).
I really: Harijan, 4/24/37.
I cannot: 1944, quoted in Fischer, 1950, p. 394.
I directed: Gandhi, 1927a, p. 70 (1948).
Page 190
I believed: Gandhi, 1927a, p. 229 (1948).

About: Gandhi, 1927a, pp. 320–21 (1948.)
We went: Gandhi, 1927a, p. 35 (1948).
Page 191
I abjured: Gandhi, 1927a, p. 36 (1948).
Ever: Gandhi, 1927a, p. 40 (1948).
My: Gandhi, 1927a, pp. 329–30 (1948).
I held: Gandhi, 1927a, p. 397 (1948).
Milk: Gandhi, 1927a, p. 401–02 (1948).
Page 192
Religious: Gandhi, 1927a, p. 436 (1948).
I was: Gandhi, 1927a, p. 477 (1948).
Lord Sankey: Quoted by Fischer, 1942, p. 20.
My friends: Yeravda Prison, 4/14/22.
Most: Gandhi, 1927a, p. 206 (1948).
Page 193
I would: Quoted by Andrews, 1929, p. 368.
Non-violence: 3/18/22, Quoted by Jones, 1948, p. 94.
Jail: Quoted by Fischer, 1950, p. 436.
I lived: Young India, 2/10/27.
The train: Gandhi, 1927a, pp. 140–41 (1948).
Page 194
I reached: Gandhi, 1927a, p. 145 (1948).
I applied: Gandhi, 1927a, p. 181 (1948).
Mr. Ellerthorpe: Gandhi, 1927a, p. 223 (1948).
I once: Gandhi, 1927a, pp. 262–63 (1948).
The word: Young India, 5/12/20.
Page 195
I assure: Young India, 6/12/24.
Often: Gandhi, 1927a, p. 4 (1948).
The woes: Gandhi, 1927a, p. 298 (1948).
Abdulla: Gandhi, 1927a, p. 353 (1948).
Immediately: Quoted by Andrews, 1929, p. 281.
My aim: Harijan, 9/30/39.
Page 196
I must: Quoted by Tendulkar, 1944, p. 362.
I have: Quoted by Tendulkar, 1944, pp. 362–63.
There: Quoted by Tendulkar, 1944, p. 362.
Experience: Young India, 11/17/21.
It is not: Young India, 11/17/21.
I am: Young India, 11/17/21.
I am far: Gandhi, 1927a, p. 5 (1948).
Page 197
Let us: Gandhi, 1927a, p. 7 (1948).
My: Gandhi, 1927a, p. 84 (1948).

My hesitancy: Gandhi, 1927a, p. 84 (1948).

I had: Gandhi, 1927a, p. 169 (1948).

All: Gandhi, 1927a, p. 184 (1948).

I never: Gandhi, 1927a, p. 411 (1948).

I claim: Quoted by Pyarelal, 1932, p. 133.

Page 198

I claim: Harijan, 10/3/36.

My writings: Harijan, 5/1/37.

I have: Harijan, 7/9/38.

There is: Harijan, 7/15/39.

My life: Harijan, 5/4/40.

I am: Harijan, 6/7/42.

My influence: Harijan, 7/26/42.

I am essentially: Quoted by Fischer, 1942, p. 102.

Life: Quoted by Tikekar, 1947, p. 39.

Page 199

I am: Quoted by Jones, 1948, p. 98.

Every: Quoted by Fischer, 1950, p. 439.

Never: Quoted by Fischer, 1950, p. 414.

I am not: Young India: 8/11/20.

I live: Young India, 4/3/24.

I lay: Young India, 9/11/24.

Page 200

A persistent: Young India, 12/2/26.

My conclusions: Gandhi, 1927a, p. 614 (1948).

To describe: Gandhi, 1927a, p. 614 (1948).

I am: Harijan, 11/17/33.

I am, indeed: Harijan, 11/17/33.

I am an: Amrita Bazar Patrika, 8/3/34.

To dismiss: Harijan, 5/30/36.

Page 201

It is: Harijan, 10/3/36.

If Gandhism: Harijan, 3/2/40.

Sometimes: 1940, Quoted by Raman, 1943, p. 37.

I have not: Harijan, 6/28/42.

I am but: Harijan, 7/12/42.

I have made: Quoted by Tendulkar, 1944, pp. 60–61.

Page 202

Truth: Quoted by Tendulkar, 1944, p. 62.

Most: Quoted by Diwakar, 1948, p. 34.

I am taking: Quoted by Jones, 1948, p. 31.

I am a born: Quoted by Fischer, 1950, p. 474.

One may not: Gandhi, 1928, p. 252.

Just: Gandhi, 1928, pp. 288–89.

Page 203

Truth: 4/8/29, Gandhi, 1949, p. 57.

Thousands: Quoted by Tikekar, 1947, p. 2.

Let us: Quoted by Tikekar, 1947, p. 4.

If I am: 1/28/48, quoted by Jones, 1948, p. 38.

I keep: Quoted by Maurer, 1948, p. 121.

If I were: 1948, Quoted in Andrews, 1929, p. 20 (1949).

He, Ram!: Quoted by Sheean, 1949, p. 65.

INDEX OF TOPICS

A CATALOG OF SELECTED
DOVER BOOKS
IN ALL FIELDS OF INTEREST

A CATALOG OF SELECTED DOVER
BOOKS IN ALL FIELDS OF INTEREST

CONCERNING THE SPIRITUAL IN ART, Wassily Kandinsky. Pioneering work by father of abstract art. Thoughts on color theory, nature of art. Analysis of earlier masters. 12 illustrations. 80pp. of text. 5⅜ x 8½. 23411-8

ANIMALS: 1,419 Copyright-Free Illustrations of Mammals, Birds, Fish, Insects, etc., Jim Harter (ed.). Clear wood engravings present, in extremely lifelike poses, over 1,000 species of animals. One of the most extensive pictorial sourcebooks of its kind. Captions. Index. 284pp. 9 x 12. 23766-4

CELTIC ART: The Methods of Construction, George Bain. Simple geometric techniques for making Celtic interlacements, spirals, Kells-type initials, animals, humans, etc. Over 500 illustrations. 160pp. 9 x 12. (Available in U.S. only.) 22923-8

AN ATLAS OF ANATOMY FOR ARTISTS, Fritz Schider. Most thorough reference work on art anatomy in the world. Hundreds of illustrations, including selections from works by Vesalius, Leonardo, Goya, Ingres, Michelangelo, others. 593 illustrations. 192pp. 7⅛ x 10¼. 20241-0

CELTIC HAND STROKE-BY-STROKE (Irish Half-Uncial from "The Book of Kells"): An Arthur Baker Calligraphy Manual, Arthur Baker. Complete guide to creating each letter of the alphabet in distinctive Celtic manner. Covers hand position, strokes, pens, inks, paper, more. Illustrated. 48pp. 8¼ x 11. 24336-2

EASY ORIGAMI, John Montroll. Charming collection of 32 projects (hat, cup, pelican, piano, swan, many more) specially designed for the novice origami hobbyist. Clearly illustrated easy-to-follow instructions insure that even beginning papercrafters will achieve successful results. 48pp. 8¼ x 11. 27298-2

THE COMPLETE BOOK OF BIRDHOUSE CONSTRUCTION FOR WOODWORKERS, Scott D. Campbell. Detailed instructions, illustrations, tables. Also data on bird habitat and instinct patterns. Bibliography. 3 tables. 63 illustrations in 15 figures. 48pp. 5¼ x 8½. 24407-5

BLOOMINGDALE'S ILLUSTRATED 1886 CATALOG: Fashions, Dry Goods and Housewares, Bloomingdale Brothers. Famed merchants' extremely rare catalog depicting about 1,700 products: clothing, housewares, firearms, dry goods, jewelry, more. Invaluable for dating, identifying vintage items. Also, copyright-free graphics for artists, designers. Co-published with Henry Ford Museum & Greenfield Village. 160pp. 8¼ x 11. 25780-0

HISTORIC COSTUME IN PICTURES, Braun & Schneider. Over 1,450 costumed figures in clearly detailed engravings–from dawn of civilization to end of 19th century. Captions. Many folk costumes. 256pp. 8⅜ x 11¾. 23150-X

MY BONDAGE AND MY FREEDOM, Frederick Douglass. Born a slave, Douglass became outspoken force in antislavery movement. The best of Douglass' autobiographies. Graphic description of slave life. 464pp. 5⅜ x 8½.   22457-0

FOLLOWING THE EQUATOR: A Journey Around the World, Mark Twain. Fascinating humorous account of 1897 voyage to Hawaii, Australia, India, New Zealand, etc. Ironic, bemused reports on peoples, customs, climate, flora and fauna, politics, much more. 197 illustrations. 720pp. 5⅜ x 8½.   26113-1

THE PEOPLE CALLED SHAKERS, Edward D. Andrews. Definitive study of Shakers: origins, beliefs, practices, dances, social organization, furniture and crafts, etc. 33 illustrations. 351pp. 5⅜ x 8½.   21081-2

THE MYTHS OF GREECE AND ROME, H. A. Guerber. A classic of mythology, generously illustrated, long prized for its simple, graphic, accurate retelling of the principal myths of Greece and Rome, and for its commentary on their origins and significance. With 64 illustrations by Michelangelo, Raphael, Titian, Rubens, Canova, Bernini and others. 480pp. 5⅜ x 8½.   27584-1

PSYCHOLOGY OF MUSIC, Carl E. Seashore. Classic work discusses music as a medium from psychological viewpoint. Clear treatment of physical acoustics, auditory apparatus, sound perception, development of musical skills, nature of musical feeling, host of other topics. 88 figures. 408pp. 5⅜ x 8½.   21851-1

THE PHILOSOPHY OF HISTORY, Georg W. Hegel. Great classic of Western thought develops concept that history is not chance but rational process, the evolution of freedom. 457pp. 5⅜ x 8½.   20112-0

THE BOOK OF TEA, Kakuzo Okakura. Minor classic of the Orient: entertaining, charming explanation, interpretation of traditional Japanese culture in terms of tea ceremony. 94pp. 5⅜ x 8½.   20070-1

LIFE IN ANCIENT EGYPT, Adolf Erman. Fullest, most thorough, detailed older account with much not in more recent books, domestic life, religion, magic, medicine, commerce, much more. Many illustrations reproduce tomb paintings, carvings, hieroglyphs, etc. 597pp. 5⅜ x 8½.   22632-8

SUNDIALS, Their Theory and Construction, Albert Waugh. Far and away the best, most thorough coverage of ideas, mathematics concerned, types, construction, adjusting anywhere. Simple, nontechnical treatment allows even children to build several of these dials. Over 100 illustrations. 230pp. 5⅜ x 8½.   22947-5

THEORETICAL HYDRODYNAMICS, L. M. Milne-Thomson. Classic exposition of the mathematical theory of fluid motion, applicable to both hydrodynamics and aerodynamics. Over 600 exercises. 768pp. 6⅛ x 9¼.   68970-0

SONGS OF EXPERIENCE: Facsimile Reproduction with 26 Plates in Full Color, William Blake. 26 full-color plates from a rare 1826 edition. Includes "The Tyger," "London," "Holy Thursday," and other poems. Printed text of poems. 48pp. 5¼ x 7.
                    24636-1

OLD-TIME VIGNETTES IN FULL COLOR, Carol Belanger Grafton (ed.). Over 390 charming, often sentimental illustrations, selected from archives of Victorian graphics—pretty women posing, children playing, food, flowers, kittens and puppies, smiling cherubs, birds and butterflies, much more. All copyright-free. 48pp. 9¼ x 12¼.
                    27269-9

LITTLE BOOK OF EARLY AMERICAN CRAFTS AND TRADES, Peter Stockham (ed.). 1807 children's book explains crafts and trades: baker, hatter, cooper, potter, and many others. 23 copperplate illustrations. 140pp. 4⁵/₈ x 6. 23336-7

VICTORIAN FASHIONS AND COSTUMES FROM HARPER'S BAZAR, 1867–1898, Stella Blum (ed.). Day costumes, evening wear, sports clothes, shoes, hats, other accessories in over 1,000 detailed engravings. 320pp. 9⅜ x 12¼. 22990-4

GUSTAV STICKLEY, THE CRAFTSMAN, Mary Ann Smith. Superb study surveys broad scope of Stickley's achievement, especially in architecture. Design philosophy, rise and fall of the Craftsman empire, descriptions and floor plans for many Craftsman houses, more. 86 black-and-white halftones. 31 line illustrations. Introduction 208pp. 6½ x 9¼. 27210-9

THE LONG ISLAND RAIL ROAD IN EARLY PHOTOGRAPHS, Ron Ziel. Over 220 rare photos, informative text document origin (1844) and development of rail service on Long Island. Vintage views of early trains, locomotives, stations, passengers, crews, much more. Captions. 8⅞ x 11¾. 26301-0

VOYAGE OF THE LIBERDADE, Joshua Slocum. Great 19th-century mariner's thrilling, first-hand account of the wreck of his ship off South America, the 35-foot boat he built from the wreckage, and its remarkable voyage home. 128pp. 5⅜ x 8½. 40022-0

TEN BOOKS ON ARCHITECTURE, Vitruvius. The most important book ever written on architecture. Early Roman aesthetics, technology, classical orders, site selection, all other aspects. Morgan translation. 331pp. 5⅜ x 8½. 20645-9

THE HUMAN FIGURE IN MOTION, Eadweard Muybridge. More than 4,500 stopped-action photos, in action series, showing undraped men, women, children jumping, lying down, throwing, sitting, wrestling, carrying, etc. 390pp. 7⅞ x 10⅝. 20204-6 Clothbd.

TREES OF THE EASTERN AND CENTRAL UNITED STATES AND CANADA, William M. Harlow. Best one-volume guide to 140 trees. Full descriptions, woodlore, range, etc. Over 600 illustrations. Handy size. 288pp. 4½ x 6⅜. 20395-6

SONGS OF WESTERN BIRDS, Dr. Donald J. Borror. Complete song and call repertoire of 60 western species, including flycatchers, juncoes, cactus wrens, many more–includes fully illustrated booklet. Cassette and manual 99913-0

GROWING AND USING HERBS AND SPICES, Milo Miloradovich. Versatile handbook provides all the information needed for cultivation and use of all the herbs and spices available in North America. 4 illustrations. Index. Glossary. 236pp. 5⅜ x 8½. 25058-X

BIG BOOK OF MAZES AND LABYRINTHS, Walter Shepherd. 50 mazes and labyrinths in all–classical, solid, ripple, and more–in one great volume. Perfect inexpensive puzzler for clever youngsters. Full solutions. 112pp. 8⅛ x 11. 22951-3

THE WIT AND HUMOR OF OSCAR WILDE, Alvin Redman (ed.). More than 1,000 ripostes, paradoxes, wisecracks: Work is the curse of the drinking classes; I can resist everything except temptation; etc. 258pp. 5⅜ x 8½. 20602-5

SHAKESPEARE LEXICON AND QUOTATION DICTIONARY, Alexander Schmidt. Full definitions, locations, shades of meaning in every word in plays and poems. More than 50,000 exact quotations. 1,485pp. 6½ x 9¼. 2-vol. set.
Vol. 1: 22726-X
Vol. 2: 22727-8

SELECTED POEMS, Emily Dickinson. Over 100 best-known, best-loved poems by one of America's foremost poets, reprinted from authoritative early editions. No comparable edition at this price. Index of first lines. 64pp. 5³⁄₁₆ x 8¼. 26466-1

THE INSIDIOUS DR. FU-MANCHU, Sax Rohmer. The first of the popular mystery series introduces a pair of English detectives to their archnemesis, the diabolical Dr. Fu-Manchu. Flavorful atmosphere, fast-paced action, and colorful characters enliven this classic of the genre. 208pp. 5³⁄₁₆ x 8¼. 29898-1

THE MALLEUS MALEFICARUM OF KRAMER AND SPRENGER, translated by Montague Summers. Full text of most important witchhunter's "bible," used by both Catholics and Protestants. 278pp. 6⅝ x 10. 22802-9

SPANISH STORIES/CUENTOS ESPAÑOLES: A Dual-Language Book, Angel Flores (ed.). Unique format offers 13 great stories in Spanish by Cervantes, Borges, others. Faithful English translations on facing pages. 352pp. 5⅜ x 8½. 25399-6

GARDEN CITY, LONG ISLAND, IN EARLY PHOTOGRAPHS, 1869–1919, Mildred H. Smith. Handsome treasury of 118 vintage pictures, accompanied by carefully researched captions, document the Garden City Hotel fire (1899), the Vanderbilt Cup Race (1908), the first airmail flight departing from the Nassau Boulevard Aerodrome (1911), and much more. 96pp. 8⅞ x 11¾. 40669-5

OLD QUEENS, N.Y., IN EARLY PHOTOGRAPHS, Vincent F. Seyfried and William Asadorian. Over 160 rare photographs of Maspeth, Jamaica, Jackson Heights, and other areas. Vintage views of DeWitt Clinton mansion, 1939 World's Fair and more. Captions. 192pp. 8⅞ x 11. 26358-4

CAPTURED BY THE INDIANS: 15 Firsthand Accounts, 1750-1870, Frederick Drimmer. Astounding true historical accounts of grisly torture, bloody conflicts, relentless pursuits, miraculous escapes and more, by people who lived to tell the tale. 384pp. 5⅜ x 8½. 24901-8

THE WORLD'S GREAT SPEECHES (Fourth Enlarged Edition), Lewis Copeland, Lawrence W. Lamm, and Stephen J. McKenna. Nearly 300 speeches provide public speakers with a wealth of updated quotes and inspiration–from Pericles' funeral oration and William Jennings Bryan's "Cross of Gold Speech" to Malcolm X's powerful words on the Black Revolution and Earl of Spenser's tribute to his sister, Diana, Princess of Wales. 944pp. 5⅜ x 8⅜. 40903-1

THE BOOK OF THE SWORD, Sir Richard F. Burton. Great Victorian scholar/adventurer's eloquent, erudite history of the "queen of weapons"–from prehistory to early Roman Empire. Evolution and development of early swords, variations (sabre, broadsword, cutlass, scimitar, etc.), much more. 336pp. 6⅛ x 9¼. 25434-8

CATALOG OF DOVER BOOKS

AUTOBIOGRAPHY: The Story of My Experiments with Truth, Mohandas K. Gandhi. Boyhood, legal studies, purification, the growth of the Satyagraha (nonviolent protest) movement. Critical, inspiring work of the man responsible for the freedom of India. 480pp. 5⅜ x 8½. (Available in U.S. only.) 24593-4

CELTIC MYTHS AND LEGENDS, T. W. Rolleston. Masterful retelling of Irish and Welsh stories and tales. Cuchulain, King Arthur, Deirdre, the Grail, many more. First paperback edition. 58 full-page illustrations. 512pp. 5⅜ x 8½. 26507-2

THE PRINCIPLES OF PSYCHOLOGY, William James. Famous long course complete, unabridged. Stream of thought, time perception, memory, experimental methods; great work decades ahead of its time. 94 figures. 1,391pp. 5⅜ x 8½. 2-vol. set.
Vol. I: 20381-6   Vol. II: 20382-4

THE WORLD AS WILL AND REPRESENTATION, Arthur Schopenhauer. Definitive English translation of Schopenhauer's life work, correcting more than 1,000 errors, omissions in earlier translations. Translated by E. F. J. Payne. Total of 1,269pp. 5⅜ x 8½. 2-vol. set.
Vol. 1: 21761-2   Vol. 2: 21762-0

MAGIC AND MYSTERY IN TIBET, Madame Alexandra David-Neel. Experiences among lamas, magicians, sages, sorcerers, Bonpa wizards. A true psychic discovery. 32 illustrations. 321pp. 5⅜ x 8½. (Available in U.S. only.) 22682-4

THE EGYPTIAN BOOK OF THE DEAD, E. A. Wallis Budge. Complete reproduction of Ani's papyrus, finest ever found. Full hieroglyphic text, interlinear transliteration, word-for-word translation, smooth translation. 533pp. 6½ x 9¼. 21866-X

MATHEMATICS FOR THE NONMATHEMATICIAN, Morris Kline. Detailed, college-level treatment of mathematics in cultural and historical context, with numerous exercises. Recommended Reading Lists. Tables. Numerous figures. 641pp. 5⅜ x 8½. 24823-2

PROBABILISTIC METHODS IN THE THEORY OF STRUCTURES, Isaac Elishakoff. Well-written introduction covers the elements of the theory of probability from two or more random variables, the reliability of such multivariable structures, the theory of random function, Monte Carlo methods of treating problems incapable of exact solution, and more. Examples. 502pp. 5⅜ x 8½. 40691-1

THE RIME OF THE ANCIENT MARINER, Gustave Doré, S. T. Coleridge. Doré's finest work; 34 plates capture moods, subtleties of poem. Flawless full-size reproductions printed on facing pages with authoritative text of poem. "Beautiful. Simply beautiful."–Publisher's Weekly. 77pp. 9¼ x 12. 22305-1

NORTH AMERICAN INDIAN DESIGNS FOR ARTISTS AND CRAFTSPEOPLE, Eva Wilson. Over 360 authentic copyright-free designs adapted from Navajo blankets, Hopi pottery, Sioux buffalo hides, more. Geometrics, symbolic figures, plant and animal motifs, etc. 128pp. 8⅜ x 11. (Not for sale in the United Kingdom.) 25341-4

SCULPTURE: Principles and Practice, Louis Slobodkin. Step-by-step approach to clay, plaster, metals, stone; classical and modern. 253 drawings, photos. 255pp. 8⅛ x 11. 22960-2

THE INFLUENCE OF SEA POWER UPON HISTORY, 1660–1783, A. T. Mahan. Influential classic of naval history and tactics still used as text in war colleges. First paperback edition. 4 maps. 24 battle plans. 640pp. 5⅜ x 8½. 25509-3

CATALOG OF DOVER BOOKS

THE STORY OF THE TITANIC AS TOLD BY ITS SURVIVORS, Jack Winocour (ed.). What it was really like. Panic, despair, shocking inefficiency, and a little heroism. More thrilling than any fictional account. 26 illustrations. 320pp. 5⅜ x 8½.
20610-6

FAIRY AND FOLK TALES OF THE IRISH PEASANTRY, William Butler Yeats (ed.). Treasury of 64 tales from the twilight world of Celtic myth and legend: "The Soul Cages," "The Kildare Pooka," "King O'Toole and his Goose," many more. Introduction and Notes by W. B. Yeats. 352pp. 5⅜ x 8½.
26941-8

BUDDHIST MAHAYANA TEXTS, E. B. Cowell and others (eds.). Superb, accurate translations of basic documents in Mahayana Buddhism, highly important in history of religions. The Buddha-karita of Asvaghosha, Larger Sukhavativyuha, more. 448pp. 5⅜ x 8½.
25552-2

ONE TWO THREE . . . INFINITY: Facts and Speculations of Science, George Gamow. Great physicist's fascinating, readable overview of contemporary science: number theory, relativity, fourth dimension, entropy, genes, atomic structure, much more. 128 illustrations. Index. 352pp. 5⅜ x 8½.
25664-2

EXPERIMENTATION AND MEASUREMENT, W. J. Youden. Introductory manual explains laws of measurement in simple terms and offers tips for achieving accuracy and minimizing errors. Mathematics of measurement, use of instruments, experimenting with machines. 1994 edition. Foreword. Preface. Introduction. Epilogue. Selected Readings. Glossary. Index. Tables and figures. 128pp. 5⅜ x 8½.
40451-X

DALÍ ON MODERN ART: The Cuckolds of Antiquated Modern Art, Salvador Dalí. Influential painter skewers modern art and its practitioners. Outrageous evaluations of Picasso, Cézanne, Turner, more. 15 renderings of paintings discussed. 44 calligraphic decorations by Dalí. 96pp. 5⅜ x 8½. (Available in U.S. only.)
29220-7

ANTIQUE PLAYING CARDS: A Pictorial History, Henry René D'Allemagne. Over 900 elaborate, decorative images from rare playing cards (14th–20th centuries): Bacchus, death, dancing dogs, hunting scenes, royal coats of arms, players cheating, much more. 96pp. 9¼ x 12¼.
29265-7

MAKING FURNITURE MASTERPIECES: 30 Projects with Measured Drawings, Franklin H. Gottshall. Step-by-step instructions, illustrations for constructing handsome, useful pieces, among them a Sheraton desk, Chippendale chair, Spanish desk, Queen Anne table and a William and Mary dressing mirror. 224pp. 8⅛ x 11¼.
29338-6

THE FOSSIL BOOK: A Record of Prehistoric Life, Patricia V. Rich et al. Profusely illustrated definitive guide covers everything from single-celled organisms and dinosaurs to birds and mammals and the interplay between climate and man. Over 1,500 illustrations. 760pp. 7½ x 10⅛.
29371-8

Paperbound unless otherwise indicated. Available at your book dealer, online at www.doverpublications.com, or by writing to Dept. GI, Dover Publications, Inc., 31 East 2nd Street, Mineola, NY 11501. For current price information or for free catalogues (please indicate field of interest), write to Dover Publications or log on to www.doverpublications.com and see every Dover book in print. Dover publishes more than 500 books each year on science, elementary and advanced mathematics, biology, music, art, literary history, social sciences, and other areas.